YOUR WORSHIP-FULNESS

PRINCESS LEIA

Starring CARRIE FISHER

JEFF RYAN

For more information contact:
Riverdale Avenue Books
5676 Riverdale Avenue
Riverdale, NY 10471.

www.riverdaleavebooks.com
Design by www.formatting4U.com
Cover by Scott Carpenter

Digital ISBN: 9781626016767
Trade Paperback ISBN: 9781626016774
Hardcover ISBN: 9781626016606
Kickstarter First Edition, 2023

To Holly,
Who's still not a Star Wars *person*

Table of Contents

Introduction

"To be honest, I think this whole biography thing is a bit silly."
—*General Leia Organa,* Princess Leia, Royal Rebel .

In the cramped toy aisle of a suburban 1981 toy store, *Star Wars* action figures lined the slat walls. Beside the various aliens and enemy soldiers hung a half-dozen Luke Skywalkers. Next to the Lukes were a half-dozen Han Solos.

I was allowed one. Would it be Luke, or Han?

My choice, like the star system on Tatooine, was binary: good guy over bad boy. I chose Luke, the Gen X equivalent of rooting for House Gryffindor. Cooler friends of mine picked Han. But we both chose wrong. Watching my wrong decision from her own peg was a third choice. This person was more heroic than Luke Skywalker, tougher than Han Solo, and sported a white plastic cape.

It was Princess Leia Organa, of course. She had a fatal flaw—she was a girl. Girl toys were for girls. Our family of mostly boys would collect dozens of *Star Wars* figures over the years, but never a Princess Leia.

We weren't the only ones. Entertainment, like Romance languages, was gendered. Most boys were like me and stayed away from "girl toys." Therefore, those toys simply didn't get manufactured in the same quantity as "boy toys." We didn't read "girl books," either—these were defined as books with female leads or female authors. This bit of pre-adolescent misogyny prompted female authors like SE Hinton, LM Montgomery, and JK Rowling to hide behind their initials.

The gendered unfairness was just beginning, though. Us boys considered male-skewing entertainment to be not male but neutral. You had to look to wrestling, monster trucks, and books about underpants for "boy" entertainment.

War movies, fantasy epics, and sci-fi films have traditionally followed the *Highlander* Rule of Female Characters: there can be only

i

one. This one girl would have to represent all of womankind: wisdom and sex, toughness and emotionality, pixie-ish delight and Mama Bear determination. Imagine what a psychological mess of a figure she would be: a princess who was also a soldier, a looker who everyone was looking for, and a love interest who was also not at all interested in love. Maiden, mother, and crone, in other words, all sandwiched between two buns.

That was the impossible role written for Princess Leia, the one female character from *Star Wars*, later subtitled *A New Hope*. It was made more impossible because Leia barely has any screen time in the script. Yet thanks to the untested actress hired to play her, Leia works as a character.

This untested teenager's acting choices, persona, and physicality made her the It Girl of 1977. She soon echoed everywhere: *General Hospital's* Luke and Laura seemed to exist primarily to be confused with Luke and Leia. The dozens of cheapo *Star Wars* knockoff films all needed a sexy, dangerous princess, blaster at the ready. Halloween costumes for every long-haired woman on the planet were set. Word got out: Leia was cool… yet she wasn't half as cool as Carrie Fisher.

Star Wars' creator George Lucas never wrote Leia as eye candy. Plenty of males would see her that way, but George wrote her as an adult in a room full of teenagers—this was despite Carrie actually being a teenager in a room full of adults. If Luke was the character in which George Lucas saw himself, Leia was the person he wanted to one day be: strong, decisive, defiant, all in a compact frame.

Carrie's life and Leia's spent the next four decades in an uncanny parallel; her life, along with her iconic hairstyle, was dual-roll. Both had famous and famously awful—dark and distant fathers. Both had big talents they hid from the world, and maybe even themselves. Both moved on from early rebellion into hard-fought wisdom. Both struggled with abuses of power. Both found huge but unheralded successes once they left the public eye. Both had those developments cut short by mercenary economics. Both were inspirations to generations of mothers and daughters—and fathers and sons not as girl-phobic as I apparently was.

"The most visible creators," poet Donna J. Smith said, "are those artists whose medium is life itself. The ones who express the inexpressible without brush, hammer, clay, or guitar. They neither paint nor sculpt. Their medium is simply being. Whatever their presence touches has increased life. They see, but don't have to draw… Because they are the artists of being alive."

* * *

Ladies and gentlemen, boys and girls, children of all ages, presenting the Carrie Fisher Sentence.

"As you get older the pickings get slimmer, but the people don't."

"This reminds me of that time I had déjà vu."

"Religion is the opiate of the masses. I did masses of opiates religiously."

"Whenever I start to talk, Harrison [Ford] gets nervous."

"What I look like now is not my fault… years of living longer make you look worse: who knew about that?"

"If my life wasn't funny it would just be true, and that would be unacceptable."

Her sentences could be one word long and still bring the house down. For instance, when she and James Earl Jones guest-starred on a sitcom together, she greeted him with "Daddy!"

Carrie spent her whole lifetime wielding her words like weapons. This wasn't rapier wit but a two-handed broadsword, accent on broad. With it she skewered, lambasted, and reproached her fellow glitterati. The world was her roast dais. She was a born-too-late member of the Algonquin Round Table, always able to make the most out of 30 seconds of attention. One quote at a time, she struck a devil's-interval chord with people. It was her version of life advice, containing the mercy of the fallen, thoughts bitter and strong. This entire book could just be Carrie Fisher Sentences, culled from her novels, memoirs, and talk show appearances.

But Carrie was not at heart a comedian: she was a writer, expressing painful truths. Spoonfuls of sugar hid the medicine: for those in darkness, her passages were lodestones. "Self-depreciation before self-destruction," her sister Joely Fisher called it. "It's easy to imagine why she chose to turn the pen on herself—to write funnier, more raw, meaner [jokes] than any tabloid scribe could."

Carrie's gift, her curse, her burden, her skill was her insight. She saw herself, from the very first, through the eyes of others. From her lithe teenage years all the way up to her womanly middle age, she was constantly aware not just of the male gaze, but the *disappointed* male gaze. She absorbed that misogyny hourly, for decades.

Carrie Fisher Sentence: "I'm someone who's very comfortable in my own skin. I just wish there wasn't so much room at times for that comfort."

Each Carrie Fisher Sentence contained a secret coded message, intended not for a rebel leader but for anyone who took the time to listen. On their surface they may have sounded like cries for help, shrugs of resignation, or venting of spleen. But decoded, they reveal road-weary wisdom. Her words speak of a hard-lived life that's still quite hard to live, full of mistakes and regrets that have left a galaxy map of bruises and scars.

Each sentence is also like an injured bird's tweet, a mordant wisecrack from a car crash victim, letting everyone know she was still here and still herself. She had a lifetime's worth of experience with depression and anxiety, which can warp remembering the past and thinking about the future into twin ion engines of shame. Many days getting out of bed or taking a shower was a bridge too far. If she could make a joke—even an off-color, mean, uncalled-for joke—that was a sign she was still fighting back against the "black dog." Her life, fissured and carried away.

This was despite her being a child of unparalleled privilege, the daughter of two of the 1950s' biggest stars. (Carrie Fisher Sentence: "I was street smart, but unfortunately the street was Rodeo Drive.") No amount of money or fame can buy a stable home life, a healthy mind and body, a happy family, and friends who won't let you down. Carrie learned this the hard way: she spent a lifetime trying to buy the peace and contentment that came to others so naturally.

Carrie Fisher Sentence: "I am truly a product of Hollywood in-breeding. When two celebrities mate, someone like me is the result."

Like many actors, Carrie learned to suggest lines for her characters on set. Unlike most, though, she kept honing this skill, moving beyond bon mots into realistic dialogue, characterization, scenework, and plot advancement. As her acting career was sunsetting—"Acting engenders and harbors qualities that are best left way behind in adolescence"—she pivoted to writing.

Carrie will of course be synonymous with Princess Leia. But what if she wasn't? If she was only known for her post-trilogy films, she would be seen as a killer supporting cast member of underappreciated gems. If she was only known for her novels, she'd be considered a melding of the Three Joans: Collins, Rivers, and Didion. If she was only known for her screenwriting, she'd be the one-woman superstar factory. If she was only known for her work on mental illness awareness, she'd be a role model.

Alas, one downside of being the world's most famous heroine is that nothing sticks in the memory like the buns, the blaster, and the bikini. Carrie always knew what the first line of her obituary would be. "Leia follows me like a vague smell," she said.

Carrie came closest to eclipsing Leia not as an actress, writer, or script doctor but as herself. Or rather a trash-talking version of herself. She would complain about men, rag on Leia, and describe her own chemical past like an archaeologist describing ancient rituals. "Carrie Fisher" was Carrie's best role.

But that brassiness was just one facet of the real Carrie, the facet she decided was her good side. "I don't hate hardly ever, and when I love, I love for miles and miles. A love so big it should either be outlawed or it should have a capital and its own currency." In her final years she became a social media star, with InstaTons of followers: even her dog became famous.

When posting online she would often write in a sort of code, picking a different emoji or glyph that resembled a letter instead of the regular keypad. This made reading one of her texts a rebus-like challenge. Only those dogged enough to see the trees through the forest could look at [tanabata tree][Pisces][information source][dollar sign] and read "THIS." The messages were often trite, but the fun came in concealing them, for to conceal is to ask to be revealed.

Fans would regularly ask Carrie what Leia was doing, and Carrie would come up with something clever or snide or wistful. But there was another way to find out more about Leia's adventures. After the *Star Wars* trilogy ended in 1983, Leia's story kept on being told. The princess of the late planet Alderaan soldiered on in novels, video games, comic books, toys—everywhere but the big screen. Fans loved the world of *Star Wars* too much to let her go.

And that fervent love, more than anything else, got George Lucas back in the directing game. He had long said he wanted to show how Luke and Leia's father became Darth Vader. So he did, in a trilogy of prequel films that created a second generation of *Star Wars* ride-or-dies. Once those were done, that seemed to be that: Leia went back to having adventures everywhere but the multiplex.

Then the band got back together in 2012, when Disney bought Lucasfilm from George Lucas, and restarted the hyperdrive engine on the Millennium Falcon. Under new hands, a third generation of fans would experience a third *Star Wars* trilogy. This time, Leia's role was not as "the girl," not as the baby born in the final moment, but as a worldly wise warrior, General Organa.

* * *

In music there's a moment where artistic and critical success coincide: this is known as the Imperial phase. Leia was no imperial, and neither was Carrie. Her greatest creative moments happened well after her youthful on-screen successes, and received much less fanfare. But Leia becomes all the stronger knowing the woman behind the blaster. And Carrie is all the more fascinating once you go beyond the space princess.

This book is about Carrie Fisher, and how she made Princess Leia such a remarkable character. Actors and their defining roles are like that MC Escher sketch of two hands each drawing the other: artists turning their lives into art, and the art in turn creating an artist. How much of Leia was Carrie, and how much of Carrie is because of Leia?

The first *Star Wars* film, and Carrie's most iconic line from it, is all about hope. There's a difference between hope and optimism. Optimism is for those who cross their fingers and walk into the street blindfolded. Optimists try to control their fate, which often isn't possible. Optimism's easy, so long as things are going right.

Hope is different. Hope is the ember that still glows after torrential bad luck. The stands of the last-place sports team aren't filled by optimists but by the hopeful. Hope isn't happiness; it's knowing there may be happiness tomorrow. Hope exists beyond reason, beyond science, beyond facts: it's a pure emotion. When everything's gone wrong, when life seems an unending assault of despair, hope is the little voice that says to keep holding on. That even the most astronomical odds are better than nothing. That life isn't perfect, but it sure beats the alternative.

This is the story of a hopeful woman.

(Content note: this is also the story of a woman who regularly and dangerously self-medicated, and one who dealt with lifelong severe mental health issues, including suicidal ideation. If you are young and inexperienced in these issues—or like me, middle-aged and inexperienced—it may feel troubling. If you are experienced in these issues, it may be troubling for other reasons. I can't leave it out, though: I'm not telling Carrie Fisher's story if I exclude it.)

Episode I:
The Princess Cut Or Rebel, Rebel

"Sometimes I do pretend I am a princess. I pretend I am a princess, so that I can try and behave like one."
—Frances Hodgson Burnett, A Little Princess .

Chapter 1: Hopefuls

Princess Leia Organa of Alderaan walks over to Han Solo and sits opposite him in a captain's chair.

"Well," she says, smoothing a strand of hair off her forehead, "the databank in Artoo is still secure." She's at ease, comfortable, high status, and speaking in a plummy aristocratic accent.

"Well then, I think we ought to have the reward you were talking about," Han says, underplaying his request. "And I hope it will be substantial, considering what we've been through already."

The princess sighs, making a not-just-yet hand gesture. "When Artoo has been safely delivered to my forces, you get your reward." She raises her head, as if conferring a blessing on her words. "You have my guarantee." She sounds like a teacher making a deal with a student.

"What's the little droid carrying that's so blasted important?"

Leia's response is a brainmelter—"The plans and specifications to a battle station with enough firepower to destroy an entire system"—and she delivers it with matter-of-fact emphasis. She shrugs her shoulders, an "isn't-this-obvious?" gesture. "Our only hope in destroying it is to find its weakness... which we will determine from the data that I stored in Artoo."

She takes a breath, leans in, and as she speaks she emphasizes with her left hand. "We captured the plans in a raid on the imperial shipyard, but we, whoo"—here she exhales her breath to shorthand the heartache of what happens next—"we fell under attack before I could get the data to safety, so I hid it in this Artoo unit and sent him off." She usually does not explain herself, but she is choosing to do so for this man.

"Yeah, and now where are you taking us?"

She nods her head and says, "The fourth moon of Yavin," like it's the solution to a riddle. "I've given the coordinates to Chewbacca."

Han protests. "Don't you understand? They let us go. They're going to follow us, they want to find your hidden bases!" As he says this she nods and nods, two steps ahead of Han.

"I know they'll follow," she says, again speaking like she's telling a juicy secret. "And they'll bring the Death Star. But our only hope is to destroy it before it destroys us." Her eyes are tractor beams locked onto Han's face.

She continues the charm offensive, repositioning herself literally and psychologically. "Hiding is useless now," she tells Han with unerring confidence. "With the Death Star, they will continue to destroy systems until they found us. We have no alternative but to, to process the information and use—"

CUT!

That is where Carrie Fisher's audition tape for Princess Leia Organa ends. Around her is not the cockpit of the Millennium Falcon but backstage at Goldwyn Studios in West Hollywood. There are rugs layered over top other rugs, mismatched chairs, and wooden cleats wrapped with taut rope against the far wall. An off-screen voice asks for her name and age. "Carrie Fisher, 19," she says, smiling to the camera. It is December 30, 1975: a *Star Wars* star had been born.

Before anyone yells "Action!," casting rooms like this are where movies live or die. Ignore the casting-couch jokes: well-written, competently produced films will fail if the casting isn't spot-on. This is arguably a film director's most important job.

Director George Lucas sat watching Carrie from a huge rattan peacock chair. The ornate chair was doing more communicating than he was: the man was as monotone and emotionless as one of the robots from his script. "He really wasn't into facial expressions," Carrie quipped later. She had seen his previous film *American Graffiti*—a big hit all about high school and fast cars—three times. It was wonderful. Now she was trying to be wonderful for him.

It didn't appear to be working.

Every actor, Carrie included, left George's audition assuming they didn't get the part. But that was George: he'd react the same to winning the lottery and having his foot run over by a cement mixer. (This quietness became an aid on set, where it transformed into unflappable confidence.)

George's problem with casting Leia came from this certitude of his. He had a finished movie in his head. He could see each shot and its specific length and camera angle and blocking. As a director, his job was to visually transcribe those images. But he didn't have a Leia in his head. He didn't know what he was looking for, so he couldn't find it anywhere.

"With film, in a close-up, you are looking into somebody's eyes," George said. "You are not only looking at the person as an actor, you are also looking at them as a human being. So I have to rely half on the human being and half on the actor." Each new Leia audition rewrote the character in George's mind, as he plugged them into the story and imagined the story playing out. Despite her meager screentime, Leia was the lynchpin of the whole film: the actress had to embody the six impossible things demanded of her in the script.

Carrie's audition scene partner was a carpenter named Harrison Ford, who handled the Han Solo line readings for each new Leia. He was doing it as a favor to George, who'd cast him in *American Graffiti*. Often actors have to read against a script supervisor, who can sound like a court reporter reading back testimony. Harrison knew how to act. He also knew, though, that George didn't want anyone from his last film in this one: Han Solo would be anyone *but* Harrison Ford. His job was to let others knock one out of the park, not homer one himself. So Harrison half-committing, playing Han with a seen-it-all laconic malaise.

The first round of Leia auditions was a real cattle call: hundreds of actresses came in, one every few minutes. There was no acting: they simply entered, said hi, made small talk, and left. For days and days, George looked for Leia in a haystack this way.

At least he wasn't looking by himself. George was sharing his star search with a director friend of his, who was also looking for young faces. The friend's film was quite different—a horror movie set in high school. Anyone auditioning for George Lucas' *Star Wars* would also be seen for Brian De Palma's adaptation of Stephen King's debut novel *Carrie*. (Perhaps hearing the word "Carrie" said over and over during casting had a subliminal influence on George.) George was supposed to give the opening speech to each actress, but DePalma soon began doing all the talking. This was fine by George.

DePalma eventually found his Carrie in Sissy Spacek, but George kept looking for Leia. "I have them do readings, then videotape tests, then film tests," George said of his casting process. "Each time, I weed people out. By the time I get down to an actual film test, I've really gotten to know that person. I've gotten to know their acting ability, and all the ramifications of their personality."

5

This process had worked in the past, but for Leia, he kept panning without finding gold. Without a Leia, he couldn't commit to any of the Hans he had seen, or any of the Luke Starkillers, since their chemistry with Leia might be off. Desperation kicked in. He started soliciting local college students to show up. He considered finding a Japanese actress to play Leia, filming her scenes in another language. He considered recasting the entire film with short actors.

Maybe going the unknown route wasn't working. George took a meeting with *Taxi Driver* and *Freaky Friday's* Jodie Foster. She could work as Leia. But she was 17, and as a minor she was required to have a tutor, which meant fewer hours on set per week. (This is one reason why teenagers in films and TV are often played by young adults.)

Leia was at heart a fighter. Storyboard drawings of her showed a comic-book Amazon, tall and strong, in an outfit of an ornate headdress and Eastern European robes. That's who George thought he was looking for: a hardened, larger-than-life warrior, a Maureen O'Hara. But audiences also had to be worried for her, and feel for her losses. If she looked like Wonder Woman, audiences would be certain she'd escape her confines. So a fighter with a vulnerable side. Oh, and also a senator diplomat princess teenager.

No wonder George couldn't find her.

If all else fails, he could do what generations before him did, and cast a Playboy Bunny. It's what the James Bond films did: they were beautiful, and who cared if most couldn't act? But he was aiming to make a family movie. That meant casting an actual teenager, who the female audience would identify with as much as the male half would with Luke.

Back against the wall, George was going to pick Amy Irving, who had auditioned well enough to also land a leading role in *Carrie*. But a casting-director friend, Fred Roos, kept pushing George to go another way. Roos had cast not only *American Graffiti* but also *The Godfather*: he knew his stuff, and had quite the track record. (Roos was also the one who sneakily convinced George to have Harrison Ford do Han's line readings, correctly figuring that it would become a stealth audition.)

Roos had a more straightforward idea for casting Princess Leia. He remembered meeting an unforgettable teenager named Carrie Fisher at a soirée. The phrase "life of the party" was coined with someone like her in mind. Wherever she was, inhibitions loosened, jokes flew, alcohol flowed, looks were exchanged, secrets came out, fun was had. She was a giant personality in a petite frame, like if Falstaff possessed Gidget.

Carrie was an aspiring actress, Roos remembered, and felt her particular brand of spunk could fill the Leia-shaped hole in the script. She was young and pretty, with a wit and a manic exuberance that seemed like how a space princess *could* be. Carrie's face, Roos felt, was the one to launch a thousand spaceships.

Carrie was, at the time of the first auditions, 6,000 miles away, studying acting in London. No one would fly across an ocean for a two-minute casting call. But as the weeks went by without a Leia, Roos kept hoping Carrie would. Once the semester ended, Roos found out she had returned to Los Angeles for winter break. He arranged for her to come in. "I thought I'd totally missed testing for it," Carrie recalled.

She went in and had her two-minute meeting, made some small talk. She explained she had had one previous acting credit, and was going to acting school in London. She stuck her foot in her mouth once or twice out of nervousness, but managed to extract it. DePalma asked what would happen with college if she got either role: Carrie said she'd probably leave.

That day, since she was there, DePalma gave her "sides"—a selection of the script—from his horror movie. Carrie was auditioning to play, as she put in, "Carrie as Carrie in *Carrie*." It was a mother-daughter scene: mild Carrie vs her evil mom.

The *Star Wars* sides came in the mail a few days later. "The dialogue for the test was even more difficult than the dialogue that ended up in the film," Carrie said. "It was space triple-talk, killer lines." There was one scene where Leia was picked up by a giant alien monkey thing, and another where she told a space captain about secret plans.

Carrie drilled and drilled the lines, running them ad nauseum. Her friend Miguel Ferrer played Han to her Leia. She didn't want to trip over a word in front of everyone, ruining her big break. "I was caught by my mother and some of my family rehearsing it in my underwear," she said. "I would come out of the bathroom and say, 'General Kenobi!' My family thought I was crazy, because the dialogue was 'A battle station with enough firepower to destroy an entire system.'"

According to *Star Wars* historian Chris Taylor, Carrie had been practicing tongue twisters all semester in London, for fun. "I want a proper cup of coffee from a proper copper coffee pot. If I can't have a proper cup of coffee from a proper copper coffee pot, I'll have a cup of tea." Challenging dialogue was her cup of tea, from a proper copper pot.

Carrie arrived for her audition with her hair tight against her head, and no makeup: she dressed for a job interview. This was also how she saw Leia: no-nonsense, tough, severe. Looking the part might help. It was more in character than bell bottoms and a feathered cut. But the audition crew took one look at Carrie and realized she had made a mistake.

Filmmaking has a shorthand: when a character coughs, you know they're dying. If two people "meet cute," they will immediately fall in love. Much of that shorthand was based in discrimination: if you wanted the part you had to "look the part." And "looking the part" was code for a sometimes monstrous series of assumptions, prejudices, and sweeping generalizations.

That conventional wisdom extended even to the attractive white people who seemed to otherwise benefit from it the most. A young woman with her hair back and no makeup does not represent regal power and determination. No, she represents manhating shrewishness. In trying to dress as a cool princess, Carrie had missed the mark, and landed on ice queen.

That wouldn't do, and there was no time to topple the patriarchy. So an ersatz glam team found a more youthfully feminine outfit for Carrie to wear, added some makeup, and let her hair down so it softly framed her face. She would act exactly as hardened and battle-weary as before, but she'd do so while looking like a college coed. The words of a warrior, coming out of the face of a debutante.

Carrie's audition was filmed in black and white from over Harrison's shoulder. She recorded a second take with more forceful confidence in her delivery, which proved she could take direction. The audition set-up helped: other Leias had to sit next to Han side by side, like they were passengers in a taxi. But Carrie and Harrison faced each other, a classic set-up for conflict. Carrie also got an entrance, which made her seem busy and vital.

"That day I think they had 10 or 15 people [auditioning]," Carrie remembered. "I didn't hear anything for about three weeks, so I thought 'Well, I'm not going to get to have lunch with monsters.'" Monsters? She was referring to the alien bar featured in the film, the Mos Eisley Cantina, already famous even in preproduction. None of Leia's scenes were set in the cantina, but if she got the part, she figured she could get George to beef up her role. "I wanted to be involved in all of it," she said.

If you watch the footage, Carrie plays up Leia's confidence, certitude, and backbone, projecting a calm majesty. She uses the soothing tone a child would use to defuse an angry parent. It made sci-fi words like "Yavin" and "Chewbacca" sound as ordinarily believable as "walkie-talkie" or "transistor radio." Hers was a kosher performance: no ham, no cheese.

She had no way of knowing this, but that was exactly George's take as well. He was going to film everything like a documentary: no sweeping crane shots that called attention to themselves, no spectacular entrances. This extraordinary world needed to be shown as ordinary. This would allow for the emotional journeys of archetypical characters—the innocent farmboy, the rapscallion, the wise old man—to feel outsized and extraordinary.

Again and again George watched the black and white clips of his proto-Leias. Cindy Williams, another *American Graffiti* alum, read Leia faster and nastier than Carrie: she was wrong for Leia, but would soon find fame as the latter half of *Laverne & Shirley*.

Another on-tape audition was Terri Nunn, spunky and energetic and all of 15. Harrison did no favors to Nunn; he muffed his lines and asked to start over, then sat away from her for the whole audition, radiating discomfort and irritation. At the end of the audition he patted her back the way you'd comfort someone who just lost a game. She'd find fame as well, as the lead singer of the band Berlin.

George now had two possible Leias, Carrie and Amy Irving. But "this other girl [Amy] couldn't do sweet and goofy. Whereas with Carrie, if she played a tough person, somehow underneath it you knew that she really had a warm heart. So I cast it that way. The princess is one of the main characters, so the actress was going to have to be able to generate a lot of strength very quickly with limited resources available—and I thought Carrie could do it."

George's description of Leia's qualities sounds remarkably like those of a director—"able to generate a lot of strength very quickly with limited resources." An introvert, he struggled on each film set, where he had to talk with 100 people a day. He couldn't really direct actors beyond saying "faster" or "more intense." He invariably got sick on set with stress-related maladies. He was in no way Leia-like.

That is, save for one personality trait: defiance. George learned it from his sisters—"we used to fight, our whole lives together"—and it had nothing to do with size and everything to do with spine. George hated the

9

Hollywood studio system, with its nonbinding deal memos in lieu of proper contracts. With his *American Graffiti* success, he fought for final cut, for casting decisions, and most crucially for the rights to sell merchandise and author sequels. The studio, Fox, was surprised—he doesn't want more money? Why not? What's wrong with him? George spent his days hobnobbing with people he hated to be around, just to get the control he needed to never have to deal with them again.

At heart, Leia was a leader, and George knew the qualities a leader needed to have were everything he lacked. "There was a very mature streak than ran through Carrie," George said. Carrie seemed to be George's exact opposite: wild and outgoing, decisive and empathetic, a lover of the spotlight. George's antipode. He would always say Luke was his on-screen alter ego—hence why Luke is named Luke, like Lucas—but Leia was his fantasy personality made flesh. His little sister, unleashed upon the world.

And perhaps Carrie's magnetic personality could imbue Leia with the polestar qualities she needed. George had—accidentally, without meaning to, completely inadvertently, won't happen again—written Leia as a three-dimensional character. Depending upon the scene, she could be a tough dame, a distraught heroine, a Katherine looking for a Petruchio, all three at once, or just an emotional teenager.

The decision to cast Carrie cemented everything. "I think if George had chosen [Christopher] Walken," Harrison said, referring to another frontrunner for Han Solo, "the princess would have been Jodie Foster." But since he picked Carrie, the die was cast for Harrison as Han: sparks flew during that audition faceoff. And Harrison had had a rapport with a young actor named Mark Hamill: Hamill's little-brother vibe clicked well with Harrison's pot-dealer chill. (Mark had in fact auditioned the same day as Carrie.) George cast Mark as well. All three had each other to thank for their roles.

The stars of *Star Wars* had finally aligned.

Chapter 2: Extreme Close-Up

Carrie's agent rang her up, got her on the line, and said two words: "They called." It was bad news, Carrie knew: no good conversation ever began with "they called."

No one except her agent. "They want you," he said.

"They do? I mean, they did?" Then she let the phone fall, and ran out into the front yard, whooping for joy. Her younger brother Todd watched from the doorway: his big sister had gotten that cheesy fantasy film after all, where she was the kidnapped princess. She was going to be the biggest film MacGuffin since the Maltese Falcon. (Which happened to be in the house a few feet away: long story.)

Carrie was enrolled in London's Royal Central School of Speech and Drama, but she couldn't be on set and at school at the same time. The point of such a school was to eventually be good enough to land acting work, right? She would learn on the job.

Accepting the job made her a college drop-out. But Carrie was used to it: she was already a high school dropout.

At age 15, after Carrie's freshman year in high school, her mom had gotten a job in New York. She was a famous singer and actress, and would be headlining a Broadway musical called *Irene*. Carrie and Todd had the choice of staying home in LA with their stepfather, or transferring across the continent for half a year. Sweetening the deal, her mom had talked the production into hiring Carrie as a chorus girl. Todd wasn't a singer, so his job would be selling programs.

Carrie had an amazing voice, a strong alto that seemed like a sight gag emanating from such a small frame. When her mom sang on the road, or set up shop in Vegas, Carrie would sometimes pop out to sing "Bridge Over Troubled Waters." Her pipes could do the difficult song justice. "Her voice is a brass band parading through her throat," Carrie would write about a fictional version of herself, "an express train to your ears."

11

Now audiences could catch that train eight shows a week, at Times Square's huge Minskoff Theater.

Irene was a Roaring '20s period piece, and the chorus singers all had matching uniforms. Carrie's stage outfit included a wide-collared shirt, and an equally wide bow holding back her hair. In a bit of literal foreshadowing, her silhouette quite resembled Leia's.

During a tryout in Washington DC, the troupe performed for a mid-Watergate President Nixon, his only such outing in five years. Nixon was a fan of Carrie's mom, and had invited her to the White House right after his reelection in 1972. Mom forced Carrie to come with her. Nixon sent her an autographed picture afterwards, writing "May all your dreams come true." (Carrie, as liberal as they made them in 1970s southern California, would hang it up in her bathroom.)

While living in New York, Carrie's mom enrolled her not in regular high school but the Professional Children's School. This was where child actors went—the "professional children" of the school's name. Carrie took a cab ride down from the Upper West Side each morning to school, to learn with the current crop of New York's child stars. The school featured special hours that catered to children who had to stay up until 11 p.m. every night singing and dancing, and individualized education that was a mix between a one-room schoolhouse and a Montessori school.

Carrie's mom had a lot on her plate at the moment. Starring in a developing Broadway show is taxing for seasoned pros: new songs, new dialogue, new choreography. This was her first time doing it on stage, so despite Mom moving her family across the country, she had little time to spend with them. Plus there was why Mom was performing: she needed divorce money.

Mom was going to sing and dance her way out of her bankruptcy like she was a Judy Garland character. She felt that pure razzle-dazzle could fix almost anything. She bent over backwards to help Carrie find acting parts. Carrie, even though she was raised in show business, did not have any burning desire to be on stage. Many nights she panicked before showtime. The price for staying by her mom's side during this ordeal was putting on a show, so she would pay that price.

This wasn't to say Carrie and her mom were buddy-buddy. "It's a teenager's job," she said, "to find her parent annoying and ridiculous." She'd barricade herself in her room at all possible hours, rarely leaving except for food, or to discreetly smoke bad pot. On shopping trips with mom, she'd pick out the most expensive items, often as gifts for other people, just to see if her mom would buy it for her. Mom never did, which made Carrie resent her almost as much as if she had given in.

Todd was the Gallant to Carrie's Goofus. He saved money by taking the subway instead of cabs, and started cleaning up selling programs. But he hated school, and with his show profits, he bought good pot. In the afternoons, he and Carrie would declaim the genius of Tubular Bells on the hi-fi while stoned. Family, 1970s style.

One night, while Carrie was at a disco that didn't card, she got a phone call from her mom. Todd was at the hospital: he had been shot. Carrie and a friend raced home to a scene out of a nightmare. No one was home, there was a recently fired gun on her mother's bed, the bedding was shredded, and bloodstains led out the door.

It had been an accident. Todd had been playing with a prop gun, and the blank inside it had discharged, clipping his leg. Carrie got to work hiding some of Todd's other guns (and flushing some contraband) before the police arrived. But a child shot by an unlicensed firearm, even accidentally, was enough for trouble. Police told Mom she had to come with them to be arrested.

The processing took all night long. By the time they got back home it was sunrise, and the press were waiting downstairs. Word had gotten out that a famous actress' son had been shot. Was that true?, they asked Carrie. "Todd wouldn't brush his teeth, so Mom shot him," she joked.

In retrospect, it's a perfect Carrie Fisher Sentence: morbid, funny, concealing, and over the top. But reporters didn't expect humor from a 15-year-old girl talking to them on the record. They ran the quote as the straight truth: Carrie's famous mom had tried to kill her own son.

If Carrie's mom was actually going to shoot a member of her family, it wouldn't be Todd. Carrie and Todd's stepfather Harry Karl had had left the family millions in debt. Carrie knew many sordid specifics about this, specifics she hid from Todd. Todd, in turn, hid that Harry was inviting call girls over every day, and paying them with their mom's money. As for their biological dad, Carrie and Todd barely had a relationship with him, despite sharing his last name, Fisher.

After *Irene* ended its Broadway run, Carrie accompanied her mom on a singing tour in Europe. While they were in London, Carrie signed up for correspondence courses to continue her schooling. She also announced she'd signed herself up for the prestigious Royal Central

School of Speech and Drama. She had to audition to get in, twice, but made the cut. Few Americans ever had.

While in London, the family received invites to Mick Jagger's birthday party. Upon entering the flat, they saw celebrities drinking and drugging. Jagger pulled Carrie's mom aside and said upstairs was even worse. He made sure Carrie stayed downstairs. It felt like a doomed party. (It was. The singer Cass Elliot was at that party that night, and despite staying clean and sober, would die a day later.)

Once they returned to LA, Carrie decided to skip drama college, and also to skip rematriculating back to high school. Instead, she would "figure out what I want to do." "Figuring out" entailed staying in bed all day, flipping through pages of everything from Fitzgerald and Hemingway to romance comics. Other days she just watched daytime TV.

Carrie hadn't meant to drop out: it was just easier than getting out of bed.

* * *

The main reason people drop out of school is academics. Carrie was quite intellectually gifted, so that wasn't an issue. Her teenage years were spent escaping into novels and writing angsty poetry, in the style of Sylvia Plath and Anne Sexton.

Another reason for dropping out is pregnancy. Carrie hadn't had sex yet, so that was off the table. Nor was she mentally or physically disabled, suffering financial distress (her family was broke, true, but rich-people broke), or burdened with caring for someone else.

That left the final reason people drop out: mental illness.

The single biggest challenge of Carrie's life, the one that set the course for everything to come, began when she was 13. That was when her mood disorder began to present. According to a study from the National Institute of Mental Illness, over 50% of teenagers will experience some form of mental illness. It's so common that *not* having a mental illness as a teenager is uncommon.

Yet it's rarely talked about, especially in the 1950s, when Carrie was growing up. Like all the other dirty laundry of life, mental illness was to be hidden: from outsiders, from family, even from yourself. Our vocabulary of insults has as one of its bases mental illness— *nuts, psycho, demented,* above all *crazy.* Why tar and feather yourself by seeking help, when you could tough it out and save face?

As a teenager, Carrie heard and understood society's message: who would want to willingly be associated with straightjackets, orderlies with butterfly nets, and people who claim they're Napoleon? In lieu of treatment, she would pretend she and her brain were fine. She was an actress: she could act sane. But neglect doesn't work any better for a mood disorder than it does for an ingrown toenail. It took her years to realize she was not just dealing with normal adolescent hormones and standard-issue mood swings.

A list of the world's great artists, thinkers, and visionaries could double as a list of those with mood disorders. Marylin Monroe and Abraham Lincoln, Nina Simone and Ludwig von Beethoven. There are thousands more. "No great mind has ever existed without a touch of madness," Aristotle said, words clung to by the off-kilter. Maybe they're just trying to describe how their interior world is different, what Virginia Woolf (another mood disorder A-lister) called "a poverty of the language."

Untreated, mood disorders can be fatal. Almost by definition, those who've died by suicide were not mentally well when they ended their life. Then there are the artists who hid their mental illnesses. And don't forget those who could have been great artists, if mental illness hadn't stopped them from expressing themselves. Society has robbed them of their voices, and we've been robbed of their art.

None of these artists were "normal," "mentally well," or even "sane." It's a bargain out of *Faust*: the ability to create, at the price of an out-of-control self. The twist on this deal is that artists don't make it, it's made for them. They wake up one day and realize they are no longer behind the wheel of their emotions.

Brains regulate and distribute potent psychoactive chemicals, such as norepinephrine, dopamine, and serotonin. Every three-pound lump of gray matter distributes a slightly different cocktail of potent potables. For the mentally ill—those hearing the "Serotonin Operetta" as Carrie called it—a subtle rebalance of that chemical mix can lessen or even resolve most symptoms. Life can go back to "normal."

Carrie fought for that control. Starting at age 15, she went into what would be a lifetime of therapy. Carrie's particular stripe of mood disorder was what was then called manic depression: nowadays it goes by bipolar disorder. But just as no one is a perfect size 6, no one is *just* bipolar. We're all "not otherwise specified," as psychiatry puts it.

The older name of manic depression delineated Carrie's two-toned condition rather well: periods of great energy and enthusiasm, chained to chasms of melancholy. The mild word "depression" suggests a footprint in the snow: to people like Carrie, it felt more like a meteor strike. Some days she couldn't start: other days she couldn't stop. The condition's newer name, bipolar disorder, suggests that it's not the mania or the depression that's the core problem but the shifting between the two. Mood weather, she would call it.

"You know that term 'I could care less?'" Carrie said, years later. "I could. I could care a lot less." She grew obsessed in her manic peaks, and catatonic in her depression valleys. Both manic and depressive episodes could last for days at a time.

In pharmacological terms, there's not much difference between a manic episode and being high on a stimulant like cocaine. When the chemical inversion hits—the bipolarity—what came up comes crashing down. Feelings become muted, like sound underwater. It's not that different from imbibing a chemical depressant like alcohol. Both the high and the low, in other words, can be replicated with drugs and booze.

Many young bipolar people try to self-medicate, to harness their mental illness. Manic for homework, depressive to get a good night's sleep. It's not always easy to alter your brain chemistry, especially via trial and error, mixing prescription medications with under-the-counter remedies. One secret thus becomes two: a person with mental illness becomes a person with mental illness and a habit.

For someone born to wealth and fame, drugs were just one more way to attempt some control to an out-of-control life: Carrie called it "putting the monster in the box." She had what everyone seemed to want: money, celebrity, famous friends, and parties that went strong into the wee hours.

Carrie turned to marijuana first: as a 1970s kid, smoking grass was practically part of the school curriculum. After that came alcohol, maybe a pill if someone had it. "I wanted to be less, so I took more," she said. From the outside she looked like just another good-time party girl. But on the inside, she was conducting experiments, placing pill against pill on the scale, trying to find a balance.

It sometimes felt like other personalities were controlling her moods. Carrie eventually decided to personify them—to get onto a first-name basis with the people in her brain. "Pam" was the introvert, the bookworm, who wrote the poetry and just wanted to do a good job. "Roy" was the extrovert, the wild child, the party animal. The quiet girl and the wild boy: put them together and you got Carrie.

"Pam" and "Roy" didn't mean Carrie had dissociative identity disorder. But for days when she wasn't in control, it helped her to be able to know who was. Some days "Pam" watched aghast as "Roy" made bad decision after bad decision. "It was like I was a car, and a maniac had gotten behind the wheel," she would write later. Other days "Roy" paced like a caged animal when "Pam" was at the wheel, doing damage control for Roy's actions. Fewer and fewer were the days when Carrie got to be herself.

People wondered about Carrie—why would she say that, treat someone that way, sabotage her plans? Carrie wondered those same things about herself.

* * *

Carrie's mom refused to let her mope around at home, not with a sterling opportunity to study acting in England. After a week of fighting—some over the phone, some in person—but her mother eventually convinced Carrie to board a plane for London. She would hate her mom for years for making her go. Once there, she found a mentor and surrogate mother in a family friend, actress Joan Hackett.

In London, Carrie learned about stage acting. Big emotions, huge across your face: opera without the music. She developed her Etonian vowels, so she could sound plummier than the SoCal gal she was. She got her first steady boyfriend. And she learned how to spend: she ran up thousand-dollar phone bills to friends back home and maxed out her charge card.

Without that schooling, she might never have had the confidence, the presence, or the experience to nail an audition, or to be trusted to hold down a leading role in a film. Now, before she knew it, the months of practicing her lines in LA were gone. She was boarding a plane to London, to report to set in a UK soundstage.

The production was saving money by flying her coach—it would be Carrie's very first time flying economy. When Mom found out, she personally called George Lucas to *demand* that her daughter be upgraded to first class. Horrified upon hearing this, Carrie ran to the phone, ripped it away, cursed her mom out, and told George that a cheap seat was fine.

Now if only she'd be allowed to board the plane.

As a student or as a tourist, Carrie could enter the UK. But not as a working actress: in her Majesty's view that was taking a job away from an English actress. They refused the princess a work visa. It took George's producers some convincing, but they explained to the authorities that over 300 UK jobs were being created by *Star Wars'* production. That would put millions of pounds into the British economy. That more than balanced out a handful of American actors, right? The UK grudgingly agreed, after being told that Peter Cushing and Alec Guinness were the leads, and that Carrie, Mark, and Harrison had small roles. *These are not the actors you're looking for.* It worked: the production got a dispensation waiver, and Carrie got her work visa.

With that settled, she was free to worry about less weighty things—like her weight. She had been told to lose 10 pounds before showing up, and had been flown to a celebrity "fat farm" in Texas. There she dined on partridge with Ann Landers and Lady Bird Johnson. But she only lost five pounds. "I thought I was gonna arrive on the set and they'd say 'Well, you didn't lose the other five, so we have this other actress waiting here.'"

Chapter 3: Leia's First Day

On the plane, Carrie read over her scenes yet again. Her first scene described her thusly: "A beautiful young girl (about 16 years old)... surreal and out of place, dreamlike and half-hidden in the smoke..." Well, that described her life so far, right on down to the smoke. But beautiful? "I didn't think I was pretty. I was a little Pillsbury doughgirl."

This would be her second movie. The first was *Shampoo*, a Warren Beatty film about a hairdresser who was bedding all the married women in Los Angeles. (Could have been a documentary.) Carrie, in an interview, said that flirting with Beatty was "a prerequisite for growing up in Beverly Hills and being female." He remembered her from a party a few years earlier: like Fred Roos, he found Carrie unforgettable.

Shampoo was a big production: every woman in Hollywood wanted a role, and the great Paul Simon was doing the music. Carrie got a small role as a Lolita type. Carrie's mom understood what *that* might mean. In full mama-grizzly mode, she thanked Beatty for hiring her daughter, then said "If you *touch* her, I will take a hit out on you." Mom may have been famous, but she was also from Texas. Beatty believed her. Carrie went untouched.

In her role, she was to aggressively come on to Beatty, dropping one of filmdom's first f-bombs. That part at least she was comfortable with: Carrie could curse like a Teamster. Her lines were frank, but that was it: all risqué behavior was implied and off-screen. They wouldn't even kiss.

When Carrie arrived on set—Warren personally picked her up, like it was junior prom—she was given a white tennis outfit to wear. She met Warren, who took a look down at her, and then wondered out loud if the scene might play better if she wasn't wearing a bra under her see-through shirt. Carrie froze. He was the writer, director, and star. She was 17. She went back to a trailer and did what her director wanted. They filmed the scene that way. It took bravery to say no to a request like that, and a different bravery to say yes.

One movie later, and now Carrie was the female lead. One of the few women in the whole production, in fact: ("I wasn't bothered being surrounded by men, no!" she joked. "God, I had no competition!") At least this time there'd be no racy scenes: this *Star Wars* thing was practically G-rated.

After countless readings, Carrie still couldn't really make heads or tails of the script. What was a Dark Lord of the Sith? A Grand Moff? Were Grand Moffs better than regular Moffs? Luckily, actors didn't have to understand the ins and outs of the story, just what emotions to convey while reading their lines.

Carrie's character Leia was a space princess. Princess of what? A country, a whole planet, a solar system? And she was also an ambassador? And a senator? And a teenager? And a rebel spy? (An earlier draft gave Leia mind-control powers as well.) That's a whole lot of backstory just to end up kidnapped: for all her job titles, her plot role was damsel in distress. Playing such an old-fashioned damsel in the era of the ERA might be... distressing.

On paper, Leia had one dominant characteristic: snarkiness. Leia mouthed off to the villainous Darth Vader, to Tarkin, to Luke and Han and Chewbacca. That was how she dealt with a tsunami of emotions: on the run, captured, tortured, rescued, then almost killed about eight times. Snark Carrie could do: years of real-world experience.

Once she landed, Carrie headed to the hotel in London, not far from her old college dorm. After that first night she'd stay at a friend's unoccupied flat in Kensington. The next morning, a studio driver whisked her off to princess her up. Her first stop was Berman's, a famous London costumer, who had been outfitting British stars for decades.

Early designs of Leia's outfit had been bi-colored and skintight, like something Nadia Comăneci would wear for a floor routine. Leia's final outfit, though, was loose and flowing, and flattering to any body type. The elegant robe, designed by costumer John Mollo, had long sleeves that suggested Renaissance-era wealth, along with a habit-like hood to hide her face. A tight belt—designers looked at Jean Harlow films to nail the particular look—cinched her waist. The dress was slitted so she could move around, and thick rubber rain boots occasionally peeked out from under her robe.

And it was all in white: whenever "a long time ago" was, it was before Labor Day. Carrie joked that she knew something new about Leia now: her favorite color. The robe's fabric was not cotton (or organdy or organza) but possibly a special nylon called qiana—sheer and shiny and able to trap heat like a puffy vest. For some promotional pictures she would wear a similar robe with a low neckline, but her on-set "hero costume" was a turtleneck dress.

George decided the technological realms of the film would be "black, white, and gray"—hence Leia, the Stormtrooper, Vader, and Artoo all being essentially monochromatic. The desert planet of Tatooine was the opposite: "tan, brown, and green." This would make the white plastic of the Stormtrooper uniforms stand out in the desert, and the rescuers seem out of place when they're on the austere Death Star.

Mollo and Ralph McQuarrie had wrestled with how much jewelry Leia should be wearing: what princess wasn't bedecked in riches? They decided on none, partly because her wrists and neck were covered by the robe. George had also said he wanted the film's clothing to be utilitarian and unmemorable—the word "nondescript" came up often. Jewelry is descript.

Carrie took some pictures in her new costume: wonderfully, she posed as herself, not Leia. Plenty of "Leia" pictures would follow, with stern commanding looks. But these first shots were Carrie, with shoulder-length hair down, playing dress-up with the uninhibited glee of a five-year-old.

After the photos came a drive up the M1 motorway to the Hertfordshire suburb of Borehamwood, about 12 miles north of London. That's where the EMI Studios were, one of several soundstages around the neighborhood of Elstree. Most people referred to all the studio spaces, under their various names and ownerships, as Elstree Studios. Everything from Hitchcock films to *Moby Dick* to Queen's music videos were filmed here. Maybe Carrie could add some Emma Peel energy to her performance—the British spy show *The Avengers* was shot here too.

Time for hair and makeup. There's a longstanding tradition that no matter the distress a woman in film is in, she always looks her best. For Leia that meant lip gloss, and lots of it. "I had so much lip gloss on you might have slid off and broken your own lips if you tried to kiss me," Carrie said. Industrial quantities of blush and eyeliner made her Death Star runway ready.

But what about Leia's hair? The filmmakers had found their Leia, but not yet her coif. Maybe they would end up copying the film's

21

storyboard artists, who drew Leia with a shaggy bob that made her look like Luke's identical twin. (Imagine that.) Or let her natural hair match Luke and Han's Me-Decade feathered do's.

Before arriving in London, Carrie had gone through multiple hair trials. "I was scared about what they were going to do to my hair, because I had so much hair put on me, two different sessions of that—I had at least 30 hairdos tried on me. And they didn't like it when I got to London," Carrie remembered. Her shoulder-length hair wasn't long enough for some of the wilder ideas, so they augmented her locks with hair extensions and partial wigs, known as flips.

When the final hairstyle was chosen, "flip" seemed the right word to describe Carrie's mental state. "I was a little afraid of it," Carrie said in a prerelease interview. "I still am a little afraid of how I am going to look in it." This had to be craziest, most distracting hairstyle in movie history. Her brown hair was twirled into two spiral chignons, and then nested on the sides of her head. Above the ears, like giant hi-fi headphones. Brunette cinnamon rolls. This was "nondescript?"

In later years, George said Leia's look was inspired by revolutionary women of Mexico from the first decade of the 20th century. More likely he's thinking of pictures of women from the Hopi Nation, whose unmarried women wore their hair in elaborate twin loops called butterfly whorls or squash whorls. The twin buns also resembled the caps that Apollo astronauts wore, nicknamed Snoopy hats. In her book about the making of *Star Wars*, Carrie described it as "17th-century Dutch school matron."

The buns needed a thumbs-up from George. If he said yes, Carrie would need hair extensions, and need to have them woven into the preposterous buns every single day of shooting. George was on set directing, so Carrie was led through the maze of sidewalks winding around nine soundstages to go find him for approval.

Through the labyrinth she wound, deeper and deeper. Past the Millennium Falcon set on Stage 3: the ship was so big they could only build half of it. Past Stage 2's Death Star corridors, row after row of hallways, like supermarket aisles. And past Stage 8, where an alleyway of the desert planet of Tatooine was built. Past there, through a door, and then—just in time for lunch with monsters—Princess Leia found herself inside the Mos Eisley Cantina.

Carrie had grown up on the studio lot: she and Todd had birthday parties on unused standing sets, and they and their friends played pretend using actual movie props and costumes. Todd would be a solider or a cop, and Carrie the nurse who sopped up his fake-blood wounds. This, though, was the first time she had even been on a stage set as an actress.

And, to be frank, some of those birthday-party home movies looked more professional. The cantina set looked horrendous, and not in a wretched-hive-of-scum-and-villainy way. The lighting seemed way too bright. Short people in bad costumes with inflexible masks milled around, like it was Halloween in an elementary school. The set looked like a bad *Doctor Who* episode. What had she gotten herself into?

She found George among this menagerie. He quickly looked at Carrie, and at her hairdo last seen in a Bavarian bakery's cooling rack. He had seen dozens of sketches and photos of Leia hairstyles, but never this. He made one of hundreds of quick decisions that day: "That's okay," he said. In Georgetown, "okay" was as high as praise got. He then asked Carrie if she liked it. She hated it—"you don't put a wide hairstyle on an already wide face!"—but she worried that hating it would get her fired. "It's nice, really nice," she lied. The buns stayed in the picture.

Carrie's next stop was wardrobe, where she got into her white robe, now purposefully smudged a bit so Leia would look rough-and-tumble. (George had a "used-universe" theory for this film: nothing should look new.) She was told, though, to not wear any undergarments. Uh-oh: was this Warren Beatty all over again?

She asked why no bra: did they want *Barbarella*? George was too shy to talk about such things directly with a woman, so a producer explained that George felt there would be no brassieres in space. Bra straps were sexy, George felt, and Leia was not to be sexualized in any way. The last thing he wanted was her to be a cosmic *Charlie's Angel*, ray gun in hand for slow-motion running shots. ("Princesses don't do that," Carrie noted.)

What George did not seem to know—a basic anatomical fact, and the primary purpose of women's undergarments—was that bras were used to *prevent* the exact sort of womanly gyrations that George didn't want to film. Keeping to the spirit and the letter of the law, Carrie's costumers used white gaffer tape to make binding strips for her every day. It wasn't very comfortable, but it was strapless. George didn't seem to notice. What a boob.

After costuming, it was time for shooting. Not shooting a scene;

shooting the blaster. "[F]rom the first day on," Carrie said, "they put a gun in my hand with charges in it, took me to a sound stage, and had me practice shooting it." This was so Carrie would stop wincing when the popcap went off: she'd already taken target practice back in the States with pistols and shotguns, but never a ray gun.

Leia's pistol was a modified Soviet Margolin, adjusted to shoot not .22s but blaster bolts. Set designer John Barry said, "George likes what he calls the 'visceral' quality that real weapons have, so there are really quite large chunks of real weapons with additional things fixed onto them." Leia's weapon was svelte, like a pressure sprayer: it would later be given the name DDC Defender.

No footage was shot her first day, but her look was now complete. She had woken up as Carrie, but by day's ends she was Princess Leia Organa of Alderaan. The robe, the buns, the pistol: almost every piece of poster art from the first film would feature all three of those elements. It was an image of fierce power and grace, especially for a petite person. Judge me by my size, do you?

If only Carrie possessed a fraction of Leia's confidence. She was petrified, still certain they'd replace her the moment she made her first mistake. The next day or so, she heard two men off to one side laughing on set. "Are you laughing at me?" she asked, tiny under her flowered hat and floor-length dress. They weren't, of course. In its own way, low self-esteem can round the horn into self-centeredness: good or bad, everyone must be thinking about me.

* * *

The day Carrie arrived, word got out that a character was going to die in the film. The character was Sir Alec Guinness' Obi-Wan Kenobi. Carrie's version of the script had the wise old man alive at the film's end, at rebel headquarters with Leia as Luke's team to blow up the Death Star. The new script's pages now had Ben dying in a duel with Darth Vader.

Guinness, one of the few "name" actors in the cast, was quite upset over the decision. But George had been swayed by his wife Marcia, an ace film editor who cut films for wunderkinds Martin Scorsese and Steven Spielberg. Marcia knew an audience's emotional reactions far better than her husband did. Without the fatal duel, the lengthy Death Star infiltration sequence had no "stakes" (in moviemaking speak), since the heroes save the princess and escape unscathed. "The villains were like tenpins: they just got knocked over... it totally diminished any impact the Death Star had," George noted. Executives thought they could save some runtime and budget by telling George to end the movie with Leia being saved, but George refused to cut the Death Star dogfight attack.

Killing Ben would solve many problems in one fell lightsaber swoop. It gave the film stakes. It beefed up Vader's villainy: right now he was Tarkin's stooge, not much more than a black-lacquered James Bond henchman. It also would be an easy change to pull off mid-shoot, since Obi-Wan had few scenes after the Death Star rescue. Besides, in stories like this wise old men existed to die, so the hero could stand alone. Obi-Wan was Luke's training wheels. Guinness accepted it: he even suggested Ben be willingly struck down in combat, like a protesting monk.

Each time the script changed, the new pages were printed in a special color. Carrie's new shooting script—the Revised Fourth Draft—looked more like a rainbow every day. In a film where everything was muted and drab, the script was sometimes the most colorful thing on set. Earlier rounds of changes had been due to budget cuts from Fox, a result of their understandable worries the film would be a dud.

Per an older script, Leia would be held hostage on her home planet of Alderaan, described as a gas giant with saucer-shaped floating cities. In the new draft, though, she'd be prisoner of the Death Star itself. This saved a planet's worth of sets, matte paintings, and costumes. Existing Alderaan sets, designed to look bureaucratic instead of imperious, became Death Star sets. This made the Death Star resemble an intergalactic airport—not a gulag but a giant DMV.

Leia also had new dialogue to learn, thanks to a husband-and-wife team of rewriters George brought in, Willard Huyck and Gloria Katz. They'd done similar work on *American Graffiti*, and saw loads of potential in the feisty Leia. In their draft, Leia becomes the one who saves herself, blasting an escape route to the garbage pit. She shoots at Stormtroopers, has more tough-cookie lines, and her sense of responsibility harshes everyone's mellow. "She's sort of a drag and she's a nuisance," George said, possibly projecting.

Plot holes are like shoelaces: sometimes the best remedy is to tie two of them together. In this case, plot hole #1 was that Leia's home planet of Alderaan was now never shown. Plot hole #2 was that the Death

Star, like Vader before he killed Obi-Wan, was not scary: it would get blown up before it fired.

So the rewriters added an interrogation scene between Leia and Tarkin… which ended with the Death Star blowing up Alderaan. Two problems solved, thanks to the single most violent act ever filmed. "Millions of voices suddenly cried out in terror, and were suddenly silenced." The audience would see the destruction from the Death Star's perspective: a cherry bomb detonating inside a Christmas ornament.

How do you act the death of an entire planet? There was no way: that level of grief was impossible to convey. It was truly unthinkable: in none of George's drafts had the Death Star ever *fired*. Carrie's audition scene of Leia blithely luring the Death Star to the rebel base was rewritten: Leia would never be so cavalier about the Death Star. In fact, she would now allow the destruction of her entire planet, just to keep the rebel base's location a secret.

Chapter 4: Pacific Princess

As the new girl on set, Carrie missed out on the bonding that most of the cast and crew had experienced during their weeks in Tunisia filming exteriors. The North African country had doubled for Tatooine, a desert planet. She had missed a big sandstorm, but also the rain and mud. She wasn't there when crew members bought, dissembled, and polished old aircraft engines in order to make fantastic-looking props on location. Worst of all, she missed a literal "come-to-Jesus" moment, when a remote-controlled Artoo rolled its way into the neighboring set of the TV miniseries *Jesus of Nazareth.*

Her fellow day players, save for two Americans, were all Brits. Playing the dog-man Chewbacca was Peter Mayhew, who joked that his entire audition was standing up to reveal his height of seven foot two. (His height had given him a lifelong back problem, so he couldn't sling Carrie over his shoulder, as was originally scripted.) Kenny Baker, a man as short as Peter was tall, crammed himself inside a rolling blinkenlights trashcan to operate R2-D2. A mime named Anthony Daniels played the effete butler robot C-3PO: his costume, resembling a bipedal French horn, was so uncomfortable he'd play many of his scenes out of his heavy copper shoes. David Prowse, a massive bodybuilder with acres of sideburns, played Darth Vader: Carrie joked that she was scared of Vader because his thick country accent might be contagious. Alec Guinness was the doomed Jedi Obi-Wan Kenobi. Peter Cushing, the other "name" actor, was the lethal Grand Moff Tarkin.

Luke Starkiller, the farmboy pilot, was played by Mark Hamill: this was his first movie. He was boyish and blond and radiated positive energy, just like his character. He snuck on set during some of Carrie's early scenes, just to see what she was like in action. True to his character, Mark had a streak of brashness that was quickly punctured. One evening Mark tried a move on Carrie, bragging how good a kisser he was. Carrie immediately called his bluff, and started making out with him before her costar could take a breath. After that show of dominance, Mark decided to be friends, nothing more.

Playing Han Solo was Carrie's audition partner Harrison Ford. He was sly and virile, a carpenter some days, weed supplier others. Now that acting was taking off, his days of hanging doors and selling baggies seemed at an end. He was in his 30s, with a wife and two boys back home in California.

That was awkward, since Carrie had started sleeping with him. She had never had an affair before, never been the other woman, barely even dated. "I began filming *Star Wars* hoping to have an affair," she said; it seemed a continental thing to do, like sipping port wine or visiting museums. A wannabe actress having an affair: Carrie was living out the plot of *Sister Carrie*.

But this was serious: she was a teenager who had fallen in love with her married leading man. It began one evening when the crew had tried to get Carrie liquored up: they succeeded. Harrison stepped in when they were escorting her barely conscious self outside. Harrison wasn't sure of their intentions, and refused to leave her alone. He and Carrie rode back to London together, and after Carrie roused she and Harrison quickly fell to what the Brits call snogging.

They hit another party with some cast members, including Mark. They both played it cool in front of the others. Afterwards, Harrison and Carrie shared a cab, made out some more as it drove to Carrie's Kensington place, and Harrison got out when she did. They spent the weekend together, and every weekend afterwards. During the week they kept their distance on set—people will say we're in love.

Harrison, never a gabber, became positively mute when Carrie brought up any real topic. He did not want to talk about work, or life back home—he lived in the cheapest apartment he could find, so that he could send all his money back to his family—or much of anything. He acted like this relationship was an immediate mistake, one he kept making day after day. He had his charms: when Carrie did her Harrison impression— she slowly moseyed into a room and looked around with disdain— Harrison shook with silent laughter.

When Todd visited the set, Carrie could confide in him, but most days there was no one around she could talk to. She turned to her diary, filling page after page with entries, poems, anything that was in her head. Writing gave her some measure of control.

She'd never let anyone know about the "showmance." It was one more unsavory truth to pack away behind an ever-present smile, a smile she dropped whenever George yelled action, and Leia's tight-lipped grit took over. A role within a role: Carrie pretending to be a put-together person, pretending to be Princess Leia.

Everything was in flux. She'd arrive at work, and the set would look completely different. Leia's lines kept changing, as did everyone else's lines. Luke's entire last name changed, from Starkiller to Skywalker, a name last seen airbrushed on a VW microbus. Leia's last name had changed beforehand, from Aquilia to Antilles to now Organa. Even the film's title almost changed, since the studio worried women would stay away from a movie with *War* in the title. No one won the on-set "NAMING THE MOVIE" contest, since no one had a better idea.

Leia's personality had evolved with the rewrites: she used to be a 14-year-old spoiled brat pampered by ladies in waiting. One early version even had Leia crowned queen at the end of the film, "her true goddess self" revealed to the masses. Now, she was a royal who had spent her life being groomed to shoulder the responsibilities of leadership. Carrie knew plenty of those rich kids, maybe even was one herself some days. But Leia was now resilient and flinty, a Barbara Stanwyck instead of a Marilyn Monroe.

Seen as a character arc, Leia's story is downright grim. She begins the film on the run, her secret life as a rebel recently discovered. She records a distress call, then gets captured. She's repeatedly tortured, then dragged before Tarkin. He blows up her entire planet in front of her, but she doesn't yield. While mute with grief, she gets rescued by the motley crew of a yokel, a dirtbag, a seven-foot dog, and bickering robots. This rescue by a poor man's *Wizard of Oz* crew goes immediately awry, forcing the ersatz Dorothy to take command.

And that was it for Leia. The movie had a third act; yada yada Use the Force, yada yada Death Star explosion. But Leia has no more lines: she just stands around looking worried. At movie's end she reappears in a pretty dress and a better hairstyle, and tosses medals around everyone's necks.

For the first hour, Leia's biggest scene is via blue hologram at one-sixth scale. Her message-in-an-Artoo packs in reams of exposition: we learn Leia's parents are part of the rebellion against the Empire. She apologizes for not appearing in person— *I've been kidnapped, my apologies*—but also requests that Obi-Wan take Artoo to Alderaan. That's an act of treason, but she frames it as a personal favor to her father. All the more remarkable is that Leia makes this exquisitely worded request spontaneously, while on the run: the words off the top of her head are an ethical jujitsu attack.

"This is our most desperate hour," she says in closing, a Churchillian statement. Then the final gut punch: "You must help me, Obi-Wan Kenobi, you are my only hope." Her message is both polite and devious.

And it will get played over and over in the film, like a skipping record. What's remarkable is the lack of desperation in her voice: despite her dire straits, she sounds like she's fundraising for a worthy charity. *Obi-Wan Kenobi, please give generously.*

George's dialogue could be a mouthful. He told his actors they had free reign to reword things. But changing lines was a responsibility Carrie didn't dare to try: she wasn't a screenwriter! Her job was to make the lines work, to alter *herself* to fit *them*. Most of the other cast felt similarly. "The script was the Bible for me," Mark said. "There were lines I just couldn't say, but I learned to say them." He approached the lines with the eagerness of a fraternity pledge during hell week.

Harrison, however, was different: perhaps Han's damn-the-photon-torpedoes attitude was contagious. He started to move lines around at will, reword them to match his own laconic cadence. For one laugh-out-loud scene he made up hilariously inadequate excuses for why there was a fight in a cell block. Han's wounded braggadocio became tailor-made for Harrison, in a way Luke and Leia's lines did not for Mark and Carrie.

"I was very impressed that he could do that," Carrie said. "I didn't know what to do with [the lines]. They seemed fine like they were. I was also being agreeable because I kept thinking they were going to realize their mistake about hiring me." She wouldn't alter any of her lines, no. But a seed had been planted.

* * *

There are two types of princesses: real and imaginary. Imaginary princesses are the stuff of fairy tales, Disney cartoons, and far-off towers. They exist to be rescued, bartered with, won as a prize. Real princesses fared worse: historically, they existed to be married off to the sons of political rivals. They were property, rewards, breedstock.

If winning a princess was the reward for boys, becoming one was the reward for girls. Pippi Longstocking and Dorothy Gale are characters who have had such royalty bequeathed on them. Lucy and Susan Pevensie from *The Chronicles of Narnia* double-jumped their competition, becoming queens. Why girls want to be princesses is easily answered: it's what society tells them is their most valued role in society.

The pulp novels of the early 20th century introduced a new type of imaginary princess. In these two-fisted tales of heroic explorers, princesses carried guns and swords. They were hypercompetent, and also hypersexualized: they often came from worlds where clothing was optional. Yet these strong female characters (such as Wonder Woman) were nevertheless plopped into stories where they were kidnapped and had to be rescued by a handsome hero.

Leia's closest fictional antecedent is someone along the lines of Dejah Thoris, the titular *Princess of Mars* from Edgar Rice Burroughs' adventure novel. Thoris is captivatingly beautiful, often captured, always stark naked, and—save for the bad habit of constantly getting abducted—incredibly competent in all human/Martian endeavors. Thoris inspired dozens of other space princess, painted in seductive poses on the covers of ratty paperbacks. Leia's name may come from one of those antecedents, Princess Alia from Frank Herbert's *Dune*.

Leia's character also hearkens back to the serious-minded, driven women who led social movements of the previous 100 years. The leaders of the tolerance, suffrage, and peace movements were all notably female. Leia the dangerous revolutionary is the sort of person Pulitzer winner Laurel Thatcher Ulrich was thinking of when she said, "Well-behaved woman seldom make history." (Carrie would later put that quote on her fridge.)

George created *Star Wars* screenplay by kitbashing all of his favorite stories together. For Leia, he combined attributes of every heroine he could remember from books, comics, movies, and real life. Leia wasn't Susan B. Anthony or Boudica or Joan of Arc or Catwoman: she was all of them.

* * *

If there was such a role as an American princess, Carrie was it. Growing up, Carrie and Todd were among the rich and famous, stars of stage and screen. The scions of famous people were everywhere, from the school hallway to the bathroom mirrors.

Her family had recently downsized due to the impending divorce: they were in a mere mansion now, not a full-on estate. It had only one pool instead of three, like the previous house. ("You know," Carrie joked, "in case two of them break.") This was one of their four homes: despite the bankruptcy, their lives were still luxurious. Carrie's bed was not just any bed but the bed Marlon Brando used as Napoleon Bonaparte in a film called *Désirée*. Her car was the red MG-TD Marilyn Monroe and Cary Grant used in *Monkey Business*.

"Be kind to the children of movie stars," Carrie wrote in a poem, published while she was walking the halls of Beverly Hills High. "Expectations to live up to/Comparisons to live down/Limelight is their legacy/Those children who tumbled from golden wombs." The school itself was famous for tumbling: Beverly Hills High contained the gym with the pool that James Stewart and Donna Reed fell into in *It's a Wonderful Life*.

She was part of a new generation of Hollywood talent, the sons and daughters of the stars of the '50s and '60s. Janet Leigh and Tony Curtis' daughter Jamie Lee Curtis starred in *Halloween*. Tippi Hedren's daughter Melanie Griffith romanced Gene Hackman in *Night Moves*. Lloyd Bridges' two sons, Jeff and Beau, joined the family business as well. By royal decree, these were the new princes and princesses of Hollywood. (Of course, that fame could double as "nepo-baby" notoriety: your parentage preceded you into every room. Michael Douglas found great success as an actor, and won an Oscar for producing *One Flew Over the Cuckoo's Nest*, but he was Kirk Douglas' kid in most people's eyes.)

Carrie's mom was a performative mom: she frequently had camera crews around documenting her love for her kids. She had reporters cover when she hosted Carrie's Girl Scout meetings. When alone, she used a spring-wound camera: sometimes it didn't even have film in it. "Affection was expressed," Carrie put it in one of her novels, "without being too frequently demonstrated." Decades before social media made it popular, her mom was a sharenting pioneer. There's no greater love than the kiss of a lens. This constant exposure made Carrie and Todd nickname their house the Fish Bowl.

The family owned a beach house in Malibu, and found out one day that their new next-door neighbor was actress Connie Stevens. Connie was Carrie and Todd's former stepmom. This coincidence allowed Carrie to grow close with her younger stepsiblings Joely and Tricia, who found in Carrie a cool big sister.

One night when Carrie was very young, the security guard caught an intruder breaking into her mom's second-floor bathroom window. After that, Carrie and Todd were always a little bit scared, for their mom and for themselves. "This subtext of fear made Carrie more fragile and edgy," Todd wrote.

She developed insomnia. If Mom sang Todd a bedtime song, he'd be out before she hit the bridge. But her nightly performance for Carrie would go on and on, song after song. "Mom would rub her back, rub her feet, sing to her, read to her, stroke her hair, anything she could think of," Todd said, "but Carrie's mind wouldn't and couldn't slow down enough to give her enough peace to doze off." What mother couldn't do, mother's little helper could: young Carrie was given over-the-counter sleeping pills to help her conk out.

Carrie would put on shows as a teenager for the regular audience of tour buses who visited Mom's house. These shows grew to be elaborate affairs, with special-effect "squibs" thanks to Todd, so they could have gunfights and death scenes.

Carrie had her mother's face, with delicate porcelain-doll features, and her mother's height, barely squeaking over the five-foot mark. She developed her mother's figure, as well as mom's pipes: she could sing to the back row without a mic. But Carrie wanted to act, not sing. "The biggest thing I did that broke my mother's heart," Carrie said, years later, "was not do a nightclub act."

* * *

One of Carrie's first filmed Leia scenes was her confrontation with Grand Moff Tarkin. Many Death Star scenes were filmed on the same set, each day dressed differently. Expensive plastic panels with industrial verisimilitude were lined up to create walls, then moved or replaced for different scenes. A Tinkertoy design, for what George called a Tinkertoy movie.

Peter Cushing was one of the faces of 1970s horror. But Carrie had grown up around actors: she was well aware that they were not the characters they played. In Cushing, Carrie saw only a kind grandfather.

33

A man who bicycled to his wife's grave most mornings before filming, and who religiously brushed his teeth before filming to ensure he never had bad breath. The "foul stench" line of Leia's was fiction: "The man smelled like linen and lavender," Carrie remembered.

How was she supposed to look at this gentle soul—who was wearing carpet slippers because his character's jackboots were uncomfortable—with hate? How was she supposed to play someone refusing to crack under pressure? She couldn't keep a secret to save her life. How many days would it be before everyone realized they'd hired a fraud? She'd only *acted* like she could act!

The filming that day wasn't perfect. Carrie kept drifting into Cushing's cut-glass British accent. Cushing mispronounced Leia's name as "Lee-uh." (Both mistakes stayed in the film.) The fault lay with George, who should have corrected his actors, the way you'd tell someone they had spinach in their teeth.

Cushing, an old pro, could turn up his calculated malevolence, and Carrie found she could respond in kind. It helped if she imagined Cushing as an authoritarian from her life, one she had a violent dislike of. (Who that person was, she never revealed. Maybe she could keep a secret after all.)

George told Carrie to deliver her lines with less sass and more anger. Leia wasn't mouthing off to a teacher: she was standing up to oppression. When she did so, the scene gelled. Soon you could almost see the history between them, the dozens of diplomatic functions where civility forced them to wear fake smiles, offer limp handshakes, pretend to not despise each other.

After her big day of filming, Carrie received no further feedback about her performance. "George didn't say anything," Carrie remembered, "which I took to mean 'he's mad.'" But that was just George. "The next day George came up to me with his hand on his beard and said 'you were great yesterday,'" Carrie said. "And from then on I knew that when he didn't talk, that it was okay—that less was more with him… I think Harrison told me that."

Chapter 5: "The Most Expensive Low-Budget Film of All Time"

Carrie had never had a proper relationship, and now she was in a very improper one.

Growing up she lived around the theater, and developed crushes on gay men. Like many girls before her, Carrie found this was a safe, nonreciprocal way to like a boy. (From her book *Postcards from the Edge*: "It's like when I was younger and I used to fall in love with homosexuals, because they had rejected me before they even met me.") But sexuality is on a spectrum, and some of the men Carrie were interested in were interested back. The crushes turned into make-out sessions. They both told each other they were practicing for men.

Mom told Carrie one day that she wanted her daughter's first time making love to be special. So, to ensure it would be, she volunteered to be in the room, for Carrie and her gay boyfriend, as a coach. Needless to say, Carrie turned this offer down.

Her only real boyfriend had been at college, and they'd taken it slow for a year. So many bad decisions, so little actual relationship experience. It all led to the moment she was in now: in bed with her costar, breaking up a marriage. If she left Harrison, the tension on set could wreck the film. She felt trapped, like Leia: different bars, same cage.

Maybe that was the key. Not to her off-screen life—that was a trainwreck—but to understanding Leia. Carrie got through each day with nerve, brusque strength, and being true to what she was feeling at the moment, regardless of the consequences. That was who Carrie's Leia needed to be: peppery, indomitable, snide. Her Leia would be toughened by life's stresses, annealed like a piece of metal, softened like a piece of leather, worn like a marble step.

Putting the buns on took two hours every morning, time Carrie usually spent asleep in the make-up chair. She got a reprieve for the ceremony scene set inside in a cavernous Yavin pyramid. It took place at film's end but was shot mid-production, in London's vast Shepperton Studios. Hundreds of extras, wearing an outrageous mish-mash of uniforms pilfered from other films, filled the hall as the rebel faithful. Carrie got to wear a new white dress for this show, with an actual neckline, along with silver flats and a necklace of chunky silver. And no buns.

The ceremony had no dialogue to memorize, just Leia bestowing medals upon Luke and Han. Carrie flashed Mark and Han a pair of Mona Lisa smiles, which meant different things to each of them. Between shots Carrie was a joy to behold: what could have been endless bore became magical. JW Rinzler credited Carrie's on-set "infectious humor and smile" for making the filming go smoothly that day.

The production had more than its fair share of technical problems. An X-Wing's canopy refused to open, forcing the actor inside to break out. The rear-projection backgrounds didn't look good: they'd all have to be refilmed with bluescreens. David Prowse kept breaking Vader's prop light sabers, and the Stormtrooper's costumes were so limited in vision as to be claustrophobic. With all those technical issues, the last thing needed was a temperamental actress.

So Carrie kept her head down and tried to make each day of filming as pleasant as she could. It was what Mom would do, why Mom had been America's sweetheart. So she'd, say, run up to Luke's X-Wing during a Yavin scene and hand him a can of beer. Anything to brighten the mood.

Some of her jokes backfired. For instance, one day between takes she started substituting the word "Jew" for "you" in song titles, like "Jew light up my life." "If you do it once or twice it's either in bad taste or not funny," Mark Hamill explained later, "but if you do 35 of them, you're rolling on the ground." Carrie and Harrison were both half Jewish, and indulged in the joke like they were *meshuggeneh*. What the crew saw were Americans being anti-Semitic. The jokes bonded the cast, but separated them further from the crew.

Carrie wasn't the only one trying to keep the mood up: Alec Guinness took the cast to a Greek restaurant one night, where a party broke out. Soon Carrie found herself outclassed as the life of the party by a 62-year-old knight, who rolled up his trouser cuffs to better dance around the room. Opa!

While in his cups, Guinness told stories of past films. He had won an acting Oscar for his role in *Bridge on the River Kwai*, but he was much prouder of the nomination for screenwriting he received the following year. Writing was a truer art than acting, he felt.

Back on set, they refilmed Luke and Leia's meeting in the jail cell, with Mark using "Luke Skywalker" instead of "Luke Starkiller." This scene changed more than most over the years. In one draft Han and Chewie were to spring the princess' cell door, only to find "suspended inside the cell by invisible rays, a bloody and mutilated Leia Organa hangs upside down." Another was described thusly: "She's a tough babe; doesn't appreciate the help... Han punches her in the face and Chewbacca carries her out."

What happened in the version they filmed is in its own way even more disturbing: Luke enters the room in his Stormtrooper disguise, and Leia begins to seduce him. It's over in a moment, but the implication is clear: Leia is flirting with him to find a way out. Her world has been literally destroyed, and she still refuses to pass up an opportunity to escape.

Production seemed forever on the verge of collapse. Even if they got through production, what would be the result? A bunch of second-rate shots of third-rate actors saying fourth-rate dialogue. When studio executives screened dailies, they almost threw in the towel then and there. Where were the establishing shots? Where were the dynamic visuals? Why spend so much on sets if audiences barely saw them? Why did everything look so beat up?

George jumped into damage control mode. This was not his film: it was at best 30% of the movie he was making. The finished film would have special effects shots, sound effects, and a score. And this footage has not been properly edited. George was at heart an editor, and intended to ground his outlandish story with cinema verité editing. Without that grittiness, the dailies came off as inevitably campy. George threw the assembly out and fired the UK editor he had hired to boot.

The suits let him continue filming. George promised he'd film all the extra shots they wanted—"masters," close-ups for all dialogue scenes, and establishing shots. But he never did. Like Leia, George had been bluffing. If he filmed what the executives wanted, then they might take away his movie, edit it traditionally, and deliver a film just as shoddy as those dailies.

No, the only way to save *Star Wars* was to never shoot anything but the right pieces. Piece that would only go together one way: his way.

Chapter 6: Epic Finale

One of the hallmarks of action-adventure is a stunt as old as silent film: the rope swing. Everyone from Tarzan to Quasimodo to Spider-Man has done it. There wasn't a natural place to insert such a scene into the Death Star escape sequence, but George took a swing at finding one.

The set-up: Luke and Leia are separated from the others. Leia closes a door to hold back Stormtroopers, but there's no walkway on the other side, just a sheer drop. Blaster fire starts raining down from open doorways on the other side of the ledge. Luke finds a spool of wire on his Stormtrooper utility belt, attaches a grappling hook, and catches a bit of machinery on the far side of the chasm.

The ledge set was built about 12 feet off the ground: a matte painting created the illusion it was a hundred feet up. Twelve feet was still a hearty distance to fall if something went wrong. Gym mats wouldn't be enough, so the crew stacked empty cardboard boxes under the ledge. "I couldn't see how the boxes were going to prevent me from breaking any bones," Carrie said. Was this worth the $750 a week she was getting paid?

To test the rope swing, two heavy puppets were attached to the rope that would be used for the filming. The puppets survived the test, so then it was Mark and Carrie's turn to be harnessed and hung. If the rope broke, they were only a foot off the ground. It held.

In the film, Leia takes out one Stormtrooper, but more pop up. Behind them, the door is being mechanically jacked open, and Luke and Leia's feet are exposed to a second front of blaster fire. She and Luke have almost no protection, yet avoid getting hit.

This lack of injury became one of George's directing problems; he kept trying to ramp up the combat and action, but the more he did, paradoxically, the less the threat grew. "I got 50 Stormtroopers shooting at three people from 10 feet away," George told Marcia, "and nobody ever gets hurt. Who's gonna believe that?"

Before the swing, Leia was supposed to kiss Luke and say "For luck." (Not that surviving hundreds of point-blank shots wasn't already lucky.) Many takes were required of that line, because Carrie kept blending the two words together, accidentally creating *Star Wars'* first f-word. Eventually she said the "for luck" as two separate words.

The swing itself, after all the prep work, was done in the first take. "I was [supposed] to hold the gun," she said, "which is real heavy, and that scared me because I thought I'd drop it." She was also scared her hair would fall off. But the stunt went off without Carrie's hair buns, or her real buns, hitting the ground.

"I was sort of sorry we got it right on the first take," Carrie said, afterward. "I wanted to do it again."

The trash compactor scene, which occurs earlier in the film, was shot after the rope swing. To protect themselves from the garbage water, the cast was given wetsuits to wear under their clothing. "I liked jumping through the garbage chute," Carrie said, "but I didn't like wearing the wetsuit." It kept her relatively dry while climbing soggy piles of trash, though. "It was under my white gown, for protection: or I was going to look like Walter Brennan from the waist down from being in the water so long."

Before the budget cuts, the characters would crawl from the compactor to the carved-out cave of a swamp monster, fight off the monster, and then escape. But the compactor scenes had themselves been compacted into one lengthy scene. The following day's shoot would be the scene directly outside the compactor: this is where Carrie and Harrison's characters really lay into each other.

Movie soundstages are often hot, due to their high ceilings, the lights, and the fact that air conditioners and fans need to be turned off before each take. Many actors perform entire films with mild to moderate dehydration, so they won't ruin a take by sweating.

"It was 105 degrees outside," Carrie said, "so I wasn't standing up straight and I was acting crazy. But George said 'Now, act more like a princess. Stand up straight.' Very black-and-white direction. Not anything weird and bizarre like other directors would say."

"I realized why directors are such horrible people, in a way," George said. "Because you want things to be right, and people will just not listen to you, and there is no time to be nice to people, no time to be delicate."

Carrie remembered George's very direct direction. "[H]e was the only one who seemed to know what was going on. He'd also refer to other scenes. 'Remember how you were in the scene with Peter Cushing? Now just do the same in this scene.' So it was never scary. I totally trusted him."

One of the last scenes in the film was chronologically first: Darth Vader's attack on Leia's cruiser. "I remember I had to shoot a gun, and that I got felled by a paralyzing ray," Carrie said. It was great fun for her, because "I know I would have to do what my mother called 'pratfalls.'"

Harrison finished filming on a Thursday in June, spent one last weekend with Carrie, then left on Monday… with Carrie flying with him back to LA. This was unintentional: the production office bought two tickets next to each other for a 14-hour coach trip. During the flight, they agreed in so many words to end their fling. "You have the eyes of a doe," Harrison said, "and the balls of a samurai."

In her second novel, Carrie wrote that maybe there weren't homewreckers per se, just… wreckable homes. Maybe the other woman can get as damaged as the other two parties, and maybe she shouldn't hoist the guilt of infidelity. Film sets are instant families, and part of that is off-camera romances. They generally last as long as production does, dissipating when the emotional energy of a shoot winds down.

Two weeks later, Carrie returned to set, gun in hand. It was a special gift she had found for George: a Buck Rogers "liquid helium" water pistol. Carrie had a knack for finding just the right gift for people. Price was no object, but it also wasn't a measure of a gift's worth: gifts had an equal chance of being from a flea market as from Gucci. In this case, Carrie felt George needed something to make him feel like a kid again. She was right. "George wouldn't put the thing down," Mark Hamill said. "We saw him in the hallways of EMI, just kinda twirling it around. Couldn't pry it out of him."

One of Carrie's final scenes was one of Leia's first: the hologram message to Luke. Mark had already filmed his side of things, gazing fondly at either nothing or an off-screen Leia model. Now Carrie would fill that void, standing on a platform that would be rotated to match the angle and distance of Luke's side of each shot. Time for her intergalactic SOS.

Alas, the message wasn't ready yet. George felt the version Carrie had memorized still wasn't right. He grabbed a pencil for a last-minute editing session. Out went a reference to Artoo being "fed" information, out went a mention of "the security of all free planets." To the last line: "You must help me, Obi-Wan Kenobi, you are my only hope" he crossed out the first two words. A demand was turned into a plea.

Carrie learned the new message: each line's change was an

improvement: less jargon, more emotion, more clarity. But right at the end of filming, perhaps unintentionally, she changed something. Until then she'd stuck with the script phoneme by phoneme. Now at the end, perhaps she felt just enough freedom to venture an idea of her own. The first script change she'd ever made was impossibly small, but crucial.

Leia's final line as scripted was "you are my only hope," but in the final film she says, "*you're* my only hope." That was it: a contraction. One simple change to make the formal sound more conversational. It humanizes Leia, helps make this pitch sound more personal than professional. It was so small a change it maybe went unnoticed during filming.

But Carrie had changed a line, and changed it for the better. Films are built from thousands of shots, and each shot is built from thousands of choices. Many don't end up mattering, but this one did. The scene played better, Leia's character was strengthened, and the movie worked better, all because she spoke up. Anytime someone quoted "Obi-Wan Kenobi, you're my only hope," she would know they were quoting words she had tinkered with.

At the conclusion of principal photography, Carrie had filmed for 37 days, less than Harrison's 42 days or Mark's whopping 70. "It was like combat shooting," Carrie said, "because we had no time, because there was no budget." The Elstree Street cast and crew received old-fashioned invitations from Alec Guinness for cocktails at the on-site restaurant.

The actors were going home and the sets were being dismantled, but the filming wasn't done. A bizarre set of pick-up shots began: one crew went to Guatemala to film jungle exteriors. Another threw a yak costume on an elephant and tromped it around the California desert.

And then there were hundreds of special effects shots to come, of X-Wings and Death Stars, lasers and light sabers, TIE Fighters and holograms. Leia's blaster needed to shoot red blaster bolts, and her spaceship's engines needed to glow yellow: those would be hand-animated frame by frame, as would all the missed Stormtrooper shots. As each FX shot was finished, it was printed out and incorporated into the working print that George and his team of editors were constructing.

After all the difficulties of production, George was back in his safe space: the editing room. The only problem there was tripping over his massive malamute, the inspiration for Chewbacca. (The dog's name? Indiana.) If films were houses, the filming process was merely ordering lumber: the editing room was the construction site. His and Marcia's relationship was built on their shared love of editing: she was better with the audience's expectations, he was better with pacing. She started rough and then "finessed" a scene down to size: George built out shot by shot. Together, they were the world's best pair of hands.

"George makes his visuals come to life with montage," his friend Steven Spielberg said. "That makes him unique in our generation, since most of us do it instead with composition and camera placement." It was the Kuleshov effect in motion: Russian filmmaker Lev Kuleshov was the first to realize each piece of film built upon each previous clip, that you could tell complex stories and evoke complicated emotions by splicing simple shots together.

Carrie went to visit George during editing, to see how he was faring. She found him sleeping on a couch, unsure what day it was, mind cobwebbed with work and decisions. When you work 18-hour days and never go outside, little things like night and day stop mattering.

Like all actors, she was surely curious to find out how much of her performance had made the final cut. One of Leia's few scenes had been cut. The first of her two confrontations with Darth Vader was gone, and Leia now went from being felled by a Stormtrooper to stuck in a jail cell. This was a smart cut. Leia already came off as strong, and if she stood up to Vader right away he'd look weak. It also allowed for Leia's first words in the film to be the hologram recording played by Luke. This cements Luke as the film's main character, important since he doesn't show up in the first two reels.

Also cut was a short scene after the trash compactor, where Han ignores what he calls Leia's "female advice" and takes a potshot at the garbage monster, which alerts the Stormtroopers to their presence. (On the day of filming, Mark was worried they looked too clean: his hair was barely damp, and Carrie's robe looked fresh from the clothesline. Harrison joked that *Star Wars* "wasn't that sort of movie." If you were looking for hard sci-fi realism, don't watch a movie with laser swords.)

Other changes included cutting all early scenes with Luke's Tatooine friends, as well as snipping out a large man in a furry cloak named Jabba the Hutt. George wanted to replace the human Jabba with a giant stop-motion slug, but there wasn't time or budget for that. Out went the first and final frames of many action sequences, for more frantic pacing. Also out went shots of blaster fire making scorch marks in people's chests: too violent.

Scenes, lines, entire subplots went out, to streamline the film to under two hours. Gone went mentions of Vader being a Sith lord, the words "Organa" and "Tatooine," and a scene of a cantina alien informing a Stormtrooper where Luke and Obi-Wan are. Left in is Luke's joyous yell at film's end as he sees Leia: it sure sounds like "Carrie!" instead of "There she is!"

Luke and Leia's swing scene was a self-contained two-minute adventure: very easy to cut for time. But it provided a defining moment of the film: me Luke, you Leia. Around the set it was called the "Lash Larue" scene, after the western star who knew his way around a bullwhip. There was no better shorthand for adventure than swinging, and despite the spaceships this was at heart not sci-fi but adventure.

More important than the runtime, though, was coherence. In *Star Wars'* case, George made the unusual choice to have the perspective characters—the ones whose journey you follow throughout the film—be not Luke the main character but Artoo and Threepio. Their journey connects the story from Vader to Leia to Luke to Ben to Han and Chewie.

Good editing also clarifies themes. *Star Wars'* main theme, it turned out, was finding your place. Luke is lonely at the film's beginning, looking for a greater purpose. Han holds himself apart from greater society, bereft of friends or family beyond Chewbacca and his ship. They both find inclusion with Leia, and in the shared fight against the Empire.

The trailer was finished by December: the first line of dialogue other than the narrator's is Leia's action-packed "Here they come!" as she and Chewbacca fly the Millennium Falcon. We also see scenes of Leia being tortured by Vader and the mind probe, she and Luke swinging across the chasm (complete with kiss for luck), and the two of them falling into the trash chute. You'd have no idea Han Solo was even in the film.

That went double for the poster, which had one of the first instances of the now-familiar *Star Wars* font, where the S's connect to the adjoining T and R. The logline read: "The story of a boy, a girl, and a universe."

Mark heard a rumor the trailer was playing up in Westwood, so he and Carrie drove up there. They convinced the theater owner to let them in for free, so long as they left before the actual movie started. On screen, for the first time, they saw bits and pieces of what they had been making with so many crossed fingers.

"Coming to your galaxy next summer!" the trailer concluded. "Yeah, and it's coming to the Late Show a week and a half after that!" yelled someone from the balcony. Mark and Carrie exchanged worried glances: *Star Wars* apparently looked like a flop.

Chapter 7: The Odyssey Begins

Thanks to *Star Wars*, Carrie now had her own money. Even for someone in the lap of luxury, earning your own bread makes a difference. It just spends better.

She could afford a place of her own, and moved into a nearby condo, in Century City Towers. (Only afterwards did she realize her stepfather, Harry, was in the same building: they didn't cross paths much.) She could afford her own illegal substances. And her gift-giving became Olympic-class, each present chosen with a soothsayer's foresight, paid for with money burning a hole in her pocket.

The distance from Mom, the cash in her bank account, and her new-found Hollywood career made her feel independent and comfortable. And finally mature enough to realize how unfairly she'd been treating Mom.

It required a performative apology. A gift so big her mom would just have to love it, so big it would say more about the giver than the recipient. Every Hollywood house was filled with these gifts, with their subtexts of "this is what I extol on someone like you." Carrie could now afford to give this obnoxiously big.

One evening, Carrie pulled up to her mom's house in a new car: a green Cadillac Seville. She asked her mom to step outside.

"I just bought it," Carrie said. "What do you think?"

"It's gorgeous," Mom said, "But green? You don't even like green."

"No, but you do." Carrie smiled. "Happy birthday. I love you, Mother." Twenty-five years earlier, Mom had bought her father a similar gift, a red 1951 MG convertible. It was a family legend. Now she was the one on the receiving end of a two-ton apology, this time in metallic Kingswood Green.

For Carrie it was a good first step, even if she still didn't quite feel the grateful daughter. "When love fails, hey, don't sweat it! Here come the gifts!" she'd write in a later novel. And besides, it might be her only chance. Once her dumb movie came out, her budding career might be nipped in the bud.

* * *

Star Wars was supposed to be a December 1976 release, between *Pink Panther* and *Dirty Harry* sequels. It lost that prime spot because special effects weren't ready. The film was pushed back to May 1977. *Jaws* excluded, summer was considered a dumping ground for B movies.

Marcia had left the production around Thanksgiving, to work on a Martin Scorsese film. She had helped shape *Star Wars* as a roller-coaster ride. Her quick cutting also hid some bargain-basement production values. She saved one bad actor by cutting around his performance, and created a huge laugh by moving a shot of Threepio tangled in wires from the opening Vader attack to later during the TIE Fighter dogfight. And she decided that Luke should only get one pass at the Death Star, not two.

Much of the first half of George's year was about bettering that one trench run. For a year he had been showing everyone a film he had made by editing together aerial combat footage from WWII films. This was what the Death Star run would be: all he needed was for the special effects house he had founded just for this movie, called Industrial Light and Magic, to refilm each one of these shots with X-Wings. Many shots were fractions of a second long: the eye couldn't even tell what was happening.

Day by day, shot by shot, George gathered his Death Star run. He also received footage of the new matte painting of an endless chasm for the swing scene, and a new inset shot of the trash compactor monster, now just an eyeball on a stalk, filmed at ILM in a replica trash pit filled with exploded TIE Fighter and Death Star detritus.

That was just half the story, though: as George loved to point out, we both see and hear movies. Sound needed 50% of his attention. Ben Burtt, who as a production assistant had escorted Carrie to hairstylists, was now told to find the sounds of sci-fi. He went wandering the streets of Philadelphia, microphone in hand, to catch ambient sounds. The groans and squeaks of the SEPTA trailers became the spaceship doors opening, the cacophony of the train became the sand crawler. Nearby power lines made an electric whipcrack sound when its tower was struck: that became blaster fire. (This outing perhaps inspired Brian De Palma, who made a thriller called *Blow Out* about a movie soundman in Philly who records a murder.)

Burtt's greatest triumph was coming up with the beeps and boops for Artoo, the mobile trash can. Beforehand, the droid had come across as an annoyance, but with sound he became wonderfully alive. He even got extra reaction shots: audiences now loved that little guy.

George's director friends flew up to watch an early cut: it was a disaster. Francis Ford Coppola suggested moving a Vader scene two reels back in the picture: he became more menacing when he was offscreen. De Palma was almost insulting about how confused he was watching it: he cowrote text he said should come before the film. That would become the famed opening crawl. Steven Spielberg offered to handle second-unit directing, but George didn't want the help.

George used temporary music tracks when editing the film, a common practice. Instead of picking synthesizers and theremins, or rock and roll like with *American Graffiti*, he went classical with the stand-in music: Liszt and Holst. Spielberg recommended a composer named John Williams to try and match the bombast of those masters. Williams had built the unforgettable *Jaws* anthem around two notes on an upright bass. Maybe he could come up with some okay melodies for *Star Wars*.

No film in history has ever benefitted from a soundtrack more than *Star Wars*. It's hard to argue against it being the single best film score in movie history. It turned Williams from "the shark guy" to the most hummable musician since the four lads from Liverpool.

Williams, leaning into the archetypical nature of the story, chose to work with leitmotifs, a highfalutin' way of saying theme songs. Princess Leia's Theme is first heard when she's on the run from Vader. It does not recur during any of her confinement scenes, but it reappears when her hologram is played. Her hologram message is truer to her nature than scenes of her stewing in a cell. And crucially, almost subliminally, the theme recurs when Obi-Wan dies. Leia and Obi-Wan never meet in the movie, but his sacrifice is to further her plans.

Princess Leia's Theme is not tied to a specific instrument: it is carried by French horn, oboe, flute, and strings, along with the rest of the London Symphony Orchestra. A complex arrangement to represent a complicated character. Williams chose D major as Leia's key, the "key of triumph," almost always personified as female in composer-speak. He worked in phrases evoking nostalgia and sweeping romance: "It really is a fairytale princess melody," he said.

As the film was being edited, others were working on tie-in releases.

Marvel Comics had been pitched into adapting *Star Wars* as a miniseries, as it had done with both *Planet of the Apes* and *2001: A Space Odyssey*. The first issue was shipped in March, and notoriously featured a neon-green Darth Vader. The promotional team even went to San Diego Comic-Con to plug the film, showing off slideshows of production stills: *Star Wars* was the first-ever film to court comic book fans at a convention.

Lucas approached pulp sci-fi writer Alan Dean Foster about novelizing his screenplay: novelizations filled the gap before VHS players allowed moviegoers to watch a movie at home. Foster chose to introduce the reader to Leia through C3PO's emotionally detached eyes: "It was young, slim, and by abstruse human standards of aesthetics, Threepio mused, of a calm beauty." He altered Leia's Obi-Wan line to the near-Shakespearean "Obi-Wan Kenobi, you're my only remaining hope." He changed most all the dialogue, in fact.

For many people, these prerelease tie-ins were their first exposure to *Star Wars*. The adaptations became bestsellers: sci-fi readers were already devouring and loving the story, before George was done editing it. Each also presents a slightly different Leia.

Marvel storytelling makes every action bigger, so the comics-Leia (drawn angularly by Howard Chaykin) yells "set blaster to kill!" before she shoots a Stormtrooper. Comics-Leia also says "And you call yourselves human!" after Alderaan is destroyed. She gives Luke a romance-novel-cover kiss before their alley swing, and another one before Luke's Death Star battle.

Novelization-Leia, on the other hand, is less superhuman. She doesn't get a shot off before being captured, but does spit on Darth Vader's helmet: it hisses like grease. Novelization-Leia says "Force will not keep the Empire together," after Alderaan is destroyed, a poor choice of words since "Force" meant something else in the *Star Wars* world. This Leia also grabs Han's hand for support in the trash compactor scene, a first inkling of the velvet hand under her iron glove.

* * *

In January of 1977, the cast did behind-the-scenes interviews. These would be followed by weeks of subsequent interviews, all asking essentially the same questions. Harrison, who had the most experience with the press, would grade Carrie and Mark after each session, as if he were their publicity teacher. The cast found diplomatic ways to say they had no idea if this movie would be any good. Carrie's was "The great thing about *Star Wars* is that when I see it, I'm going to be as surprised as anyone, because I've not seen any of the effects… I'm very curious to see… what I look like flying through space."

She also added "Are they going to have my planet blow up?" to a reporter. In a more contemporary film climate, such revealing of plot points would be verboten. But Carrie loved to give and receive gossip: as Mark would later joke, the three ways to disseminate information widely were to "telephone, telegraph, tell-a-Carrie."

These interviews may have been where the Carrie Fisher Sentences began in earnest. Adopting a tone of voice used to thank a grandmother for a birthday card, she'd spout out absurd, inane things, such as "Leia was unconscious a lot, and I wanted to be unconscious. I have an affinity for unconsciousness. I thought I could play that very well." She would toss off jokes like this with a blow-dried airhead affect, and they sailed over reporters' heads like Stormtrooper fire. The interviewer often didn't realize until typing up their notes later on that the vapid pretty face they'd interviewed had been funny.

Blame misogyny, sure, but few were prepared for the young lady behind Princess Leia to be a smiling, passive-aggressive jokester. Reporters who were used to the typical softball answers lobbed by most celebrities were flummoxed by her fastballs. Especially since she never paused after a joke: Carrie just kept talking, all the time wearing her Miss California grin.

It was Carrie's own version of Leia's distress call: is anyone out there actually listening to me? Do the words I say just get ignored? And she got her answer. Reporters smiled and grinned like she was speaking a foreign language.

* * *

Before *Star Wars* opened (and people found out it was a bomb), she filmed a television movie for the BBC, *Come Back, Little Sheba*, with Joanne Woodward and Laurence Olivier. It was a supporting role, but there was no better acting school that getting paid to do scenes with living legends.

After filming, she flew back to Los Angeles and had a low moment.

Carrie's life was going rather well, considering. But one of the nastiest things about mood disorders is they can be unconnected to external reality. No one wins a fight against depression with logic.

Carrie tried medicating her way out: she took mood stabilizers, Percocets, and acid. Todd checked on her a day or two later and found her knocked her out on the floor, still as a stone, covered in cold vomit. She tried to make a joke of it—"it's a wacky, mod-a-go-go world," she told him, her breath horrid—as he got her to the nearest emergency room. They kept the episode quiet—perhaps not even Carrie knew if she had partied too hard or had been looking for an end to her pain.

* * *

Star Wars wasn't supposed to have a big premiere—it wasn't shaping up to be the sort of movie you bragged about being in. But another film was a month late for release, so *Star Wars* took its timeslot for a grand opening at Mann's Chinese Theater on May 25, 1977.

Nearby, George had finishing up the film's stereo sound version, but was still knee-deep in the version for mono sound. He was meeting Marcia for a meal nearby—"my breakfast, her dinner" since he was working nights and she was working days. At Hamburger Hamlet, they saw the lines and limos outside the theater across the street, and wondered what film it was for. "It never occurred to me that my movie was out," George said, "because *I was still working on it.*"

Carrie knew about it: she had practically broken the record for Most Cigarettes Smoked in an Hour before the premiere. Here was where the moviegoing public would find out exactly what sort of B-movie pulp cheesefest she had made, and how she was the worst part of an awful film. This was going to be the night she became uncastable, the moment when her career stalled after one leading role. She snuck in after the fanfare and the opening crawl, taking a front-row seat.

Over the next two hours, her life changed.

She had been to plenty of film premieres, and knew the standard reaction she'd get afterwards: everyone would stop talking to congratulate her, then resume their conversation. But the cheering and applause she heard, from the opening chase on, was something else. For two hours, electricity was in the air. And afterwards, people *talked about the movie.* That just did not happen.

One and all were blown away by the technical prowess that had been married to such a simple premise. It was a B movie, yes, but made with the flair of an A picture, like a Michelin chef serving grilled cheese and tomato soup. Try not to cheer when Luke blows up the Death Star. Try not to walk out of the theater feeling 10 pounds lighter. Had there ever been a movie so exciting?

Mann's Chinese Theater sold around 4,800 tickets that Wednesday at $4 a pop, making it the biggest single day in the theater's 50-year history. By that summer's end, Darth Vader, Threepio, and Artoo would all have their handprints in the cement in front of that theater.

Most actors go their whole lives without a hit: those who get one are seldom lucky enough to play a memorable role. The rare few who deliver iconic performances in iconic films become as permanent in our collective psyche as the lights in the sky: hence the term stars.

Carrie had fallen into a star-making role before she could legally drink. Her acting choices at age 20 would be with her for her whole life. Her and everyone else. "Remember when I'd never been Princess Leia before?" Carrie mused to her brother that night. "Now I'm going to be her forever."

Likewise, *Star Wars* quickly became the film that eclipsed all other films that summer, the movie you had to see, then see again. When the first batch of reels had gone out to theaters, it was bundled as part of a deal: if you wanted the surefire hit *The Other Side of Midnight*, an R-rated WWII romance, you had to take the cheesy PG fantasy. Soon enough, movie theaters were begging distributors to give them a *Star Wars* print, at any expense.

Acting was never first on the list of the film's praises. The special effects, costuming, makeup, creature effects, set design, and above all the meat-and-potatoes storytelling were all praised. Rare was the film where almost all parties, from lighting to set designers to prop masters, got to tap into their whole imagination.

Those Stormtroopers who couldn't hit a bantha at point blank turned out to be a masterstroke: four-year-olds could easily identify the "bad guys." They fell down dead with no blood or gore when shot, were easily fooled, and were as dispassionate as truancy officers. The biggest threat to the galaxy: stupid white men.

The Stormtroopers' clear Nazi presence muted the existing Vietnam parallel of guerilla heroes fighting the oppressors. (George had been slated to direct *Apocalypse Now*.) The heroes were also called "rebels," which for any American versed in the Revolutionary War equals "good guy." *Star Wars* encompassed all wars, all conflicts.

The scourge of *Star Wars*, feared even by the Empire's worker bees and bureaucrats, was Darth Vader. Vader was a villain out of medieval times, a black-cloaked Torquemada. When people say to fear the man who believes in only one idea, Vader is that man: fanatical, uncompromising, savage.

Star Wars did more than just enter the national conversation: it literally became the language of that conversation. Words like "The Force," "Stormtrooper," and "Jedi" became commonplace. If a building was imposing and foreboding, it might be nicknamed the Death Star. The Bible gave us phrases like "forbidden fruit" and "good Samaritan," Shakespeare gave us "love is blind" and "heart of gold," and as of May 1977, *Star Wars* gave us "Use the Force," "These are not the droids you're looking for," and "let the Wookiee win."

People started saying goodbye with a "May the Force be with you." Catholics would instinctually respond "And also with you," and then laugh, realizing they had mixed up their religions. Some fundamentalist Christians were taught that Carrie and the other *Star Wars* actors had to sign contracts denouncing their own religions in favor of the Force. They hadn't, but others took that pledge voluntarily: census workers around the world were stymied to find out how many people began to list their religion as "Jedi." By year's end, *Star Wars* was omnipresent.

The Social Security Administration compiles yearly lists of the 100 most popular names. "Leia" had never made the list before, but starting in 1978, it did. As of 2021, it's the 299th most popular girls' name in America, in between "Angelina" and "Paige." Even more popular is Leia's regnal descriptor: "Princess." "Princess" had never made the list either, but started its reign in 1979, and has been there almost every year since.

Chapter 8: Bunheads

Star Wars was the #1 movie in America, for seemingly every week in 1977 since its release in May. Pity any other film released that year, all ignored so moviegoers could watch Luke and Leia swing across the ravine one more time. "*Star Wars* got an amazing response," Carrie said. "I used to drive by and look at the lines and think 'What?' I haven't had a chance to absorb the madness."

By September, five months after the premiere, the film broke an astounding record: it was now the single most successful motion picture of all time. This was partly thanks to inflation: if you adjusted for the difference in ticket prices, *Gone with the Wind* was still the champ.

By the end of summer, Carrie had been on more movie screens than anyone since Scarlett O'Hara. A cast picture ran on the cover of *Rolling Stone*. In a Topps trading card series, made from the film's stills, she showed up dozens of times. The film was only in America so far—the crew at Elstree still hadn't seen it yet—but soon Leia would be world famous.

"When the film came out, I seemed to do publicity for ages, which meant a lot of travel," Carrie said. Each new market came with more requests for Han, Luke, and Leia to answer the same questions from different reporters. Harrison became glum, but Mark and Carrie got silly. In Toronto, due to cinnamon buns being on the pastry tray, the trio decided to recreate their poster pose. Luke held up a butter knife in lieu of a lightsaber, Harrison fudged a blaster with the remaining utensils, and Carrie squinted yearningly into the distance, holding the buns over her ears.

She was treated by reporters as a celebrity, but by kids as a new kind of spunky, modern princess. Girls saw Leia as cool: she shot laser pistols and stood up to both Darth Vader and the bad boy on her own team, while rewarding the good boy with a chaste kiss. "I only got a sense of *Star Wars'* importance when a child recognizes me and becomes speechless. Kids don't think I'm from this planet. Very little children even believe Princess Leia is a real human being who lives in outer space."

And what about the superfans? The first person Carrie ever met who recognized her as Princess Leia had seen *Star Wars* 12 times. This was only a few weeks into its run: 12 times. She quickly joked that the prize for that much commitment was "a free date with a princess and a bucket of popcorn." For months, when she received fan mail, she'd reply to each letter: wasn't that what you were supposed to do? (Those were the letters to her: the ones sent to Princess Leia—anyone know the zip code for Alderaan?—were answered by Lucasfilm.)

Everyone around the globe now knew Carrie as Princess Leia. One of the also-rans who didn't get the role of Leia said in 1978, "I'm glad I didn't do *Star Wars* because it was a nothing part. I would not want to get famous because of that movie."

Leia didn't just make Carrie famous: it made her rich. George Lucas gave the principal cast and key crew members a percentage of the profits. JW Rinzler places the value of the gift of a "point" at $320,000, which would have made her a millionaire in today's money. (Lucasfilm later reached out to all point-holders, offering large one-time fees to buy them back.) Carrie bought a house near Laurel Canyon, an area of LA home to more countercultural folk than an issue of *Creem*.

"I became more financially independent," Carrie said. "It made me more conspicuous," she added, an odd statement considering she was the star of the biggest movie of all time. But now she had the funds to live a lavish lifestyle: clothing, travel, parties… and party favors.

Money plus youth plus entertainment plus 1970s plus Los Angeles equals cocaine. People then assumed it was a "clean" drug that kept them thin, active, and inspired, with no downsides. Inhalable coffee. The only problem with cocaine was running out of it, since that meant you were no longer rich.

* * *

While editing his film, George had set up meetings with every toymaker he could. Most, like dollmaker Mego, passed. Kenner said yes, though, and designed a series of plastic dolls small enough to fit into vehicles. The company took its time on production, since back then movies rolled out regionally, not nationally. Some time in 1978 they'd ship the toys to stores.

This slowwalk was a disaster: every kid in America wanted *Star Wars* toys for Christmas. Kenner, who had lucked into the grand slam of all grand slams, was now unable to even take first base. No matter how the company rushed, it couldn't manufacture toys before 1978. It could only ship empty boxes to stores.

In an act of pathetic desperation, that is exactly what they did. The "*Star Wars* Early Bird Certificate Package" was a cardboard box with pictures of eight *Star Wars* toys on the cover. Buy it, and sometime next year you'd receive via mail an R2-D2, a Luke, a Chewbacca, a Leia, and four others. Other characters—Stormtroopers, Han, Obi-Wan, Vader— would be sold separately.

The toy industry learned the tragedy of an unprepared hit: in the future, toys would hit stores in the weeks before a film's opening, not the months after. This preparedness would double as advance marketing for the film itself.

As the millions and millions rolled into Lucasfilm's coffers, Hollywood slavered. There was exponentially more profit in toy licenses, it turned out, than in box office receipts. (May the forecasted projections be with you.) Toy licenses would start to dictate movies: characters would have costume changes and use cool vehicles not for plot reasons but because it allowed for more injection-molded vehicles and action figures. "One word: plastics" was right on the money.

Just as McDonalds makes more money from real estate than cheeseburgers, Lucasfilm, once it got going, became a licensing powerhouse with a small moviemaking subsidiary. George needed a lot of accountants and lawyers and sales-people to handle all the deals. The company's mostly female staff was originally based in a giant Park Way mansion in San Anselmo nicknamed the Parkhouse, atop a hill guarded by a gate with a security code. The women of the Parkhouse were nicknamed the Park Way Princesses. (By contrast, George's FX division ILM skewed so male it grew sordid with frathouse antics, such as miniscule pin-up girls hidden in spaceship cockpits. In the future, Lucasfilm would purposefully try to hire female ILM employees, just to reduce the grossness quotient.)

Over the years, Leia has been the face of over 75 action figures. She is the second most prolific female toy character of all time, behind only Barbie. Memorable Leia toys include a 1995 Leia nicknamed "Monkeyface" since the sculptors did a woeful job capturing her likeness, a 2005 San Diego Comic-Con exclusive of hologram Leia that's translucent and blue, and the Walmart-only Baby Leia collectible from 2007.

Those are simply the action figures. If you add in the various Lego figures, the bobble-heads, the Funko dolls with oversized heads and black-marble eyes, the Leia Barbie dolls, the statues, the Minnie-Mouse-as-Leia figures, the Christmas ornaments, the "Expanded Universe" figures—then the number pulls way into the three digits. (Carrie especially loved the Leia Pez dispenser, joking how you could now eat candy from a hole in her neck.) Lucasfilm refused to put out a Princess Leia makeup line, though: sorry, lip gloss addicts.

The original Kenner dolls were made from molds that became damaged over time, resulting in imperfect faces. More careful craftmanship would go into subsequent products: Leia could look cartoonishly bold and vibrant, her features exaggerated like a caricaturist's. And her outfits could be made of real cloth—or in the case of her *Revenge of the Jedi* wardrobe, real little cloth. Carrie disliked these creepily realistic dolls of her in undress: "I told George, 'You have the rights to my face,' you do not have the rights to my lagoon of mystery!"

This largesse of Leia figures is notable for two reasons. First, the number of Leia toys is, believe it or not, way too low. Toymakers butt up against deep-seated gender preferences: boys don't want to buy figures of girls. Girls, on the other hand, are sold girl-only toys, found in the pink aisle. As a result, all those hundreds of Leia figures represent a massive undercount in demand. Generations of girls who grew up loving Leia never owned her toy, never even saw one.

Second, Carrie Fisher never received a cent of the billions in revenue these toys generated. George gave her a point for the film, yet for her likeness she received nothing. None of the actors did: the idea of their face on anything other than a movie poster was hard to imagine. Actors' licensing rights would soon be a bone of contention for blockbuster franchises. A big-name actor might get paid extra for such rights, or refuse to sign at any price.

What's more, all of those Leia dolls represented Carrie Fisher at age 19. The dolls—along with the character onscreen—would never age. The popularity of *Star Wars* meant Carrie would spend the rest of her life aging, while her trapped-in-amber (or maybe trapped-in-carbonite?) lookalike was fresh as a daisy. "Why couldn't I get the Dorian Gray thing?" she quipped.

* * *

The comic and novel versions of *Star Wars* had helped seed the soil for the movie's popularity. George wanted them to continue to print new adventures. However, to prevent them from using plotlines he might want for future films, he walled off all character backstory, and character development. That was reserved for his sequel screenplay, which he'd been putting off. (He didn't like directing, but he *hated* writing.)

To postpone that arduous task, George arranged to be interviewed about his characters and their history. He role-played as each person, answering questions in the first person that would be transcribed as a backstory bible. One day he channeled Threepio: "Actually, [Artoo] was quite a nuisance, though I wouldn't say that we have any feelings for each other... he might have feelings for me because, obviously, I'm a great help to him." Another day he was Han Solo: this consisted mostly of gearhead talk about the Millennium Falcon's modifications.

When George was Leia, he very rationally described Alderaan—everything from its geology to its political structures. His rationality, when transcribed and attributed to Leia, sounds very much like denial. He casually mentions Alderaan's doom because its fictional: she does so because it's the only way to move forward and defeat the Empire. This emotional suppression becomes her character's attitude: I'll grieve later.

Alan Dean Foster's work on the *Star Wars* novelization was as purple as grape cough syrup, and George loved it. Before the premiere he asked Foster to write a second *Star Wars* novel, based on a subplot from an earlier draft. It had a smaller cast (no Han or Chewie), fewer spaceships, and just a few locations on a bog planet. If the first film underperformed, George figured this sequel novel would be a good springboard for a smaller-budgeted second screenplay.

Foster's name would appear on this book, titled *Splinter of the Mind's Eye* and written in the *Star Wars* font, over an imposing painting of Darth Vader. The actual words *Star Wars* would not appear, though, since Fox owned the rights to that. Carrie and Mark hadn't yet signed their no-money-down, no-money-ever licensing paperwork, so Luke and Leia are shown from behind.

The plot is straightforward: Leia's on a diplomatic mission, with Luke as her bodyguard, and they crash on a swamp planet settled by miners. They learn that somewhere in an ancient ruin is the Kaiburr crystal, which gives Force-sensitive people superpowers. They have to track it down before the Empire can.

Luke and Leia's relationship is given full weight: "I was actually more interested in the character of Leia than I was with Luke," Foster said. Leia puts duty before her feelings, something the brash Luke can't do. To help then blend in, Luke pulls out Leia's buns, and pretends she's his servant. He has her misbehave in public, so he can slap her. Leia understands the abuse is necessary for the ruse, and that it hurts Luke more than her.

There's a boat passage scene, made perilous because Leia can't swim. Leia also suffers post-traumatic stress flashbacks from her torture at the hands of Vader: at one dark point she tells Luke to kill her if it looks like she'll be captured again. Later, in a moment of resolve, she says her one goal in life is to personally shoot down Vader. She gets her chance, but only hits his cloak. Then she attacks him with Luke's blue light saber.

A daily *Star Wars* newspaper comic strip began running as well. It was a perfect fit for the breakfast table, since many of George's influences were action-adventure strips like *Terry and the Pirates* and *The Phantom*. Luke and Leia star in the first months-long storyline, about a casino planet. Per instructions, Leia's characterization never drifted beyond permanent feistiness.

The *Star Wars* comics continued the story as well. The final issue of the comics adaptation of the film was #6, released in October of 1977. Issue #7 began an original storyline—a quest to find a new rebel home base. A ban on character development was not a problem for comics: Archie has been deciding between Betty and Veronica since before WWII. So Han and Chewie meet a space pirate who has stolen an Imperial Destroyer, Luke gets trapped on a water planet while searching for a new rebel home planet, and Leia goes to rescue him… but alas gets captured.

This repetitious storytelling showed the gaps in Leia the character as established in the first film. Luke was recognizable as the earnest, innocent hero, and Han the world-weary defensive type. (Han and Luke in fact used to be one character, before George divided the role. Luke also was briefly female, since there were so few females around.) Adventure after adventure clarified Luke and Han's attributes. Chewbacca was loyal and violent, Artoo sarcastic and bold, Threepio frightened and courtly.

Who was Leia? What is she like when she's not acting tough under various forms of duress? Not even her look changed: the comics always portrayed her in her floor-length white gown and double-whelk hairstyle.

It took until issue #30 for Leia to get a solo issue. She sneaks onto a cruel factory planet that makes munitions for the Empire. Hard sci-fi ideas abound: she received sleep-imprinted information about the planet's layout, for instance. She fails in her short-term mission of sabotage, but succeeds in introducing the idea of revolution to the downtrodden factory workers.

Leia's primary character flaw was that she was unflawed. She was a two-dimensional perfect specimen, always bold and heroic, right where the action was. This made Carrie sometimes feel upstaged by her own updo. What really would strengthen her as a character was a weakness, a vulnerability, something that humanized her. A mistake to live down, the bigger the better.

Luckily, a big mistake was right around the corner. 1978 was the year of the *Star Wars Holiday Special*.

Chapter 9: "I Have a Bad Feeling About This."

Star Wars was a hit on movie screens, bookstores, comic stands, and toy aisles. What about the TV set?

Maybe the idea started with a holiday newspaper ad that ran in December 1977, reminding moviegoers that *Star Wars* was still in theaters. It featured photos of the cast, each signed as if they were Christmas cards. Artoo's was in a punch card language, Han's said, "Best Wishes and Happy Holidays," and Leia's said, "All my love, Princess Leia." Apparently, the *Star Wars* world celebrated holidays.

George had designed *Star Wars* to be vast, so future storytellers could venture into fantasy or horror or action. One angle he had not considered, though, was the televised comedy variety show. But hey, it was the '70s: everyone from Johnny Cash to the Brady Bunch had such shows.

In a *Donny and Marie Show* tribute to *Star Wars*, the Osmond siblings played Luke and Leia—imagine that, Leia and Luke being brother and sister!—and lip-synched a disco song called "Lost in Space." It got stranger from there: Redd Foxx appeared as Obi-Ben Okefenokee, Kris Kristofferson out-grumped Harrison Ford as Han Solo, and Paul Lynde played Grand Moff Tarkin with a watercolor paint set on his chest. If camp is your thing, this is a jamboree.

Lucasfilm sent a massive number of props and costumes over to Utah, where *Donny and Marie* filmed, to make the sketch feel more authentic. Four Stormtrooper armatures, various Cantina alien costumes, Darth Vader's costume, Threepio and Artoo and Chewbacca, plus Anthony Daniels, Kenny Baker, and Peter Mayhew.

Carrie didn't make it: she was busy filming another cheesy TV one-off. In the hour-long special *Ringo*, the ex-Beatle Ringo Starr switches places with an identical stranger. Ringo gets to experience the life of "Ognir Rrats,"—"Ringo Starr" spelled backwards—and Ognir gets to be the celebrated drummer. Carrie played the love interest, Marquine, and got to sing "You're 16, You're Beautiful, and You're Mine," as a duet with the legend. She also starred in a music video with *Monty Python*-style collage animation.

Ringo wasn't a hit—backwards or forwards, "dud" is spelled the same—but the Osmond's' *Star Wars* parody was. CBS executives met with George Lucas, to discuss a *Star Wars* TV movie. George saw another opportunity to tell some of the *Star Wars* tales he had dreamed up over the years.

One such tale was about Chewbacca, Han's seven-foot Wookiee friend. George imagined a tense low-budget chase film as Chewie tries to reach his family before they are killed by Stormtroopers. Han would be involved because—backstory time—Han was secretly married to a Wookiee, and Chewie was his brother-in-law. That was the premise: a high-stakes gritty nail-biter. The CBS crew greenlit the project, and hired writers who had experience writing with mimes (mimes, Wookiees, same diff).

Preproduction started off well: the costumes and set design were first rate, and most every prop and costume in the Lucasfilm warehouse found its way back onto the sound stages. The Wookiee home planet of skyscraper-like trees and treehouse dwellings was wonderfully realized. A thrilling animated sequence from Japan featured a new bounty hunter character, Boba Fett. The *Star Wars* feel was imbued in the project: this was no cheap knockoff, like the *Battlestar Galactica* show.

Then the tone began to change. New writers from *The Carol Burnett Show* were brought on board to add comedy, which would be worked into the show as TV programs the Wookiee characters watched. As more and more sketches were written, the Wookiees (now named Itchy and Lumpy) became seven-foot framing devices, wandering from one screen to the next. The special threatened to turn into two hours of grunting bigfoots watching Harvey Korman skits.

That is precisely what ended up being filmed. Astonishingly, Korman starred in three separate sketches, playing an alien cook, a robot salesman, and a man with a blowhole in his head who is serenaded by sultry bartender Bea Arthur. Many of the storylines seemed inappropriate for a family show: one subplot has a Wookiee grandfather watching cybererotica starring a birdwoman: another was a performance by Jefferson Starship into a glowing microphone that resembles a radioactive sex toy.

It was not an easy shoot. The actors in costume needed to be cooled down regularly or risk fainting; many did faint under the hot lights. The gorgeous treehouse set proved impossible to use for a TV-style multi-camera shoot. The first director quit after just a few days.

The script includes short scenes for the three lead actors. Mark Hamill signed on because he felt obligated to help out the franchise. Carrie, still on the fence about a singing career, agreed to do it if she could sing. (Mark insisted that Luke NOT sing.) That left Harrison, who grouchily agreed because "it was in my contract. There was no way to get out of it." All three appear via video screens on separate sets, which maybe explained their phoned-in performances.

Carrie's scenes in particular are notable for her seeming to be blitzed out of her gourd. The opening shot is of her staring blissfully into the middle distance, like we've caught Leia grooving at a Grateful Dead show. She gets a video call from Chewbacca's wife Mala, interpreted by an ever-patient Threepio. "Mala, it's so good to see you," Leia says. Her words are slurred, her gait altered, her makeup troweled on. She seems five seconds behind the conversation. "Happy Life Day!" she says, vapidly, cheerily, out of nowhere.

Leia has more to do in the Boba Fett cartoon, which is properly tense and exciting. This was Carrie's first voicework, a job many actors find difficult. So much of an actor's toolbox is visual—facial gestures, body poses, hand movement, even pauses and silences. Carrie acquitted herself well in the cartoon's few lines, as did Mark, who'd later find a lifelong career in voicework.

The final segment was the last filmed: the big Life Day celebration, which doubled as a cast reunion, and tripled as Carrie's song. (Because it was the Holiday Special she had pitched singing a Christmas carol, and because she was Carrie she wanted it to be Joni Mitchell's "River," the saddest Christmas song ever written.) Arriving on set, Carrie found there was no budget left, so the "set" was an empty stage filled with candles, dry ice, and actors wearing Halloween costumes. It looked like a New Wave music video.

"This holiday is yours," Leia says, embracing Chewbacca like a shy kindergartener on her first day of school, "but we all share with you the hope that this day brings us closer to freedom, and to harmony, and to peace." Her syrupy, hooray-for-everything monologue continued in this vein, the director having nothing to focus on in the bare room but Carrie's seemingly tripped-out face.

She then sings instantly forgettable lyrics set to the melody of the

Star Wars theme. The song isn't in her range, but she tries to sell it. Again the camera lingers on her face, and the iris slowly shrinks around her, like an impending blackout, as a starfield is clumsily superimposed. The psychedelic effect is the final bizarre choice of a wholly bizarre show.

The special aired on a Friday, November 17, 1978, on CBS: ratings dipped in the second half of the first hour as viewers tuned out. Many switched to ABC, which was airing a Mickey Mouse 50th anniversary tribute that also featured Chewbacca and Artoo. The *Star Wars Holiday Special* became a quickly forgotten piece of 1970s kitsch, like Spiro Agnew watches or earth shoes.

But if you missed it that Friday, you weren't out of luck. Some early adopter recorded the imbroglio via a state-of-the-art top-loading video cassette recorders. They passed around copies via the "sneakernet" of friends and relatives. Over the decades, samizdat recordings were sold in the back of comic book stores, along with Hong Kong action movies and bootleg concert recordings. One VHS copy was so low-rent it included commercials from the tristate-area CBS station it was recorded from, including period ads for unions, McDonalds, pantyhose, and a robot toy named Tobor. (As Ognir Rrats surely knows, "Tobor is 'robot' spelled backwards."). To *Star Wars* fans, it is the guiltiest of pleasures. We love it all, they say, even the misfires. May the farce be with you.

What seems most shocking is the extent to which the "story" introduced in the special became a legitimate part of the *Star Wars* mythos. The *Star Wars* daily comic strip would retell the Life Day story the following year. All subsequent stories about Chewbacca and his world are based off the same treehouse planet, the same itchy, lumpy family. The *Star Wars Holiday Special*, to use geek language, is canon. In its own way, it succeeded in showing the breadth of the *Star Wars* storytelling universe.

The same appeared to be true for Carrie; all doors seemed open to her. She was invited to guest-host *Saturday Night Live*, airing on November 18, 1978, one day after the *Holiday Special*. As she joked in her monologue—after a near-unrecognizable picture of her with her hair down was shown—people didn't know what Carrie looked like, only Leia. Hence why she was wearing her Leia get-up on stage.

That led to imagining if she had been in a popular movie from the '50s instead of the '70s, cueing a *Beach Blanket Bingo* parody. "Hi, everybody!" Leia cheers, as her hologram joins the beach scene. "I'm from another galaxy and another time… and another movie." (This was quite the in-joke, referencing the novelization's opening lines: "Another time, another galaxy.")

Leia rips off her white gown to reveal, in what seems like foreshadowing, a gold two-piece swimsuit underneath. The sketch ends with Carrie singing "I'm a Teenager from Outer Space," a rousing cheesy anthem. Before the first commercial break she had showcased her acting, humor, bravery, commitment, singing, dancing, charisma, and midriff. This was what the *Holiday Special* had been reaching for.

Being an SNL host is a demanding job—you have to be flexible, fast, incredibly funny, up for looking the fool, and often cast in subpar sketches. Carrie did all that so easily she practically fit in like an eighth Not Ready for Prime Time Player. By this time, she owned a place in New York, and she often hung out with producer Lorne Michaels, the writers, and the cast.

This sparked some interpersonal drama. Gilda Radner, for instance, was standoffish to Carrie, who had attracted the attention of castmate Dan Aykroyd. Gilda and Carrie were both women whom all men seemed to fall in love with, and it's basic middle-school science (and middle-school cafeteria behavior) that two magnetic attractors will repel each other.

The cast partied hard, and so did Carrie. "These were people who were abusers," she later said, "people who liked to drink and use and stay up all night. Once one got into that little society, you were well in." Writer Terry Southern said that he'd covered two Rolling Stones tours, yet "I've yet to see anything comparable to the sheer quantity of [cocaine] heaped and stacked in the writers' wing of *SNL*!"

Hanging out at *SNL* brought her into the sphere of another friend of the show, Paul Simon. He made light of his humorless troubadour air in a Thanksgiving episode, while singing "Still Crazy After All These Years" in a humiliating turkey suit.

Just like Carrie, the Paul Simon of 1978 had the world in the palm of his hand. He had released three hit solo albums since parting ways with Art Garfunkel, with whom he'd helped define the folk genre of the '60s. He'd acted, writing his own lines as a sleazy LA agent in *Annie Hall*. Now, after a decade of writing and touring, a marriage and a divorce, he held court every night in midtown as the reigning Prince of New York. He wasn't sure what his next move would be: another album? A novel? A screenplay?

His next move turned out to be starting a conversation with Carrie. The conversation that began between the two of them was a party line chat, one either person could pick up or drop off. It started in April of 1978. By that summer they were an item, getting photographed at celebrity birthday parties, him in a bucket hat, her with a can of Tab.

"You have to understand," she would write in a novel, "that once you open a line of communication with me, that line may be interrupted, but it's never entirely closed." Like Carrie, Paul was slim and compact, and secretly funny. Both had a long line of suitors: hers included Mike Nichols, Richard Dreyfuss, and David Geffen. Together, they seemed like a matched set: "Don't stand next to me at a party," she once said, "people will think we're salt and pepper shakers."

If Harrison had been too closed off, Paul was the opposite: empathetic instead of stoic, vocal instead of mute. He was more "boy next door" than "tall, dark, and handsome." And he was intellectual: he had been in *law school* when Simon and Garfunkel hit it big. Carrie had been taking private philosophy classes from a Columbia professor to be a worldlier conversationalist. For someone longing to be taken seriously—to be really heard and understood—he seemed perfect. He was even good at sports!

"I think I have a Jewish demeanor and a Protestant ethic," Carrie said. "I think my extroversion is the Protestant manifestation [read: Mom], but emotionally I am Jewish [read: Dad]. And I was always drawn to people who looked like I felt: a little upset, a little like an outcast, uncomfortable, ready to leave…"

Paul also fed into Carrie's downbeat view of herself: he was Mr. Perfect. Being with Paul meant Carrie's hobgoblin of self-doubt always reminded her that he was better than her. He'd been passive for the last year, but within months of meeting her he was writing and producing his first feature film, *One Trick Pony,* complete with soundtrack.

Their relationship was sometimes a love affair, sometimes an argument, sometimes sweet nothings, sometimes a full-throated duet. Their conversation would last for the next seven years, and span multiple breakups, more than one marriage, more than one overdose, life, death, music, screaming, and everything else that happens between hello and goodbye.

Chapter 10: "Would It Help If I Got Out and Pushed?"

In the summer of 1978, Carrie, Mark, and Harrison all signed on for more *Star Wars* sequels. Carrie and Mark's deal was for three sequels each: however else their lives went, they'd probably always be known as Luke and Leia.

George was already rich when he made *Star Wars*: now he was wealthy. But wealth wasn't enough to let him call his own shots in Hollywood. "The only way I can do it," he said, "is to create a company that will generate profits." In a move just slightly less tense than a Death Star run, George would attempt to build a multimillion-dollar film facility hundreds of miles from Los Angeles, while also financing and filming the *Star Wars* sequel. Normally the studio takes out the loan to bankroll a film's budget. George borrowed it himself. He was now broke, having risked everything on *The Empire Strikes Back.*

The licensing arm made sure this time around there would not be any shortage of child size bedsheets, Dixie cups, trading cards, Burger King glasses, model kits, puppets, coasters, watches, and above all toys. Action figures, dolls, playsets, vehicles: may he who dies with the most toys win. Excess was all over *Empire*: the name of the author of the new novelization—a film-school friend of George's—was Donald *Glut.*

The only way to remain a down-and-dirty filmmaker, George felt, was with filthy lucre. In 1978 Kenner alone brought in $100 million in sales. By March 1979 toy sales were $200 million. Imagine what would happen when toys for the sequel were available from day one of its release! In a way, it would be like a company going public: George was betting the masses would pay a premium for rulers, pens, slide projectors, piggy banks, and erasers, all branded with Han, Luke, and Leia.

Everyone wanted to know what would happen in the second movie. So did George. "I want to have Luke kiss the princess in the second book," George had said back in 1975, before the first movie had started filming. (He often referred to his films as books.) "The second book will be *Gone with the Wind* in outer space," George continued. "She likes Luke, but Han is Clark Gable," referring to Gable's debonair smuggler Rhett Butler. This had been the plan before everyone saw the flying sparks whenever Carrie and Harrison shared a scene.

George's sequel story would be one catastrophe after another, as Leia and Han fall in love while rat-a-tatting insults at each other, all while the Empire was striking back at them. This premise solved a huge problem: who Leia was. The second film would define Leia as someone who takes charge in a crisis. Falling in love was low on her priority list, an irresponsible act made worse by the irresponsible person she was developing feelings for.

George decided to outsource the directing duties for the sequel to one of his film teachers, Irvin Kershner—when you're rich, you can hire people to do the jobs you don't want to do. George would produce from the Bay Area, a continent away from "Kersh" and the production. And he hired Leigh Brackett to write the *Empire* script: she had decades of screenwriting experience and a background in sci-fi novels to boot. George also signed her up to write a Princess Leia spinoff book.

Brackett, strangely, didn't focus much of her attention on the character of Leia. In her draft, Leia does little more than kiss Han and Luke, and then get kidnapped again. Luke carries the film, trains under a little swamp-dweller, and communes with the ghosts of Ben and his father Anakin about killing Darth Vader. Cancer claimed Brackett soon after she handed in her first draft, but her early work set the epic space fantasy on the right path.

George edited Leigh's script, scrapping some ideas, and saving others for a possible third film. He added some clever new dialogue: Han says he doesn't have time to run his decisions past a committee, and Leia barks back "I am not a committee!" His biggest single change, though, was cutting the visiting ghost of Anakin Skywalker. He made this cut because—spoiler alert—he had decided Darth Vader *was* Luke's real father. Anakin *was* Darth Vader.

This reveal is indeed a stunner, but one that doesn't hold up under scrutiny. Vader clearly didn't know Luke was his son in the first film: when did he find out? If Luke was in hiding, why wasn't he using a fake name? Why didn't Obi-Wan seem to know who Luke was? Wouldn't either Luke's *or* Vader's Jedi powers kick in if a blood relative was nearby? "I'd have laughed on camera if Mark had told me for the first time on camera," Carrie said. The entire cast was kept in the dark about this twist.

Enter screenwriter #3, Lawrence Kasdan, who'd recently written a romantic comedy for Spielberg. What George needed was some Bogie and Bacall, some Hepburn and Tracy. Kasdan's revisions added grit and grunge: Brackett's ice castles were changed to ice caves. Ships now malfunctioned, per the used-universe idea. And third-act conclusions were left dangling. George and Kersh went over every line of the new draft, to ensure they delivered on character development.

One of the exchanges between the ghost of Ben and Yoda involved searching for "another" Jedi. "We must find another," Kasdan had Yoda say. George changed that to "We must search for another," a more adventurous word choice. But in the final film, a very dramatically lit Yoda says "no... there is another."

This seemed to be a preview of the plot of the third film: another Jedi! But it was actually an escape pod.

In postproduction of the first film, driving to a pick-up shot location in Death Valley, Mark had been crashed his car, and required some reconstruction surgery. Rumors spread it was near-fatal: George worried whether he would survive. Mercenarily, he then wondered how the Luke-centered franchise could continue without a Luke. Solution: start telling the story of another Jedi.

Mark of course pulled through—the wampa attack scene may have been written to explain any residual scarring—and he had a multifilm contract. But George was a belt-and-suspenders guy, and wanted to plan for all eventualities. If Mark didn't come back for a third film, the stage was set for this other Jedi to take over. George had also written Han out rather dramatically at the end of the sequel, because Harrison made it clear he wouldn't do a third film. At least Carrie was on board: no Hoth feet for her.

As with the first film, the tight timeline and various writers left a few plot holes. On Hoth, for instance, Vader has the rebels pinned down, yet by personally invading instead of bombing he allows everyone to flee. It's almost like he wanted them to escape: hmm. Yoda was different as well: he was such an eleventh-hour creation, he's described as blue in the novelization and drawn as small as a shampoo bottle in the Marvel comic. And how much time does the film take place over? Han and Leia seem to be on the run for a few days, while Luke is in training for months.

Just as there were desert and jungle worlds in the first film, the second film would have ice worlds, cloud worlds (what Alderaan was supposed to look like), and in a nod to *Splinter of the Mind's Eye*, swamp worlds. This reflected George's microclimate-laden Bay Area, where the joke is if you don't like the weather, walk a few blocks. It could be foggy by Golden Gate Park, warm and sunny in Noe Valley, and cold and windy in Candlestick Point. *Star Wars'* planets shared that variety: if you didn't like Dagobah's humidity, walk to Tatooine.

Kershner, an actor's director, knew nothing about special effects. George, as producer, would look after that side of things, shepherding the second unit work. He wanted Kersh to get great performances from the actors. This echoed the ways of the past—William Wyler, the director of *Ben-Hur*, had little to do with its famed chariot race sequence. And it set another template for the future, where a film's director was responsible for the actors, not the postproduction dragons and wizards and whatnot.

John Mollo, who won one of *Star Wars'* seven Oscars for his costuming of the first film, kept Leia in white. Her snow outfit for the ice planet of Hoth featured a tan vest over an off-white jumpsuit, with a toque-style hat. Her "Hoth couture" was drastically tailored, but did not photograph like she was shrink-wrapped.

If we're talking cut and color, though, let's talk hair: was Leia still going to sport the buns? No, her new hairstyle was a crown of braids described as "1930s Nordic" by the production. This hairdo required more hair extensions, this time down to Carrie's waist. It seemed as sturdy as a bird's nest, and the right choice for a tense film where she wouldn't have much time to look in a mirror.

Chapter 11: Adverse Events

Mark, like Carrie, had found it hard to find work after *Star Wars*. His TV work dried up once he became known worldwide as Luke. He eventually found a starring role in the WWII film *The Big Red One*, but it wouldn't hit theaters until after *Empire* came out. Their success was like a monkey's paw wish; actors become rich and famous, with the fine print that they'll no longer be allowed to act.

Harrison took a different path: he signed up for films he disliked, so long as they were leading-man roles. He had held down war romances and westerns this way, and George and Steven Spielberg were grooming him for an action adventure where he would be a debonair grave robber, with a lot of Lash LaRue bullwhip scenes.

Carrie seemed a perfect fit for a romantic comedy film, but the roles weren't rolling in. Perhaps it was her second career as a mainstay of the LA party scene, where the choice was between the A-list "upstairs cocaine" or the pedestrian "downstairs cocaine." It was exhausting to keep playing this role, and possibly sabotaging her career. Word was getting out about Carrie's habits: she was poised to be yet another actress who sent her life up her nose.

Three years ago, no one noticed when Carrie flew in to the UK to start filming in Elstree. Now, the sequel choosing to film its snowy exteriors in the treeless mountain town of Finse, Norway, was Norway's biggest news. At a press conference, she and Mark wore matching blue anoraks with *Star Wars* décor on them—never too early to display the merchandise—to announce that *Empire* has officially begun its filming.

Mark told reporters that making the films was "fun": Carrie chimed in with "And terrifying." She played coy when asked if Leia would end up with Luke or Han: "I can't decide!" And when asked about the reception from *Star Wars*, Carrie said "I've had a lot of dating offers from 12-year-old boys." Every joke got a laugh. She and Mark then posed for playful pictures in the snow. (A reporter snuck onto the set and pressed Carrie for plot details. This level of hounding was new to her. Despite the reporter being female, she said it felt like an assault.)

That first night, she, Mark, and some production members from the first film dined in an Oslo restaurant that left them speechless. Or something had left them speechless: they just weren't clicking yet. The fabled group energy connecting them all had yet to kick in.

Carrie never got to film in Tunisia, but was glad to be part of location shooting this time around. She didn't have to be there: Leia didn't actually have any exterior scenes. But if someone *were* to write her such a snowy scene, *hint hint,* she was ready to go! No one did. So Mark and Harrison spent their days freezing in the snow, while Carrie partied in hotel rooms, venturing outside only to take more promotional pics. Other days she went sightseeing, but seemed fatigued by it.

Leia may have had no lines, but Carrie had plenty. This was the beginning of what she called being the "crew mascot." She fit the cheerleader bill better than earnest Mark, and certainly better than Harrison Bored. She was little and lithe enough to climb up camera members and walk across their heads and shoulders, maybe crouch on top of a camera.

Even for Norway, the winter weather became brutally cold. The camera lens had to be cold, otherwise snow would melt on it, but the camera itself had to be warm, otherwise the film inside would snap. For days everyone was snowed in: many of the Han and Luke snow scenes were filmed just steps from the hotel lobby. At nights, everyone asked around for who had booze. Once the roads became passable Carrie left for London, but she was in Scandinavia long enough to help cement the bond the cast and crew were developing.

Back in London, she stayed at a rented home in the ritzy St. John Wood section, featuring the famous Abbey Road crosswalk. A flat in the city gave her nightlife options beyond BBCs 1 through 7. The whole cast would sometimes head down to her place in the evenings to hang, maybe hit a disco afterwards. She mingled with other actors: all set visitors were given themed "Intergalactic Passports." Dan Aykroyd and John Belushi, visiting from New York, wanted to film cameos as space aliens. They didn't, but other actor friends did.

Her first filming day at Elstree was her reunion with much of the crew from the first film. "You did a film for a few months," she would write in *Postcards*, "and you got a family. An intimate family with its own dynamic, its own in-jokes, its own likes, dislikes, and romances. The intensity of it was heightened by the knowledge that it was all temporary. Not only did you know that it would end but, give or take a week or two, you knew when." The Elstree crew had just finished *The Shining*, and some were also working on a spaceship movie greenlit in *Star Wars'* success, Ridley Scott's *Alien*. (Ripley, the film's survivor, was originally going to be male, but the film's producer Alan Ladd Jr—who also produced *Star Wars*—realized the horror film needed a Leia.)

And just like last time, Carrie would begin filming by kissing Harrison. Rather, Leia would kiss Han. The old on-screen chemistry needed to be at its hottest, and it was. They worked with Kersh for a few alterations of the kiss-scene script: one or two lines were dropped, and Threepio interrupted much earlier, adding a comical button to the scene. Carrie chose to have Leia—who was plenty strong against intergalactic supervillains—wilt like a flower over Han. Not at his advances—those she fought off like womp rats—but at his insistence that she shared his feelings.

Over in the Hoth sets, all sorts of tricks were used to approximate actual ice: salt everywhere for white reflective gleams, magnesium sulfate on top for sparkle, and aerated mineral oil in the air to approximate fog. After an action shot blew scorch marks on the walls, painters would slather another layer of eggshell over top for another take. It could be over 100 degrees on set, which made for some real cognitive dissonance: it looks cold but feels hot. The set was designed to crumble for scenes of bombardment. The stage itself was brand-new, and not even finished: builders would hammer on exterior walls between takes because only parts of the vast room were finished.

On this set, dozens of extras in winter wear were gathered, all standing around Carrie. Cheerleading was one thing; acting was another. Leia had to speechify a few choice mouthfuls of far-off galaxy jargon, and her "proper cup of coffee" training was failing her. Appropriate for the setting, she froze. "[A]ll I could say was '…mumble mumble,' and then I walked off exactly as thought I'd said it correctly."

Carrie had fainted once on set from the heat and paint fumes. Her perpetually empty stomach didn't help keep her blood sugar up. She didn't like pub fare, nor the craft service offerings, so some days she only drank. "At one point I only weighed about 85 pounds, because we were working 12 hours a day," she said. She was told by worried crew members to gain weight.

Keeping things light became a heavy responsibility for her. When called to set, she'd ask to be carried on a chair, or be given a piggyback ride. When a contest winner visited the set, she ran lines with him. She hopped in Peter Mayhew's arms for one goofy photo after another. Once, she even told Mayhew to put his Chewbacca-furred hand on her chest, so she could act shocked for the camera. She posed with tape over her mouth. She teased Mark about Luke not having his own leitmotiv music, and Harrison for not having a puzzle with his face on it. This was all fueled by cocaine: she was now regularly using on set, and it was affecting her acting.

For a *Rolling Stone* cover, she was hoisted by Mark and Harrison, an elbow around each of their necks. A near-identical pose runs alongside the article, this time with her wearing a fashion-forward sideways baseball cap.

"There is something very childlike about being an actor," she said in the profile, "because you go in and they dress you, they put your makeup on, they do your hair, they bring you something to drink when you want it, they drive you there and they drive you home." At age 22, Carrie was having a second childhood.

But this one, too, was being gobbled up by pills. She would fall asleep on set, mix up her human and robot costars, and dream of cyborgs and androids. "So I had these violent nightmares, dreams where you keep trying to impose your reality and you can't. It gets you crazy." Carrie missed more and more days, claiming a cold, then the flu, then bronchitis; in reality she was too altered from the previous night's activities to function. She took a weekend vacation to Ireland, then jetted back home to California. Half the crew believed she was stricken with malady after malady; the other half had been around the block, and knew what they were seeing.

"I used up so much energy," she wrote in *Postcards from the Edge*, "explaining why I was late, why I didn't show up, how I wasn't really loaded, I was just tired, I had jet lag. Avoiding looking people in the eyes because I couldn't stand how I felt when I saw the disappointment in their faces. That ate up a lot of energy."

George was a straight-and-narrow guy—one of the reasons why he hated Los Angeles—and his vices ended at soda and chocolate bars. He refused to license *Star Wars* to vitamin companies, for fear of associating his characters with any type of pills. He was rarely on set, figuring that if he was, no one would treat Kersh like the film's director. But as producer he was surely aware that Carrie's perpetually altered state was affecting production.

"Kersh directs us actors more than George did," Carrie said. "But in *Star Wars*, George didn't really have to. There weren't as many scenes that called for character portrayal." Kersh moved his camera around more, and used stronger visuals, but like George he did not shoot coverage. This was a conscious choice on Kersh's part, to make both films feel structurally related to each other.

With *Empire's* script and Kersh's direction, Leia finally felt like a real person. "I'm open to suggestion," Carrie said. "I would be stupid to be otherwise. Leia is not a real character. She is more of a caricature and is somewhat one-dimensional. It's not really possible to write out a list of Princess Leia's likes and dislikes... In this film, though, Leia develops more."

Develops into what, though? All three leads saw their roles be as tailored as their costumes. Harrison's bruised-ego insensitivity and Mark's overeager rashness were now defining character flaws for Han and Luke. How could Carrie's own flaws echo in Leia? Carrie was madcap instead of stalwart, but where they overlapped was that they both tried way too hard.

For the Cloud City scenes, Leia got a new costume—one with colors other than white! Looking for the first time like she was in a proper sci-fi movie, Leia now wore a wine-colored knee-length tunic, with separate matching leggings, and over it a dun-colored macramé coverup. She resembled a futuristic nun. She also availed herself of Bespin's beauty shop, switching her crown of braids for a bun with two long twisty cables of hair. From the back it resembles a daisy with all but two petals removed: he loves me, he loves me not.

As for the actor's most important prop—her face—Carrie relied on a sophisticated make-up team to give her the no-makeup look. They erased any evidence of hard partying the night before. (Want Leia's look? Visit the London Cosmetics Museum. Framed on a wall is the Max Factor Make-Up Chart used for *Empire Strikes Back* to pretty Carrie up via base, shadow, and powder into a camera-ready Leia.)

Secrecy was important this time around: many actors were only given their pages, or sometimes just their lines. David Prowse was so notorious for leaking that he was given a dummy script: Darth Vader was clueless about this false flag operation, and that any plot twists he leaked were fake. Combine that with filming out of order, and frequent rewrites, and the status of reality was as up in air as Cloud City itself.

But back to that final Hoth scene, in what was becoming a real pressure cooker of a day. Carrie knew that as soon as she nailed another jargon-y monologue in front of 100 sweating extras pretending to be shivering, the whole set was going to be torn down, and Dagobah erected in its stead. The production had drifted weeks over schedule, millions over budget. And right now she, and she alone, was the sole remaining delay.

Nothing around her was what it seemed. Cold was hot, Leia's supposed longtime allies were brand new extras, and every second the camera wasn't burning film, construction crews were hammering like mad. All led to a final paradox: the indomitable princess in front of them was actually helpless, weak, and defeated.

Twice Carrie had to leave the set, to avoid the cacophony and the pressure. She knew the lines, but they were coming out in the wrong order. She kept doing the math in her head; how many hundreds of thousands of dollars did that flub just cost the production? The final shots, with extras looking very tense as Leia gives them their marching orders, was no doubt sweetened by the real struggle it took to attain.

Most big films feature a "second unit" to work at the same time as the first. For *Empire*, Carrie, said "they were working two and three and maybe four units at a time. And you were going from set to set and you had to sort of regroup your emotions for that particular requirement of each scene." While the Kersh-directed scenes felt "fun," the second unit could be a boiler room of tension.

John Barry, the first film's Oscar-winning set designer, was brought in as second unit director. A few weeks into filming, he felt ill and had to leave the set. Within 24 hours he had died, of meningitis. Barry had decided to power through his symptoms, and that decision had killed him. Production didn't stop; it couldn't, they were just too far behind. Nothing in Hoth was colder than the phrase "The show must go on."

Then came the cockpit.

For day after day, the principals all sat in the Millennium Falcon's cockpit—built larger than the first film, a small blessing—and looked out at nothing. They pretended to fly, to avoid obstacles, lasers, and other spaceships, all while staring at a blue wall that would be spaced out in postproduction. "The worst is when we're in the cockpit and you're supposed to see stars or asteroids or whatever special effect, but we don't see anything," Carrie said. "We're looking at a corner of a camera and screaming 'What are you going into an asteroid field for?' or 'There's something out there!'"

After so many stressful days, being stuck in a small room with each other did a number on everyone. Carrie and Mark fought almost daily: by day's end, neither of them could remember what it was that had made them upset. Harrison once got a stagehand's saw and start hacking apart the set in anger, while the rest of the cast debated who, if anyone, should stop him.

Rewriting went from being done daily to being done hourly. Kersh ended up spearheading much of this, improving an already solid script. One exposition scene began with Leia saying "Not bad, hot shot, not bad: then what?" to Han. Kersh crossed out everything but "Then what?" since Leia at this point in the film was in no mood for chit-chat. Out went many of Leia's small-talk moments, always getting her right to the point. These changes made Leia tenser, more direct, more, well, Leia-like.

There was scripted misunderstanding a bit later: Han says they're going to see Lando, and Leia thinks Lando is a planet, not a person. As scripted it was a bit wordy: Kersh boiled it down to three words: Han says "Lando," and Leia says "Lando system?"

These changes made the scenes more effective, more true to character, more informative, and most importantly shorter. Actors may angle for adding a clever line, or ask for a close-up, but few think about the scene as a whole, and how it in turn relates to the picture as a whole. Carrie saw how rewriting could be done well, and on the fly, provided you could see both the forest and the trees.

One day she bowed out of filming early, claiming to be ill. That evening she hosted an infamous party where Eric Idle brought a drink nicknamed "Tunisian table-cleaner." Table-cleaning ensued. "Well, Harrison came over," Carrie said, "and the Rolling Stones came over, and I think we stayed up most of the night." She showed up late the next day, received some "medication" from the crew, and then was "relaxed" enough to film.

That was their first day filming with new cast member Billy Dee Williams, who played Lando, the person not the system. Lando was Han if he had better luck with cards, ladies, and life. Billy Dee played him like a riverboat gambler. Perhaps to ensure Carrie played Leia as equal parts

77

intrigued and repulsed by Lando, he kept whispering dirty things to her on set that day. She whispered dirty things right back.

"She's not quite a disciplined performer yet," Williams said, hinting at her bright young thing antics, "but she could be, I think, in the future." The crew was reportedly "anxious" to get Carrie's scenes wrapped, so they could focus more on Mark, who had a light saber fight with Darth Vader and all of Dagobah still to film.

In Leia and Han's goodbye scene, her final scripted line was "I love you. I couldn't tell you before, but it's true." To which Han would respond "Just remember that, 'cause I'll be back." But in an impromptu story conference with Kersh, Harrison suggested a change. "But if she says 'I love you,' and I say "I know,' it's beautiful and it's acceptable and it's funny." Kersh readily agreed: it would become one of the best moments of the film. It works for Leia because she's finally brave enough to admit the truth to Han, and it's true to Han that it gives him the courage to face his demise, and to needle her one last time.

But getting to the "I know" was tumultuous, and required from Carrie a bit of *Jane Eyre*-style "I have as much soul as you" spirit. When Harrison told Carrie about the script changes, she grew incensed that she hadn't been part of the conversation. And possibly that it was reflective of their past relationship: her head over heels, him flatfooted. To her, it felt like this wasn't Han getting the last word over Leia, it was Harrison getting the last word over Carrie.

Then Kersh and Billy Dee Williams came over. Carrie started pitching the director her ideas: Leia can maybe slap Lando, which would give her and Williams something new to do in the scene. She demonstrated by slapping Billy Dee Williams, hard, out of nowhere. "Don't hit me like that!" he cried out, and she apologized.

But she was still irate for Kersh treating her like a "day player." "Harrison was here while you were making changes, and I always feel like it's behind my back... I always feel like 'it's the bimbo again.'...I would just like to be there. I don't even need to say anything."

Kersh told Carrie that he gave Harrison carte blanche for the scene because he felt it was Han's scene, and Harrison was "very insecure" about making suggestions. "He's not *insecure*— *I* barely even speak!" Carrie retorted.

Carrie then realized that while she was no longer angry at Harrison—it had burned out of her system—he was now angry at her.

"As you can see," she said, "he is very angry, as he has a total right to be because I would not speak to him. I'm sorry. So it may play well for the first part of the scene, but if we have to kiss each other, there might be some trouble."

Kersh then warned his assistant director that "Everybody's furious with each other. Carrie went crazy." Carrie went to apologize to Harrison, but he waved her off. She warned Kersh that "Harrison and I will probably not be speaking with each other for another couple of hours." A few minutes later she grew distraught over things. When filming, Harrison asked to use Carrie's stand-in: Carrie herself sat off-camera, dejected, on an orange and black staircase soon to be immortalized in a lightsaber fight.

"I think Carrie in her way is very dedicated," Kersh later said. "I think she hides it. It's not stylish to be that dedicated." Everyone says they want passionate people, but few are prepared to deal with the passion they can bring to a project.

Harrison got over it, and filming resumed with Carrie. On dailies that night, Carrie's off-camera body mike recorded her "I love you" at the correct volume. Harrison's reply was an "I KNOW" that sounded screamed by a giant through a megaphone. It prompted a huge release of laughter, the surprise breaking the tension of the day. Fittingly, the final scene would do that exact same thing: the audience's emotions would need an outlet for their grief.

* * *

After burning through $25 million of the bank's money, George got an unhappy phone call: he had a new contact there, and the new contact was turning off the money spigot. George was faced with going to Fox to get the remaining money to complete the film. If he did that, they'd surely demand ownership over the picture. All his risk would have been for nothing.

Things looked dim for weeks, right up until another bank happily agreed to finance the *Star Wars* sequel. But to get the loan George had to put all of Lucasfilm on the line. "If it isn't a success not only could I lose everything, but I could also end up being millions of dollars in debt, which would be very difficult to get out from under." This exact thing happened to his friend Francis Ford Coppola, destroying both his film studio American Zoetrope, and his friendship with George, who couldn't (or wouldn't) lend him money to stay afloat.

He kept these fiscal worries from Kersh and the cast: they had the movie to worry about. (Keeping the secret also let him stay at home.) The footage arriving to be edited was often superb. Kersh had dreamed up many wonderful little bits, like Artoo getting up on tiptoes to look in Yoda's window. "There's also a point when Lando's driving," George said. "Something goes wrong with the ship, and Leia and Chewie turn and look at each other. It's just a funny little moment for me, between a woman and Wookiee."

Chapter 12: New York State of Mind

Empire Strikes Back's filming never seemed to end, especially after Mark injured his thumb, forcing him to be out for weeks. Each cast member had missed some work due to stress-related ailments. And all that on-set rewriting and directing made the already expensive film $10 million over budget. Vacations helped with the stress, but the miracle cure to all their ills was wrapping up filming.

Carrie finished filming *Empire* after 68 days, many more than on *Star Wars*. A few days before she left, a phone call from Mom warned that there was a kidnapping threat. It was probably a false alarm, probably nothing, but Carrie had bodyguards on set for her final few days of filming. So much for no stress. To bring a little bit of Los Angeles to the set, on her last day of filming she hired London's only Mexican restaurant to cater a taco and enchilada lunch.

Returning to New York, she spent some of the fall watching Paul and his former partner Art Garfunkel get ready for a reunion gig in New York City. It would be the first time in years they'd performed together, from a specially built stage in Central Park. Half a million people watched that show from the Great Lawn: Carrie watched it from backstage. (That wasn't even her best seat for a Simon & Garfunkel reunion. Her friend Penny Marshall had started dating Art, and Penny goaded them into an impromptu concert in their living room. Neither singer had the energy to fight their girlfriends, so their first reunion show was for an audience of two.)

* * *

When Carrie was in the sound booth doing *Empire Strikes Back* ADR, she was given lines for an 800 number. All the cast were recording 30-second sound bites, which teased what would happen in the upcoming film. And they were written in character. "'But the Rebel Alliance must and will succeed in forever ridding the galaxy of their… scowge?' What the hell is that?" Carrie was told the word was "scourge." "Why do you give me this ancient dialogue to say? 'Scourge?' Do we all say 'scourge,' and I missed it?" She eventually defeated the scourge, and posed for a photo of Leia holding a telephone receiver.

The second time around, George's FX team at ILM ran a much tighter ship. George again timed each shot he wanted down to the frame: this saved time and energy, since an 11-frame shot didn't require an A-list effort. For some pick-up shots of the bog planet, George filmed his own half-dug back-yard pool, which sadly enough could double as Dagobah very convincingly.

To help with editing this time around, George had crude stick-figure animations of the attack scenes made. Everyone could now visualize what the final scene's actions were supposed to be, and how best to craft each shot to take its place in sequence. This style of "pre-visualization" would become standard in moviemaking. He also brought in Marcia, busy shepherding the construction of Lucasfilm, to "guest cut" a Han-and-Leia scene.

Audio guru Ben Burtt collected over a thousand new sounds, including the stomp of a metal-cutting machine, to serve as the calamitous AT-AT footsteps, a slowed-down sea otter as the cries of the tauntaun, and the power windows of a Cadillac Eldorado for Threepio's joints. He collected loads of animals sounds for the denizens of Hoth and Dagobah, among them tree monsters and snow squirrels, but most were cut from the final film.

John Williams returned to write new themes, most notably Darth Vader's Imperial March. For the new love theme, which he called Han Solo and the Princess, he again turned to the rising-sixth D-major of Leia's theme from the first film. This love theme plays when Han and Leia first kiss, and again when they say goodbye.

The only thing uplifted at the end of *Empire Strikes Back* is a very soggy X-Wing. Luke gets his hand cut off, and finds out Darth Vader is his father. Han is freeze-dried, then floated away to a gangster's confines. Leia is betrayed by Han's supposed friend Lando. Threepio is dissembled to pieces. Audience was captivated: was Han coming back? How did Leia hear Luke's Force distress call? Was Luke really Vader's son? Who was the other trainable Jedi Yoda mentioned?

Fox made theaters promise to run the film for up to half a year straight in order to claim a print: strongarm tactics work when you have a strong arm. Early marketing included a trailer narrated by Harrison Ford in an unrecognizable gee-willikers voice. Lucas wanted the poster to promise romance, so Han and Leia were posed a la Rhett and Scarlett in *Gone With the Wind*. As a poster girl, Leia had gone from bang bang to kiss kiss. (Marketing was also aided by dumpster-diving thieves, who would grab bits of rubbish from ILM, including snippets of film, and sell them to magazines as sneak peeks.)

As long as filming was, the press tour seemed longer. At a London department store, the cast signed autographs under a banner proclaiming "LUKE SKYWALKER & HIS FRIENDS." Carrie did one interview in a room filled with merchandise from the first film, the sci-fi equivalent of a doctor's ego wall. Every day more men with microphones and notepads arrived, to capture Carrie's particular style of sweet nothings.

Each junket, each interview and profile, revolved around a paradox: actors weren't supposed to actually discuss the film, especially its ending. Instead they were supposed to entice people to see the film, but never in a way too huckster-y or desperate. A bit aloof, a bit befuddled, like Dean Martin two scotches into the evening.

Carrie was in her glory. They wanted quotable but inscrutable lines? Welcome back, my friends, to the show that never ends. She joked about the gaffer-tape bra from the first film, and recycled her old jokes about calling David Prowse "Darth Farmer." Regarding a cut scene of torture: "I loved the idea of having yellow eyes and being beaten and carried." Regarding her less-than-stellar career outside *Star Wars:* "I function exclusively in space, it seems."

On Leia: "Lucas always had to remind me to 'Stand up! Be a princess!' And I would act like a Jewish princess, and lean forward, slouching, chewing gum." On Chewie: "If she had her wits about her, she would have fallen for the big, strong Wookiee." On Vader: "Darth Vader having an affair, making the princess do awful, kinky things. Then afterwards, you could shoot a scene where you see her sleeping contentedly, and have him lying there, smoking a cigarette."

She described herself as "a strong girl with a low voice and self-righteous nature." That wasn't how others saw her, she knew. "[Being Leia] changed my name from Carrie '[movie star's] Daughter' Fisher to Carrie ' *Star Wars'* Fisher. I don't think I'll have to change my middle name again."

"I'm way under the weather today," she told a New York alternative weekly reporter, apologetically. "I feel bad that I can't articulate… that I can't properly represent myself and the film. I love the film… because you can be transported. It's very childlike so you can be very childlike."

She was feeling physically better but emotionally vulnerable for a *Rolling Stone* reporter, who talked with her in her New York apartment. Death was on her mind. "When we all kick off, we will be the princess and Luke and Han," she admitted.

"How does that make you feel?" the reporter asked.

"Her smiles vanishes and the color drains from her face," the reporter wrote. Carrie's response? "Helpless."

The film had a pair of premieres. The US premiere was in Washington DC, attended by members of the Kennedy family: First Daughter Amy Carter looked starstruck as she posed for pictures with the cast. The world premiere in London was attended by Queen Elizabeth's daughter Margaret: two princesses for the price of one. Carrie brought a pair of dates, Paul Simon (visiting from the set of *One-Trick Pony*) and Art Garfunkel.

Then the rest of the world got to see *Empire Strikes Back*. It broke first-day box office records to a preposterous degree: how do you improve upon selling out every seat of every show, as many theaters did? It made the cover of *Time* magazine. The novelization sold two million copies in its first week alone: the *Empire* strikes paperback.

George needed the second film to hit at least $60 million to not lose his studio: "It has to be the biggest grossing sequel of all time for me to break even." *Empire* ended up making over $200 million, putting it #3 on the all-time list, behind *Jaws* and *Star Wars*. The merchandising for the sequel alone was revolutionary: everywhere you looked, Vader's steampunk samurai eyes looked back. Every Christmas tree would have an AT-AT and a Snowspeeder under it. George was, for the third time in a decade, set for life: his big bet had paid off.

Lucasfilm had a smut squad, who regularly sued anyone trying to market pornographic parodies. The office assumed, likewise, that *Mad Magazine's* parody "The Empire Strikes Out" deserved at least a cease-and-desist warning letter. *Mad* sent the legal team back a fan letter from George Lucas himself, who said he loved both the magazine and the parody: oops. The squad stuck to threatening merchandise bootleggers from then on.

The second *Star Wars* film was critic-proof, which was a polite way of saying its initial reviews were mixed. From the 21st century this seems shocking; everyone knows *Empire* is the best of the trilogy. But back then critics were true cineastes, and *Star Wars* was understandable by five-year-olds. Therefore, it's no Fassbinder. The bad reviews were from highbrow aesthetes, fighting a losing battle against the low- and middlebrow.

Empire's reputation would soon match its box office. As the entertainment of the 1980s continued to level-set to the lowest common denominator, *Empire* began to be seen not as weak Shakespeare but as great space opera. Like *Godfather Part II* before it, it proved that sequels didn't have to be cheapo cash-ins. Each successful film had the potential to start a whole licensing and merchandising emporium, with sequels, novels, and everything else that came with a multimedia platform. Any successful film, handled the right way, could become the next *Star Wars.*

All through the summer *Empire* struck back. It was too bad for any other film that came out, such as Mark's movie *The Big Red One*. Or Dan Aykroyd and John Belushi's *The Blues Brothers*. Their black-suited alter egos had been the musical guest the night of Carrie's SNL hosting gig, and she had a recurring role in the film as a gun-toting, potty-mouthed mad bomber. In any other movie that would be a memorable role. But *Blues Brothers* was a riot of overkill: cars demolished entire malls, Volkswagens fell from the sky, and a traffic accident causes a Brobdingnagian three-story pile-up of police cruisers. Oh, and it was a musical.

Carrie stuck around during filming, even on nights when she wasn't needed on set: *Blues Brothers* notoriously had cocaine as part of its budget. Even without the drugs, John Belushi was a bulldog of energy and affection, while Dan Aykroyd preferred to let his mouth do the motoring. She became friends with them both, tagging along not only in Chicago, but also LA and New York. In Malibu, they surprised Carrie's 13-year-old sister Joely, wandering into the house all wearing sunglasses, then all collapsing on the couch.

Dan was her ex, but during filming she fell for him again, despite still being with Paul. "Danny was adorable, he was lovely," Carrie said. "He's just your classic codependent and caretaker." Dan offered a nice hot-and-cool balance to Carrie, unlike Paul, who was a fellow spitfire. Dan got her to stop using cocaine: she was energetic enough without it.

"I was set up with Danny by John," Carrie said. "John invited me over and then passed out. That was the set-up. That was a blind date, John style." Dan felt she was too thin, so in his movie trailer he made her eat. Mid-meal, Carrie started to choke on a Brussel sprout. Dan did the Heimlich maneuver and saved her. Minutes later, he proposed marriage. Carrie thought: "Wow, I probably better," since a spouse could be the safety net she apparently needed. Right after that she went clothes shopping for Dan; if they were going to be together, she wanted him to look good. Plus, retail therapy is better than no therapy.

Carrie and Dan moved in together into Dan's Chicago place, in Astro Tower, a modernist aluminum box that resembled a three-dimensional computer punchcard. Carrie disliked its coldness, and Dan apologized on behalf of his apartment's architectural flaws. When the *Blues Brothers* shoot was done they flew to Martha's Vineyard, where John's wife had bought Dan and Carrie a house. Carrie disliked this house as well, saying it "looks like it was abandoned by Fred and Wilma Flintstone." (She hadn't liked her childhood home either, saying it resembled a post office.)

Dan was nevertheless in love with her: he gave her a blue sapphire ring, and they had pre-marriage blood tests done. But all Carrie's architecture criticism masked something deeper: she wasn't ready for this. One day she left Martha's Vineyard, returned to New York, and resumed life with Paul. That was that. For Dan, Carrie was the one who got away.

Chapter 13: Kudos

Not for nothing was one of Paul Simon's definitive songs called "The Boxer": he was a man in constant conflict. The course of his life seemed to be set when he was 11, and struck up a friendly rivalry with another boy in a school play of *Alice in Wonderland*. That boy—the Cheshire Cat to Paul's White Rabbit—was Art Garfunkel. The next 30 years of their life was one-upsmanship: who sang better, who had the better solo album, who was more respected, who'd lost less hair. They'd always forgive each other, and always resume feuding a bit later.

This seemed to set up a template in his life: every interaction was a proving ground, every relationship a chronicle of the wills. He'd never seriously dated someone as successful as he was: with Carrie he found someone who shared his celebrity asymmetry. Carrie had grown up in this world, though, and thrived in it. This younger, less accomplished person was somehow better at being herself in public than Paul was.

Paul had the very thing he wanted—an independent, strong, smart, funny, successful, beautiful woman. Carrie was even game to step up and, at an age other women were finishing college, be a surrogate stepmother to Paul's young son Harper. Coming from the home that she had, she knew the longing a child had for parental figures—and the damage a partner could do if they weren't committed. She would become a second mother to Harper, and love him as if he were her own, regardless of how she was feeling toward Paul at the time.

Despite all of this, Paul and Carrie couldn't stop fighting. A lot of it was about partying: he had seen his fair share of rock and roll excesses, and Carrie couldn't stop. She couldn't even go to sleep without pills. Her behavior was erratic in ways that drugs alone didn't account for. They had not enough bridge, way too much troubled water.

Carrie prepped for her *Empire* success by landing a leading role in a Broadway musical set in a nightclub, with the odd name of *Censored*

Scenes From King Kong. The farcical plot is about hidden spy codes in the cut scenes of the giant ape film. Carrie's *Playbill* biography claimed that "[s]he is well known to audience through her performances on film and in television," giving equal weight to Leia and her British TV role in *Come Back, Little Sheba.* In terms of word count, much more is made of short films she made for *SNL* than *Star Wars*, or the "soon to be released *Empire Strikes Back*." She ended her bio with a Carrie Fisher Sentence of a joke: "In real life Ms. Fisher is surprisingly tall."

This is who she wanted to be: a working comedienne, a trained actor, a singer, a Broadway star... anyone but Princess Leia. Alas, *Censored Scenes* was performed at what had been the 22 Steps Theater, but which had recently changed its name... to the Princess Theater. There was no escaping Leia, it seemed. Especially not via this particular show: it closed after five performances. This may have saved her money in security: Mark was appearing on Broadway down the road in *The Elephant Man,* and his hired security cost almost as much as his salary.

Carrie's next film role seemed a perfect opportunity: a zany hotel comedy. She was the female lead in *Under the Rainbow*, a slapstick period piece about Nazi spies, Japanese spies, and the filming of *The Wizard of Oz.* Carrie played a chipper, wavy-haired production assistant, and Chevy Chase was a Secret Service agent. Chase towered over her as much as she towered over the dozens of short actors playing Munchkins.

But she didn't get along with Chase, and her drug use was escalating. Her mom, trying to help, assumed Carrie was only using hallucinogens, not opioids as well. She called a friend she knew who had experience with it. Carrie probably felt like she was on acid when she got a phone call from Hollywood legend Cary Grant, warning her about bad acid trips.

"By then I was supercrazy," she said about the *Under the Rainbow* filming. "I mean, my behavior was really... it wasn't just the drugs. I was really nuts then. I think I was taken from that set in an ambulance." Mom met her at the hospital, mother and daughter both still wearing their wigs, costumes, and makeup form their mutual days of filming. The Hollywood farce came and went from theaters faster than the madcap hotel's doors slammed. "I didn't have that much fun making *Under the Rainbow*," she said on *The Tonight Show*.

All Carrie's life she had said yes: yes had gotten her where she was, for better or worse. But movie stars must learn the power of saying no:

no to interviews that stripped away the glamorous mystique, no to most scripts coming their way, and no to most public appearances. Carrie kept saying yes, and because of that Hollywood started to say no.

Carrie's antics became notorious. At LA gatherings she'd go through people's medicine cabinets, claiming to be Robin Hood "taking from the straight, and giving to the potentially stoned." When with Paul she'd sometimes jump up on stage to sing songs like "Bye Bye Love" with him. And she and Penny Marshall, who shared October birthdays, began throwing legendary joint parties that became one of the coolest invites of the year.

Carrie appeared on Penny's show *Laverne & Shirley* in its sixth season, dressing up in a Playboy Bunny outfit and singing a showtune. That was the week Penny's daughter left for college: she was on set for some last moments of mother-daughter bonding. Carrie saw Penny, also in bunny ears and a bathing suit, and joked to her daughter "Study hard, and one day you can be as successful as your mother."

Both this guest spot and *Under the Rainbow* featured Carrie in states of undress. Like many actors cast in wholesome roles, Carrie gravitated toward racier fare, perhaps just to show that while *Star Wars* was PG, she was not. She never felt she was attractive, so costumes that didn't skimp on the skimpiness was a way to, in her mind, give men a reason to look at her.

She had no idea what the third *Star Wars* movie would entail, but reporters kept asking anyway. When one asked what she wanted to happen to Leia in the third film, she joked "I'd like to have a door open and you'd catch me with of my buns off. And I'd say 'Look, my planet's been blown up, my boyfriend's been frozen, I've been tortured, I've been chased around in space for years now, I'm just gonna take so much.'"

In the *Star Wars* comics, Leia was still having new adventures: with Han in deep freeze she went from barely appearing in most issues to becoming the comic's main character. One issue she's stuck on a neutral no-weapons planet and has to defeat Darth Vader through wits alone. Another, she's blowing up a mobile Death Star called the Tarkin. In a third, she's saving another planet from an Alderann-like destruction. Leia was now all about take-charge versatility.

That versatility would be reflected in a third movie, which had to live up to perhaps more expectations, both financial and critical, than any film before ever had. Both *Star Wars* and *American Graffiti* had been films "where people felt better coming out of the theater than when they went in."

That was due to the three-act structure: set up stakes, heighten the stakes, resolve them. *Empire* was made to be incomplete: it was an installment of a story, not one with an actual end. Harrison joked that the even without a proper ending, the film had "at least $11 worth of entertainment."

This meant that the third film had to both resolve *Empire's* cliffhangers and serve as a proper conclusion to the three-film cycle. And set up the next three-film sequence. At least George had all his cast available. Carrie was of course on board, as was Mark. Surprisingly, Harrison said he would finish the trilogy. Too bad he'd been written off!

Star Wars was always going to be a trilogy, George knew. "In the end [of the second film], I want Han to leave," George said, back in 1975, during the first film's preproduction. "Han splits at the end of the second book [he referred to the movies as books], and we learn who Darth Vader is."

"In the third book," George went on, "I want the story to be just about the soap opera of the Skywalker family, which ends with the destruction of the Empire." He also wanted Leia to end up with Luke, and Han to sacrifice himself. Harrison was on board for that story: Han's story would end well if he gave up his life for his friends.

Production staffers scoured the globe looking for locations with breathtaking geography and access to nearby hotels. They ended up in their own backyard: sequoias and redwoods in Northern California. The Tatooine scenes would be in the epic sand dunes of Yuma, Arizona. Both locations were told that a horror film called *Blue Harvest: The Ultimate Evil* would be filmed there, not the third *Star Wars* film. This was to keep spoilers from leaking, and also to avoid price gouging.

Like with the first two films, George locked himself in a room to write it with pencils and yellow legal pads. Draft after painful draft came out. He kept moving around big story beats—Leia on a hoverbike, Luke fighting Vader over lava pits, a furry tribe of forest dwellers, a pleasure barge sailing over sand. At one point Ben Kenobi was going to not only resurrect himself but resurrect Anakin Skywalker.

For one of these happy final beats—a victory celebration—George wrote "Han & Leia confront Luke" in his notes. Then he drew a connecting line and wrote one word: "Sister!" It was the shoelaces thing: two independent plot strings, tied together in a perfect bow. In this case, the two strings were how to resolve the love triangle, and who was the other Jedi Yoda hinted at. George's brainstorm solved it: Leia Organa and Luke Skywalker were long-lost brother and sister—twins, in fact.

This doubled down on Darth Father-style plot twists: Vader was now a deadbeat dad to *two* kids? And he had kidnapped and tortured his own daughter without realizing it? And that scene where Leia kisses Luke to spite Han: she was kissing *her brother*? It roped in yet another character to the Skywalker family drama, but at the expense of credibility.

Here's how George saw the backstory playing out: "Luke's father gets subverted by the Emperor. He gets a little weird at home, and his [pregnant] wife begins to figure out that things are going wrong." Obi-Wan fights Anakin, who falls into lava but survives. Ben tells Anakin's wife that her husband has survived. But "Mrs. Skywalker has had these kids, the twins, so she has these two little babies who are six months old or so. So everybody has to go into hiding." They separate, Ben taking Luke, and "Mrs. Skywalker" taking Leia. "She died shortly thereafter, and Leia is brought up by her foster parents. She knows that her real mother died."

More ideas from the first film populate the third. The Sarlaac pit, a vast tentacled mouth buried in the sand, is essentially the garbage monster from the trash compactor scene. The seedy scenes in Jabba's palace expand upon the creepy welter of the Mos Eisley Cantina. Jabba the Hutt, cut from the first film, finally appears, as an immense disgusting worm. A battle between forest aliens and imperial forces, first written in 1974, would become the Ewok climax of the film. George admitted much of this film was similar to the first, except with the time and budget and know-how to do it right.

Rehashing these leftover ideas would be another new director, Richard Marquand. George had gotten into a row with the Director's Guild of America, and quit in a huff. Now anyone who worked with Lucasfilm would be similarly kicked out of the DGA, or at least fined. Since Marquand was English, and thus not able to be a DGA member, this wasn't an issue.

One of the things that drew Marquand to the film—besides the accomplishment of directing a *Star Wars* film—was how George had handled Leia. "I talked about the way that Carrie Fisher was portrayed—she meant a lot to me in *Star Wars*—that she was this perfect little doll-like creature, and how terrific it was."

Marquand was added to the regular meetings with George and returning screenwriter Lawrence Kasdan, to hammer out the script. How could they make this story seem like it was the conclusion they'd envisioned since 1977? As JW Rinzler wrote in his *Making of Return of the Jedi* book, "while [Han and Leia's] love affair had been central to *Empire*, the couple was given only a functional task in *Jedi*." "I think you should kill Luke," Kasdan suggested in a story conference with George and Richard Marquand, "and have Leia take over."

"You don't want to kill Luke," George replied.

"Okay, then," Kasdan said, "kill Yoda." George objected to this as well: he was a toyseller as well as a storyteller now, and no one wanted a doll of a dead character. He eventually relented, and Yoda was given a peaceful exit.

The three devised an elaborate rescue plan for Han, which would put all the players in action. Marquand suggested Leia wear a bounty-hunter disguise, pretending Chewbacca was her prisoner. It was the same exact story beat from *Star Wars*, George pointed out. But it worked once, so it would work again.

When Leia thaws Han out, she finds out he's blind. "It could help the scene when he comes to life and embraces Leia, and he just feels her face," Kasdan said. George then suggested a line Jabba could say upon discovering them—"So you like to kiss. I like to kiss, too." Considering Jabba had green goo coming out of his nose and brown goo coming out of his mouth, the line was ultimately too repellant to be filmed.

Leia's capture by Jabba—he would put her in a "dancer" outfit, they decided—would be visually indicated by a metal shackle she had on her ankle. This would allow Luke to visually free her by slicing it with his lightsaber. But the three quickly realized Leia was a character who had to free herself: the chain would become the weapon she used to choke Jabba to death.

Once the main cast was rescued, a reunion scene on the Millennium Falcon seemed mandatory. But there was so much ground to cover—Leia and Han's reunion, Luke and Han's reunion, Chewie and Han's reunion, etc.—that it would take forever on film. "I don't want to do this," George groused, "and I've struggled and got myself in all these drafts because I wanted to avoid this moment." They would end up moving individual reunion scenes to Jabba's palace, expanding the opening segment to nearly 45 minutes.

Leia was always set to befriend the Ewoks: an earlier draft had her also save some captured rebels, but that role was given to Threepio. A solo-mission subplot of hers was scrubbed, as was Luke's adventures before he arrived at Jabba's palace, and an escape plan involving a sandstorm.

Luke's showdown with Vader was going to be on the previously unseen Imperial homeworld of Had Abaddon, with spaceship battles through the city planet's streets. But it was too hard to pull off, so just like with the first film's Alderaan scenes, this confrontation was moved to the Death Star. Oh, yeah, there was another Death Star. Third verse, same as the first!

* * *

"They think I'm some kind of space bitch."

Carrie was discussing the third film with Marquand—though venting might be the better word. This was the cast's chance to affect the screenplay. Mark lobbied to give Luke a girlfriend, since Leia was obviously off the table. Harrison lobbied for Han to die—but he didn't know about the secret twin reveal, or that Han and Leia were going to sail off into the sunset together at lightspeed.

For her sake, Carrie wanted booze. "I asked George for some sort of drinking problem," she said. "I said, 'Leia lost her parents and planet in the first film, and in the second a very close friend lost his hand and her first boyfriend was frozen. By the third movie, I must be totally exhausted. I've been chased for who knows how many years.' I figure, I'm ready to go 'Hey guys, I can't do this anymore. I'm going to get my hair done. You handle it!' And I book myself into a convent."

It was an astute observation: Leia goes through the most peril, loses the most by far, yet seems to suffer the least. To Carrie it was inconceivable: the *robots* had more emotional responses than Leia did. Actors normally love when their characters suffer, since it lets them emote. But the suffering without the emoting was, to Carrie, a sign that Leia was burying her trauma in a deeply unhealthy way.

"If only I could just break down," Carrie told the director, referring to Leia as "I" instead of "she." Right after making that mistake, Carrie did break down, sobbing in front of her director, over how wrecked Leia must be, and how deep she's had to bury her pain for the greater good.

Marquand couldn't give Han a death scene, or Luke a girlfriend, or even Leia a breakdown. He commiserated with Carrie about Leia's diminished emotional spectrum. In his mind, what he liked least about *Empire* was Leia's steeliness. "In the last movie, the princess became such a bitch, she really was a drag," Marquand said. "It became very boring. I was sure there was a lot more depth there we could use, and more comedy too." Leia, in other words, should smile more.

Carrie referred to the *Star Wars* cast as crew as "a club," and in this club her role was the Cool Girl. Per Gillian Flynn, the Cool Girl is a woman who pretends to be who men want her to be. A Cool Girl would accept that in a film like this, her role was to shut up and look pretty. Carrie was very much the Cool Girl, swapping dirty jokes, staying thin, dressing to please others, and never bringing down the party mood by asking for better treatment for herself.

But it was one thing for herself to be demeaned. It was different when Leia was slighted. Carrie felt protective of her, this fictional warrior. This bastion, this powerhouse, this woman who never needed any protection. Carrie would take all sorts of bad treatment. But don't dare mistreat Leia.

Chapter 14: Ending Battle

Moviemaking, like trucking and mining, was a male-dominated business. But that was finally changing. Lucasfilm employed women in most departments now, including many leadership roles. A sign posted during *Revenge of the Jedi* production by one woman's office read "PLEASE... NO SLEEZY [sic] GEEKS TODAY." Communication between departments always seemed a little smoother when there were women involved, leading to fewer screw-ups and wasted effort. (There was still wasted effort. The male-dominated ILM built a huge lava pit for the third film, only to be told the lava-pit scene had been cut weeks ago.)

Despite this push for more inclusion, most of the "women" of Lucasfilm remained the wives and girlfriends of the male staffers. The mothers in the group (including Marilou Hamill, Mark's wife) would take turns hosting lunches every Monday. The Park Way Princesses who were moms were invited to join as well. Marcia Lucas was invited to stop by: she had freeze-framed her editing career to raise a family. Amanda Lucas was adopted in 1981, and Marcia's days were now divided between baby care and design work for Lucasfilm's in-construction buildings.

One of the new moms in attendance was costume designer Aggie Rodgers, who'd worked with George ever since *American Graffiti*. During some of the staff meetings, if it was her son's feeding time, she would breastfeed him. "I'm rather bossy," she said later, "but I'm also very nonthreatening." One of the producers complained: Aggie shrugged. "Well, what am I supposed to do? My son is hungry." Because of actions like this, she said, Richard Marquand didn't consider her an employee so much as a burden.

Marquand had a duty, he felt, to reinvent *Star Wars* for a new audience. Fans of the first film had appreciated the second, darker installment, he explained to reporters. Now that audience comprised teenagers and young adults, and they deserved something appealing to them. Sure, Ewoks would bring smiles to the eight-year-olds, but other parts of the film would reward older audience members with "a lot of excitement and a lot of showmanship."

He was talking mostly about Leia's harem-girl outfit, usually referred to as slave-girl Leia, or just Slave Leia. It would introduce a whole generation to bondage fantasies, and somehow eclipse even Leia's cinnamon-bun look in people's minds, especially boys and men. *Star Wars* was a fantasy film, after all, but *this* wasn't the type of fantasy George was intending. "I may have been naïve," he said later, "but I sort of missed that angle."

"I couldn't believe the way Princess Leia was dressed in Cloud City," Marquand said. "It was a disgrace: this beautiful girl in this terrible brown and white outfit." For his film, he wanted Carrie to be in a risqué outfit, because she was "a very sexy girl… she was very embarrassed to try it on the first time, which is not surprising."

Instead of John Mollo, a new team of costumers was working on *Jedi*. Nowhere was that more apparent than with Leia's slave girl outfit, which dispensed with the worn, utilitarian, nondescript idea. This new look was inspired by Frank Frazetta, painter of barbarians. George had a Frazetta original hanging behind the desk. Frazetta's women wore flowing silken sashes alongside metal bikinis that were as modest as they were comfortable. They were invariably posed kneeling in submission next to warriors with muscles smooth and ovoid as stones from a creek bed.

The original design suggested the top be brown leather, with filigreed spiderwebs of gold connecting it to a choker and Vegas showgirl headpiece. The outfit's bottom half looked like a necklace that had gotten tangled into a feather boa. Costumers found a wax material that, if held to the body, softened and molded to the form around it. It made for a brassiere closer to jewelry than swimwear. They also experimented with swirling fabrics, and ended up using a queen-size bedsheet's worth of crimson.

Carrie travelled to San Rafael with Penny Marshall, for preproduction costume fitting. The designers explained about the wax bra, which Carrie had to put on while it was cold to create a custom fit. "Penny was looking at me like I was making all this up," the costume designer said. "She was shooting daggers from her eyes." Carrie agreed to slip on the chilly piece of clothing—so long as the (male) designer first turned around.

It was the buns all over again. After two movies, Carrie still didn't feel confident enough to make the demands that other stars routinely made for their characters. If she did, she probably wouldn't have ended up looking like the cover of *Heavy Metal* magazine. But that wasn't the Cool Girl way. Carrie could make wearing this fun, even if it demeaned Leia. The biggest challenge at the moment was her hair, actually: what looked good on a Polaroid in California required a new wig in England to match.

Her weight that particular day would become what she had to weigh for all of the shooting: gain or lose any curvature, and the fit would be off. "They didn't want me to have any lines on my body," Carrie said. No stretch marks, no loose skin, no cellulite. "In those days there was no working out, but I bought these weights that you put around your ankles to do leg lifts." A youthful metabolism was her greatest calorie-burning tool: "Thank God I was only, like, 23."

Carrie had a record number of costume changes for *Jedi*, including a disguise as a bounty hunter named Boushh. She had complained about acting like "a boy in girl's clothing": now she was a girl in boy's clothing. The small but mighty Boushh stands up to Jabba with a grenade device called a thermal detonator. Layers of armor and a bulky headpiece gave the audience no clue that it was Leia in disguise.

For the Endor moon finale, Leia would be made up to look like an Earth mother: two long braids interlaced with ribbons framing her face, her hair hanging long and wavy. You can practically feel the crushed leaves in there. Another Endor outfit was of oversized forest-colored fatigues, so loose as to seem like post-Jabba Leia was burying herself in layers as a coping mechanism.

Filming began in Elstree the first day of 1982: it was supposed to film in 1981, but script delays had pushed the date back. Carrie flew in with Harrison (now divorced) and his new girlfriend, screenwriter Melissa Matheson. The three had vacationed in Hawaii before the long plane ride across two oceans to report for work. This time around they'd film on sets first, and then the location work.

The first day of filming, for a sandstorm sequence, was nasty: sand got in everyone's eyes and noses and mouths, no one could see or hear each other, and the begoggled, blanket-draped cast looked identical. Yet it was better than Carrie's night before: her heating system had started blowing toxic fumes. If she hadn't noticed, once she was asleep she

97

would never have woken up. (The sandstorm scene was later cut, so the cast's misery was for naught.)

After that came all the interior scenes with Ewoks, whose furry costumes put the *bear* in *unbearably hot*. "You'd be doing a scene with them, and sometimes they would just fall over, fainting from the heat," Carrie said. She almost got KOed as well, but from a slipping boom mike, a big deal when you're on a wooden catwalk suspended 25 feet in the air.

Then came the day Marquand filmed the Luke-and-Leia twin reveal. The actors were given scripts, which were shredded as soon as they were done memorizing. Mark joked that it was like working for President Nixon. "The days when we'd shoot the secret scenes, they would ask the crew not to *listen,*" Carrie said.

Carrie wasn't happy with her acting that day: she wished she had taken "maybe an extra beat or two during that scene with Mark," to have Leia process her emotions. "So, this is my father, who tortured me in that little room?" But instead she played acceptance and joy at being sister to Luke, instead of horror at being daughter to Vader.

Joy was not a very Leia emotion. "I couldn't get into the swing of things, so I couldn't find my way into the character fast, because she was different. All of a sudden I was someone who loves you, and, you know, all that stuff." She had asked for more emotional range, but now she was practically a flower child. "My hair was down and I'm wearing this hippie dress… I felt like a Barbie doll. And I got insecure. I felt really uncomfortable."

She also felt uncomfortable because she had resumed her *Empire Strikes Back* routine of hitting the nightclubs, dancing and drinking and drugging. The next morning she'd pound 6 a.m. cans of Coke to give her a sugar rush, but it wasn't enough. The cast and crew noticed her exhaustion.

The third film's secrecy also meant that Carrie couldn't edit the wording. There would be no Kersh-style daily script sessions; the words were the words. Carrie couldn't find Leia as a character by rewriting her lines, scribbling out what didn't ring true and replacing it with what did. Only Marquand rewrote—removing lines that weren't focused on Luke's mission to fight Vader. Marquand also crossed out a passage of Leia reacting to the news, and instead had her only worry about Luke's safety. Doing so altered the scene's weight: Leia was now a supporting player in Luke's story, her life-changing revelation given second billing to Luke brooding.

The new line was "I know. Somehow I've always known." It sold an unsellable moment, by back-burnering Leia. "That discussion [scene] is one of the things you never want to have to write," George said. "It's a real challenge to come up with dialogue that is sincere and believable." Carrie had the bigger challenge of selling it.

"All of the sudden it was like 'I know somehow—dah-dah-dah—I've always known.'" Carrie told a reporter, mimicking her own worldly-wise delivery. "I think [selling that line] would require acting, and I'm not much of an actress. I can play something close to myself—and I'm not putting myself down so you can reassure me that I'm really great. I'm, you know… serviceable. But it was hard to say, the dialogue was hard to—it was sort of sentimental and stilted, but somebody who's a good actress could probably do that."

Marquand called himself an actor's director, and preferred to film without rehearsals. He was pleased with Carrie's acting: "She really has some emotionally deep scenes, which she handles wonderfully well."

Dialogue would not be a problem for the Jabba the Hutt scenes: after being captured, Carrie had to lie next to Jabba's side, motionless and uncomplaining. "The thing that killed me about this set-up was, Okay, you put me in this bathing suit—but then I have to stop talking from here on? Strip me—and I'm silent?" Leia used to be brassy: now only her outerwear was. "I am defiant with everyone else—Tarkin, Darth Vader—but this slug really shuts me up. Any defiance I had in the other movies—all gone."

There was still acting to be done, though. The Jabba puppet was even more disgusting in person, but quite immobile. Carrie kept having to learn forward to keep her chain taut, since the puppeteer operating Jabba's three-fingered hand could barely grasp it. "Hey, pull the chain," Carrie would request, "I want to feel that I'm really being captured."

Another time, the same puppeteer was supposed to rest his hand on Leia's shoulder. In an even-tempered tone, she informed him "that's not my shoulder." He let go. Another day of filming, Jabba's slimy tongue was supposed to waggle by her face. Instead, it slithered directly into her *ear*. She was asked if she wanted her stunt double to strangle Jabba. "I said ' *really, really* not. I *really, really* want to kill him myself.'" Of all the scenes Carrie would ever film, strangling Jabba was her all-time favorite.

Carrie's outfit was the cause of quite a few wardrobe malfunctions. "This was no bikini, it was metal," Carrie said. "It didn't go where you went. After shots, the prop man would have to check me… so I started checking for any bounce or slip after takes. Then it was 'Cut, hey, how they doin', hooters in place?'...I was embarrassed at first with a hundred guys going crazy over my revealed self. Dignity was out of the question."

At least she was dressed appropriately for the temperature, which could soar to triple digits. This was during a winter with a record coldsnap in England: some days there was almost a hundred-degree difference between inside and out. Cast and crew were shocked when they moved from the Jabba's palace set to the barge, which was somehow even hotter.

One aspect of the rescue scenario always bothered Carrie. The heroes brave death in order to rescue Han and Luke from a death sentence... but before that, Leia was turned into a harem girl. Shouldn't *that* have been when everyone jumped to the rescue? "Don't worry about me... I'll be fine!" Carrie imagined Leia saying.

The problem was that men had written this: no woman would see sex slavery as an acceptable price, not even an iron-shouldered sort like Leia. Men were very good at putting themselves in Luke's shoes, but not Leia's gray suede boots. (At least her *footwear* was comfy.) What men knew about women was always going to be secondhand information.

After the first film spiraled $10 million over budget, George decided to be a more hands-on producer for the third film. With an even less experienced director at the helm, George ended up staying on set most days, sometimes as a second unit director. In the mornings he'd sometimes add extra cameras to certain shots, to give himself more freedom in the editing room. By the end of filming he and Marquand were joking about the oddness, George yelling "Cut" and Marquand yelling "No, don't cut!"

"Only once did I get conflicting directions," Carrie said. Marquand wanted her to stand upright for a scene, and George told her not to do that. When he found out he had publicly contradicted Marquand on set, he let the matter go. Carrie, though, did the scene George's way.

"[Marquand] did the wrong thing when trying to become one of the members of the club," Carrie said. "He would try to assert himself, but certainly not ingratiate himself, so then it would be like 'I'll show you who's boss.' He would be sort of grand and very British." Carrie learned her job on set was to hit her mark and say her lines, nothing more.

Mark had no problem with the new director: they gelled quickly. He was surprised to find out that Carrie had been butting heads with him. "He might've been someone who wasn't giving Carrie enough information," Mark guessed, charitably.

Marquand was starstruck by Harrison, Carrie guessed—wow, Indiana Jones, in person! Hey, where's your bullwhip?—and generally let him have his way with scenes. This brown-nosing made Harrison acutely dislike Marquand, since he felt all three leads should be treated equally. At least that was Carrie's read. "That was my impression: maybe I'm wrong," she said.

Carrie had off for a few weeks, while Mark did more fencing training and stuntwork, so she Concorde-ed it back to her home in New York. While she was away, John Belushi died. After a decade of heavy usage, he had overdosed. John was a prodigious talent, and like Carrie lived his life to extremes. The night he died, he had been talking with friends at a bar about how distraught he was that Carrie and Dan had broken up.

His death shook the worlds of entertainment. Expensive drugs were supposed to be free of consequence: so long as you were rich, you could stay elevated all the time. Drugs being the cause of an actor's death was like finding out that Oscars were radioactive.

"Cocaine is God's way of saying you're making too much money," Robin Williams famously joked. Williams was with John that night, and he became one of many people who would change their pharmaceutical ways. "The thing I regretted about John," Carrie said, "was that he hadn't had a scare, he hadn't had some sort of overdose, or hospitalization or something, some warning. He just went straight to death." John wasn't even the person on *SNL* who did the most coke!

Scares are not enough to stop an addict. Carrie had had multiple scares, and it hadn't stopped her. She was one of the last people to see Mama Cass alive, and it hadn't stopped her. She'd had multiple near-death experiences, and it hadn't stopped her. *Addict*, noun, from the Latin for "to be enslaved."

Carrie Fisher Sentence: "There but for the grace of overdose go I."

In one of their final conversations, John had warned Carrie that she had a drug problem. This was like Liberace telling someone their clothes were garish. "All these people who I'd seen do drugs with him," Carrie thought, while attending John's memorial service on Martha's Vineyard—looking around the room at his friends, sober in attitude if not blood alcohol content—"[Y]ou know what they're thinking. Hoping? That what he died of was not what they liked to do best."

Changing was hard: far easier was drawing a line in the sand and calling it a day. "When in doubt, I floor it," John had said, "I let my lifestyle play itself out." And it did. Carrie's line in the sand was syringes: she decided never to inject anything. Since John's fatal dose was intravenous, if there was no needle, there would be no damage done. Carrie described this self-delusion this way: "those were other people, careless people, guided by different stars, subject to different rules, marked for sadder destinies."

After some more UK filming, it was time to go on location. First was the Sarlaac Pit sequence, in the Arizona desert. Mark Hamill's stand-in was a local boy, completely star-struck by Carrie. Now here she was next to him, wearing a whole lot of almost nothing. The Luke stand-in told her that he had had a crush on her since the first film. "Yes, well, don't get fresh," she replied.

These sorts of encounters were happening to her with increased frequency; boys of all ages telling her how she was their dream girl. Now this guy was leering at her like it was his job. In a year's time, she realized, everyone in the world would be looking at her just like this. Great.

Carrie and the Luke stand-in were on a disguised scaffolding, high up near what she called the "sand vagina." ("Pauline Kael is gonna have a blast with that.") The stand-in was told to put his arm around Carrie's "precious self" for a shot. He kept her from falling in... and then his arm stayed around her. "I think they're finished now," she said, removing his arm for him.

"The stuntmen were hilarious," Carrie said. For them, taking a leap into the Sarlaac pit was an irresistible urge. "We had stuntmen breaking things daily," Carrie said. "I'd come on the set and there would be this kind of silence, which was unusual—and you knew that meant something bad... three stuntmen had gone into the sand genital."

Carrie had a stuntwoman for the desert shoot, and she said they were the Double-Mint Twins when they stood next to each other. For one gag picture they sunbathed in identical harem costumes. The double was four inches taller, and healthier—Carrie had lost weight again, and her tight costume hung loose. (Some scenes of *Jedi* show Leia with a left index fingernail longer than her other nails. Carrie denied it was a "coke nail," saying she only used "dollars or tiny spoons," not her fingernail.)

Some of Carrie's best acting happened off set. She hit the local bars and restaurants for a bit of dancing, but grew frustrated when she was inevitably mobbed by fans. One night, when a group of girls crowded her, calling out her name, she put on an English accent and said "What do you mean? Who is she?" She stopped Marquand: "Do you know who Carrie Fisher is?" Marquand played along, and said that no, he didn't know. "Well, I don't know. But these girls here keep asking for Carrie Fisher. Somebody is making a film here—do you know about it?"

Sandstorms kept filming time to a minimum: to entertain themselves, the filmmakers devised a plot for the phony horror film *Blue Harvest*. It would star killers in dune buggies who stalked Carrie (in her harem outfit, of course) around film trailers. George suggested they actually film it: he said it was what low-budget king Roger Corman would have done.

The travelling circus then moved to the redwoods of northern California, doubling for the forest moon of Endor. The cast was split among hotels, and one was reserved just for the little people playing Ewoks. This was due to the rumors of little-person debauchery, a la *Under the Rainbow*. Almost all of the Ewoks had in fact filmed *Under the Rainbow*: when the bus pulled up the first day, one by one they all filed by Carrie, saying hi to their former costar.

Whatever the producers worried might happen in the hotel carried over to the set. One time the Ewok actors pegged Carrie and the rest of the cast with water balloons. Another time they set off a squib (a small explosion) next to her as she was talking to someone. The grandest prank was the "Revenge of the Ewoks"—they even had shirts made—when all the little people pretended to have quit en masse and gone back to the airport: they were actually hiding on set.

As an extra layer of security, in case a call sheet got stolen, the principals were listed as "Martin," "Harry," and "Caroline." When "Caroline" reported to set to work with Kenny Baker one day—the man inside Artoo was doubling as a lead Ewok—she found out he was sick. Montezuma's revenge wasn't just for Mexico: Carrie had been sick for all three UK shoots, and now the British actors were all getting sick in America.

Filling in for Baker was "Just the most darling, adorable boy in the world," 11-year-old Warwick Davis. Davis had been a huge *Star Wars* fan, and now he was in it! Carrie mothered him with cookies every time he nailed a scene. "He had a born instinct and did everything right, right away... the whole crew just stood, hushed, and watched the scene. It was like in theater."

Warwick picked up the lingo fast: he'd say "Am I in frame? Is this a two-shot?" Compare this with the local lumberjacks hired to play the Stormtroopers: some had never seen *Star Wars*. Or compare with Luke's handsy body double in Arizona. Couldn't everyone be as professional and nice as this kid? (The whole cast fell in love with Warwick: they filmed video of him wandering the sets in his Wicket costume, trying to find where to go. He has since appeared in eight more *Star Wars* films.)

The scene they played, of Leia befriending a forest creature, was in its own way as out of place as her mute acceptance of Jabba chaining her up. "The princess is sweeter in this last episode. I've been a testy space soldier—so single-minded I'm nearly mean—for six years. And now I'm so nice and feminine, it's almost confusing."

She could have used some of the gentleness herself. "There was a shot where I had to shoot a gun and run up a hill, and I was never good at that stuff. I'm not a particularly feminine girl, but I'm not the opposite." She fumbled with her actions during the elaborate shot, and Marquand yelled that she was ruining "his" shot. "I burst into tears... So then that took like a half hour to redo my makeup." She didn't say much to him for the rest of the day.

"After a while it was very difficult for me to do action sequences," Carrie said. "It really wasn't my thing. You pretend you're punching and shooting people, and you're upset and you're crazed all morning long. So I'm revving up this thing in me which is not innate—and I'm a pretty intense broad—and after a certain amount of time, I was done. But you can't be done. You have to keep going."

The last day of location shooting was greeted with a *Blue Harvest* wrap party. The crew, many of whom had been together for the whole trilogy, got wild: "We had fun," Carrie said. "People had fun. We'd known each other a long time and we had fun." The morning after, Carrie woke up to find a crew member passed out on her floor: he'd downed an entire bottle of NyQuil, and his mouth was, in accidental Jabba homage, leaking green.

After that was Carrie's first ILM scene, for her and Mark's elaborate speeder bike chase. In a new method of previsualizing a film, action figures of Luke and Leia had been placed on scale models, and filmed racing through model trees, recycled from FX work on *E.T: The Extraterrestrial*. They included loads of clever bits of action. When George saw it, he added the final beat: a dismounted Luke slashes the last enemy bike with his lightsaber.

Carrie and Mark were to do the filming that would, shot by shot recreate the doll scene in real life. Mark had plenty of bluescreen practice, but it was new for Carrie. New, and difficult, and boring—she frequently described boredom as "unenthusiastic hostility." When ILM crew members asked for her autograph—for their kids, they said—she turned them down, and seemed like a diva. She was photographed reading a book of French poetry on her speeder bike during downtime.

Once the FX shots were completed, ILM decided to fudge its other Leia shots with stand-ins. Certain long shots and close ups are not of Carrie but ILM staffers who most resembled Carrie in frame or hand size. They'd be easier to work with, less acidic.

Speaking of acid, around this time Carrie started expanding her drug territory to include LSD. (Sorry, Cary Grant.) She'd organize parties of people going on trips. They might freak out, but for her, she wasn't going anywhere her brain didn't already take her every day.

Chapter 15: Nineteen Eighty-Four

George had purposefully not shown any of the *Jedi* footage as it was shot to Marcia. He trusted her judgement implicitly, and was keeping her eyes fresh for later in the process. She'd helped edit *More American Graffiti* and *Empire Strikes Back*, both unofficially. Officially, she'd been unemployed since picking up an Oscar for editing *Star Wars*.

For *Jedi*, George was cutting film mercilessly: he'd become an expert on pacing, on ratcheting up suspense. If a just-completed special effects shots that ILM had spent weeks on threw off the pacing, out it went. Or he would request an element change: reshoot, and add two X-Wings so it will match up with a previous shot. Marcia was near-tears with worry that all these new FX shots wouldn't be completed in time.

George could only push the envelope so much, demanding everyone around him work the same insane schedule. (One ILMer joked that George worked a daily 5-to-9: 5 a.m. to 9 p.m.) To ease the building tension, one staffer changed a hallway into a mock Italian restaurant. Marcia took one look and walked right out, announcing "I have too much work to do to bother with this."

They hadn't told anyone, but George and Marcia were getting divorced. She told him in the beginning of editing, and they kept it quiet through production. It came out of the blue for George: they had just adopted a baby. But the baby was Marcia's breaking point: success and fame and wealth and now fatherhood hadn't changed George: he was the same morose workaholic he'd always been, and always would be. This was who he was, and Marcia couldn't change it. An editor knows what to do with a scene that's not working.

A series of fake *Jedi* scripts was made for leaking purposes, each with a different false ending. It was like a Choose-Your-Own-Adventure novel: here's one ending where Luke kills the Emperor, and another where Leia never finds out her parentage. The important secret scenes had been blue in the screenplay: the fake scripts often had everything but the blue harvest of those revelations. The film's title also changed from *Revenge of the Jedi* to *Return of the Jedi*, because Jedi aren't supposed to want revenge. The change prompted a fan theory that this was done to stymie the legions of bootleg merchandise, which would now be branded with the wrong title.

Carrie did some additional dialogue rerecording in December. That would be her final time playing Princess Leia, and she would do it standing in a studio in front of a microphone, wearing street clothes, trying to tap into the emotions of a year ago.

Then she flew back to New York to start her post-princess life. She was playing the lead in the tense Broadway drama *Agnes of God*, about a young nun who claims an immaculate conception. It was a juicy dramatic role, requiring the range of emotions she had been denied as Leia. This was her chance to show how much more she had in her.

She had 10 days to prep for the huge role. There were only two other women in the cast, and each night she would have to run a gamut of complicated emotions, none of which ever lets the audience off the hook.

Such raw performances require great sacrifices of an actor. Some go into a cocoon-like seclusion in their apartment, building a reservoir of strength to deplete on stage. Once the show is over, back to the cocoon. Other take vows of silence, saving their voice for 8 p.m.

Acting as Agnes for two hours every night, Carrie would rip her guts out on stage, thrash around, and commit fully to the performance. But she refused to turn down a party in order to go to bed before midnight. So she would hit the bars afterwards, and then wake up well past noon, exhausted. She was burning the votive candle at both ends: in later weeks her Agnes was low-energy and defeated.

And that was if Carrie showed up at all. She'd sometimes miss her call entirely, and crew members would have to run to her apartment to rouse her. She joked that people who talked to her must have heavy hair, since they'd always tilt their head as they asked "How are you?" Her understudy began to prep for every night, just in case. Carrie's movie-star casting was a big deal—TV commercials specifically said to go see Carrie as Agnes. After one too many nights of no-showing, she left the production early, most likely after being fired.

Just a few months later, it was back to the buns, this time to promote *Jedi*. If there was a venue in New York or Los Angeles that wanted to interview a *Star Wars* cast member, Carrie made herself available. She made her first appearance on *The Tonight Show Starring Johnny Carson*—with a special "princess footstool" so her legs wouldn't dangle from the guest chair like a school child's. She even flew to Australia in October for the Down Under premiere.

Carrie was used to seeing herself as a drinking glass, a bedsheet, and of course an action figure. Now she could add Pepperidge Farm cookie to that list—the cookie was an image of her with buns, not the gold bikini. Action figures of her alter ego Boushh were hard to come by: making one with a removable helmet would give away one of the movie's surprises. Malls across the country had pop-up Jedi Adventure Centers, which looked surprisingly like gift shops. Ironically, Kenner refused at first to make an Ewok stuffed animal, claiming it was too close to a teddy bear. Besides, *Star Wars* was for boys, and boys might not like a female-friendly toy.

The *Jedi* novelization by James Kahn went further than the film did in hinting how Leia was able to strangle Jabba—he outweighs her 30 to 1— and to fly a speeder bike. Kahn said she was unconsciously using her Force powers. The *Jedi* comic, on the other hand, was only four issues long, and to get that slim it left out 1/3 of the plot points. Both were released after the film: building buzz was now secondary to avoiding spoilers.

Fans made their third mecca in six years to the theaters. *Jedi* somehow did better than *Empire*: happy endings bolstered the *Return's* box office returns. Seemingly powerless critics took potshots, occasionally deserved, about how rushed and repetitive the storytelling felt. "Princess Leia even seems to have shrunk," *Newsweek's* reviewed griped. "She's no longer a commander, just the whiskey-voiced damsel in distress in a harem outfit."

Carrie agreed, of course. "I thought it was the weakest one," she said later. But she never lost her bond with the actors, with George, or with the cast. "We have a shared history, which is a bond for a friendship. Even if it's a bad history, it's still something."

Carrie Fisher Sentence: "We went through a war together—three of them."

Viewers now had not just a third film to watch but a trilogy. And seen from that tripartite perspective, it becomes a different story. Han Solo's taming of the screw-up routine is complete by *Empire's* end: for all his screentime in *Jedi,* he does little that other rebels couldn't have done. Luke's arc appears to be the true hero's journey, but his third-film dark-side turn felt inauthentic, necessary to the plot but false to his character.

And Leia? Leia began as a hero who refused to break under unfathomable stresses. In the second film she taught a selfish man to believe in something bigger than his next payday. In the third film she slays a monster, saves her man, makes friends with teddy bears, leads a rebellion, and did so in a two-piece. Hands down, Leia was the best character of the trilogy. And Carrie had delivered the most consistent performance to boot.

Leia's growth was problematic for the comics, who once again didn't know how to write for her: an earth-mother space-warrior? Mostly they did not; Leia went back to being a supporting character to Luke and Han. When the comics did include Leia, it was often for embarrassment; she had to wear a slinky nightclub outfit and sing on stage, or receive a faceful of mud from protesters, or attend a reception wearing a very ripped dress. Now that the galaxy was saved, her biggest role in the Alliance of Free Planets seemed to be as a target for humiliation.

Post-*Jedi*, everyone's careers moved in different directions. George rolled into producing *Indiana Jones and the Temple of Doom*, a darker, more violent film that spurred the Motion Picture Association of America to create the PG-13 rating. Harrison starred in that film, of course. Mark claimed the lead role in the Los Angeles production of the play *Amadeus*.

Carrie signed up for a low-budget BBC adaption of *Frankenstein*, which let her use her British accent, and work with more Royal Shakespeare Company pros. She then worked with Anne Bancroft in *Garbo Talks*, a Sidney Lumet movie about the last wish of a dying woman in New York. It would be one of the first PG-13 films, allowing Noo Yawkas to talk the salty, peppery way they talk in real life.

One of her best performances wasn't seen by adults: it was the title character of *Thumbelina*, for Shelley Duvall's star-studded *Fairy Tale Theatre*, airing on HBO. Carrie was—how's this for casting?—a tiny, singing, captured princess. Shelley happened to be not only Paul Simon's ex-wife, but the person who introduced Paul to Carrie. Shelley wasn't the jealous sort, though: relationships end. Carrie wasn't the jealous sort either—Paul was worried Carrie would be upset after he wrote a song about Shelly, but Carrie simply found it "sweet" that he thought she'd be worried. Thumbelina was bigger than that.

For all the ways Carrie and Paul were a matched set, they kept fighting: her 20-something LA lifestyle vs his 40-something New York attitude. It didn't take a psychiatry degree to see that Paul had found in his new partner a sparring partner, just like Art. And that Carrie, little girl lost, had maybe found in Paul a father figure.

"Whenever there was a big problem I'd go off on a job or something, and Paul interpreted that as the job being more important to me than he was. He wanted someone by his side." But the reverse didn't hold true: Paul always put music and songwriting first: that was his life's passion. He didn't feel a relationship could survive if both partners were ruled by such passions, and wanted Carrie to step back from hers. It'd be different if she felt about acting the way he did about music, but many days she didn't even *like* acting. If the doors were closing on her, why not let them?

After *Jedi's* premiere they were ready to end it. Carrie was already on edge because her psychiatrist had wanted to prescribe her a mood stabilizer, for hypomania, but she refused to accept that diagnosis. Now she and Paul were fighting: they'd agreed to break up, but were butting heads over the *how*. Sometimes it takes two smart people to make one dumb decision. That fight somehow turned into a decision to get married instead of splitting up.

Carrie and Paul wed in August of 1983, in his ritzy duplex overlooking Central Park. He had proposed at a Yankees game five days earlier. Despite the last-minute nature, over a hundred people crammed into Paul's place for the ceremony, included George, Penny, Art, Robin Williams, and both of Carrie's parents, who hadn't been in a room together in years.

"We partly did it to save the relationship," she said. "It was a relationship based on a great conversation. It probably should have stayed a conversation." Now if they decided to break up, it would take lawyers. Marrying didn't fix anything: they reportedly fought their very first night as husband and wife. But that was on the "for worse" side of the ledger: on the "for better" side, Paul wrote lots of songs while with her.

Pictures of the wedding made the front cover of the *New York Post*: the rumor was they got married because she was pregnant. Waiting in LaGuardia Airport for a flight a day later, Carrie pretended to be shocked by the front-page coverage. A posed picture of her pretending to be shocked by a previous posed picture: Carrie was turning the paparazzi into a modern art statement.

Their honeymoon in Egypt and Israel was not a romantic getaway: they invited the better part of a dozen friends along. Despite being married they still didn't seem to want to be alone together. But Penny

111

Marshall's international fame saved them from getting recognized: Egyptians saw a man without a guitar holding hands with a woman without buns… and they were next to the brassier half of *Laverne & Shirley*. "Laverne! Laverne!" the crowds yelled at Penny Marshall— giving Carrie and Paul some rare anonymity.

Their fights even made it onto prime-time TV: Lorne Michaels (who was also on the honeymoon) cast them as a feuding couple for his *SNL* follow-up sketchfest, *The New Show*. This time, the sight gag was Paul in an Abraham Lincoln costume. In another sketch, Carrie played a frumpy middle-aged woman so well no one knew it was her, other than her scene partner John Candy.

Carrie and Paul would joke about how often they fought, which then turned into actual fighting—"not only don't I like you, I don't like you *personally*!" she once yelled—and that would double back to laughing. It was the sort of unsustainable that could go on forever.

Paul would divorce Carrie in 1984. She would take no alimony from him: some things are not worth fighting about. "There are so many things that make a relationship go wrong," she said. "He was smart in areas I was not," she said. She saw in him one of the all-time great songwriters, and in herself a high-school dropout.

"One and one half wandering Jews/Returned to their natural coasts," Paul wrote in "Hearts and Bones," a breakup song about the relationship. He's called it the single best song he's ever written: boiling down a 7-year contentious relationship to five minutes. She's wild, he's practical, she feels unloved by him, he can't love her the way she needs to. "This is how I love you, baby," he says, singing with a resigned delivery, like a rope inches short of crossing a chasm. "It's a rare moment in pop music," Paul Simon biographer Cornel Bonca writes, "when a song marks the end of a relationship not with tears or rage or acting out, but with a clear, mature understated recognition that two people have no business being together: they aren't compatible."

The divorce did not mean they stopped being in each other's lives, stopped seeing each other, or indeed stopped fighting. It was Art all over again: "I am leaving, I am leaving," but the fighting still remains. The girl who was stuck as Princess Leia and the boy who was stuck singing "The Sounds of Silence" were stuck together, two of a kind.

Or three: "They were together from when I was five years old," Paul's son Harper said, years later, "and they divorced when I was 11.

They got back together when I was 14, and broke up again when I was 17… she's like my stepmother." Carrie would keep Harper in her life, which meant Paul always had a presence in her life. And Carrie was great at presence.

Tabloids that used to pay big money for candid shots of Carrie and Paul now had a new goal: get Carrie to say something mean about Paul. "I call myself the Hunted Beast," she said, "everyone is trying to get me to say something negative, sensational, and awful about a family member or an ex-husband." Telephoto lenses wouldn't do: this required gossip. Anyone who knew Carrie—and who didn't know Carrie?—knew they could cash in if they passed on a negative bon mot she thought she was saying in private. Her life was now like a Cold War spy novel: assume every room is wired for sound, and anything you say will be front page news. Or maybe an Orwellian surveillance state: it was 1984, after all.

She could handle being silent about Paul—it wasn't her style to be nasty. But she couldn't handle being silent, full stop. Like literature's Carry Fisher (from *The House of Mirth*), she was now a petite divorcee with a lot of opinions. She had something to say. And just as she decided she wasn't going to sing it out, she decided she wasn't going to act it out either.

She would write it out.

Episode II:
Another Galaxy Or Old Soldiers Never Die

"To a fatherless child, all things are possible, and nothing is safe."
—Anderson Cooper

Chapter 16: Oil and Water

Carrie's mom was *Debbie Reynolds*.

Debbie Reynolds the *beauty queen*: her parents moved from El Paso, Texas to Southern California, where teenage Mary Frances Reynolds was crowned Miss Burbank.

Debbie Reynolds the *triple threat*: shortly after winning that title, Mary Frances signed with Warner Brothers and began cranking out movie musicals, with a new first name: Debbie. Debbie almost became a different personality, a professional kewpie doll that Mary Frances played. She learned the ropes of movie dancing from the likes of Gene Kelly and Fred Astaire. And boy could she sing: several songs she recorded from her early films went gold.

Debbie Reynolds the *film icon*: 1952's *Singin' in the Rain* launched Debbie to a new level of movie stardom. From then on, any woman in a yellow raincoat evoked Debbie Reynolds, the same way any woman in a tuxedo evoked Marlene Dietrich. The film also cemented her cheerful, sweet, good-girl image. (Later, Doris Day and Sandra Dee were seen as "the Debbie Reynolds type": small, perky, and energetic.) By 1960, Debbie had a star on the Hollywood Walk of Fame, and in 1964, she earned Oscar and Golden Globe nominations for *The Unsinkable Molly Brown*. A year later, the astronauts of the Gemini 3 christened their ship the Molly Brown, in honor of her indomitable title role. She sent them a scarf for luck, and they took it into space.

Debbie Reynolds the *preservationist*. When her studio MGM was sold, all its props were auctioned off at fire-sale prices. She camped out in an auction house for five days, buying racks and racks of old costumes and movie paraphernalia. Carrie's childhood home held the ruby slippers from *The Wizard of Oz,* Marilyn Monroe's little white dress from *The Seven-Year Itch*, and the titular *Maltese Falcon.*

Debbie Reynolds the *sainted wife*: In 1955, Debbie married a handsome Jewish crooner from Philadelphia. Four years—and

two children—later, they were divorced. Her husband had been having an affair with Elizabeth Taylor, the world's most beautiful woman... and Debbie's best friend. After the divorce, Debbie didn't rush into another relationship, but focused on charitable work, motherhood, and learning from loss. In 1960, though, she married shoe store magnate Harry Karl. That marriage lasted 13 years, but Harry wasn't exactly the perfect husband either.

Debbie Reynolds the *devoted mother*: She doted on her children, stepping back from the big screen to become den mother to Carrie's Girl Scout Troop. (She said she wanted to become the world's oldest living Girl Scout.) She was famous for movie nights, everyone munching on the one dish she could cook—popcorn. During her second marriage, Debbie took in two of Harry Karl's children from a previous marriage, after their mother died of an accidental drug overdose on Carrie's ninth birthday. She tried to integrate them into her family, having Carrie share her room with her stepsister, who was the same age. But the Karl children had been through a great deal of trauma and were emotionally disturbed. When it became clear that it wasn't working out, she paid to send them to boarding school.

Debbie Reynolds the *tough broad*: Over the years she learned to fight for her proper share of income, and respect. She walked out on millions from a TV deal because she didn't want to be sponsored by a tobacco company. Sometimes her fighting was not metaphorical: little Debbie would sock people in the nose if she caught them ripping her off.

Debbie Reynolds the *workhorse*: As her on-screen roles began to dry up, she took to the Las Vegas stage. She was smart enough to realize she still had loyal fans who would flock to see her perform two shows a night, seven nights a week.

Carrie admired her mother's work ethic. Instead of taking the Norma Desmond route of kvetching and kvelling about her fate, Debbie was out there singing and tapping her heart out every night. "My mother," Carrie joked, "was the only person I know who had a nervous breakdown without getting nervous or breaking down: she just moved right through it."

But Carrie knew other sides of her mom too, ones not captured in gauzy, posed photographs. There was Debbie Reynolds the *eccentric*, who had had let young Todd keep a pet alligator that nearly devoured

Carrie's hand when she tried to feed it. There was Debbie Reynolds the *lush*, the *vain*, the *fame addict*, the *name-dropper*. And there was Debbie Reynolds the *blind optimist*, who couldn't see how much damage her second husband's habits were hurting them all.

Harry had expensive tastes: his dress shirts were monogrammed, fastened with shirt studs instead of buttons, and he discarded them after a single wear. He wasn't much of a husband or a father—he was more of a permanent houseguest. His general disinterest extended to his own children. When Debbie was fretting over what to do with her troubled stepchildren, he refused to help. And then there was his gambling—after losing all of his own money, he started gambling away Debbie's as well. "I'm slow at seeing what I don't want to believe," she confessed in her autobiography.

Carrie and her mom had been close, but a rift began to grow as their lives got more complicated. Attempting to protect her from the truth of Harry's gambling, Debbie started keeping more secrets from her daughter. At the same time, teenaged Carrie kept Debbie in the dark about the storm clouds brewing inside her head.

When she was 14, though, Carrie took a chance at communication. She wrote her mother an impassioned letter on a small hotel-room notepad. Carrie's "large, loopy letter" gushed on for page after page. "Read this," she said to her mom backstage in Las Vegas one night. What she needed to tell her mom, what would be so hard to get right in person, could be said in ink.

It was not about her mental health, or their relationship, or boys: it was about Harry. Along with his money, he had lost all his self-respect. And continuing to enable his misdeeds by not kicking him out or confronting him would destroy Debbie the way it had already destroyed Harry. He was going to lose his family no matter how hard she tried to save him. "Both you and Harry are miserable, so why drag it out? It only makes all of us unhappy. Todd and I included." Her mother was attempting to absorb the hurt as the price of a happy home. But there would never be happiness with Harry. And "sacrifice for sacrifice's sake," Carrie wrote, "only gains your own depletion."

Debbie had no idea Carrie felt this way, no idea she knew so much about the gambling, the other women, or the doubts she had. Her little girl was now giving her advice, wise advice at that. She could hardly dispute Carrie's all caps declaration: "I AM CORRECT NOT IRRATIONAL OR EMOTIONAL JUST ACCURATE AND ANGRY."

In addition to its maturity and insight, Debbie recognized something else in that letter. "The talent was evident from the beginning… I knew then that she would one day have a career as a writer," Debbie wrote. And she soon drew a line with Harry: no more money, no more sharing a bed.

* * *

A decade later, Debbie was backstage for the first night of Carrie's debut in *Agnes of God.* She made her appearance a performance in itself, since she dashed away from the theater as soon as the show was over. *Playbill* magazine quoted Debbie as saying she ran because she "just didn't feel that Carrie's moment should be diminished." She was then there for Carrie's second show. The article about Debbie not wanting to overshadow Carrie runs almost 200 words, and does not quote Carrie.

"I went into musicals and she went the dramatic route—our careers are kind of comparable," Debbie noted, proceeding to reel off dueling filmographies like a *Jeopardy* champ running the category. "Then," she concluded, "when we were both barely 18, Carrie did *Star Wars* and I did *Singin' in the Rain*—two hugely successful cult classics."

Debbie was chuffed at the mother-daughter parallels, but Carrie less so. Teachers in Beverly Hills had called Carrie "Debbie" growing up: her mom was so famous Carrie sometimes didn't merit an identity of her own. And now when she was independent, her mother was tying their fates back together. You see, Debbie had agreed to star in the musical *Woman of the Year*. Mother and daughter would be headlining rival Broadway shows!

* * *

"Hi, dear," came the voice on the phone. "It's your mother. Debbie."

It was a few months later. Debbie was calling her daughter in London from Miami, Florida. It was the day of her third wedding. She had recently met a man who had proposed on their first date: she eventually accepted. The marriage was timed to occur before a cruise-ship gig she had lined up, which would now double as her honeymoon. She had invited Carrie to the wedding, but Carrie had never met this new man, didn't trust him, and knew her mom's optimism made her susceptible. She couldn't support the marriage.

Debbie still wanted to connect with her daughter on this day, though, so she called Carrie's London hotel room. Carrie answered the phone sounding sluggish. She claimed she was just suffering from a cold, picked up from one of her recent trips. Debbie wasn't sure. This was how life with a drug user was: even on the happiest day, you were worried about the worst-case scenarios.

From the reception dinner, Debbie called the front desk of Carrie's hotel to send someone up to check on her. The hotel, attempting to protect privacy, couldn't confirm that Carrie was a guest there, even to a woman claiming to be her famous mother. Debbie then asked if they would check on Carrie if, say, Ava Gardner stopped by. The desk clerk stammered and said yes. Debbie called in a favor. Half an hour later, Ava Gardner stopped by. The clerk sent someone to check in on Carrie.

Carrie was found face down, unconscious on the floor. The television was on full volume, and the windows were open. She had overdosed, again.

She had recently suffered an ectopic pregnancy, which occurs when a fertilized egg implants outside the uterus. Ectopic pregnancies can't be brought to term, and endanger the life of the mother. It was Paul's, but Paul had not been by her side while she was recuperating. They'd broken up again. (In a novel a few years later, Carrie wrote that "I guess that's how guys are thoughtful in the eighties—they accompany girls to their abortions.")

The Carrie found lying on that London hotel room floor had lost her baby, lost her sanity, lost her husband, lost her career, and was now losing her mom. Losing her life, at that point, seemed a technicality.

Chapter 17: Bile

Pumping a stomach isn't a gentle process. First, a thick plastic tube goes into the patient's mouth, or in some cases down their nose. Saline or water is injected and then retracted, via a large syringe. This happens over and over, until all stomach contents are washed away. In the final step of the process, the doctor who pumps your stomach will send you flowers and ask you out on a date.

At least, that was the final step for Carrie: the physician who prevented her overdose propositioned her. At her darkest moment, the people trying to help her not die still saw her as Princess Leia, quite dateable if she survived. She would recreate this moment in her first novel, calling it a meet cute over a thrown-up dinner of "scallops and Percocet."

A day or so after the overdose, she took a plane back to Los Angeles: Todd was waiting at the airport for her, having flown there directly from their mom's wedding. After embracing, Todd berated her into tears. She had gone once again to the very edges of life: why? Her small frail frame was again more dead than alive: why? What reason was there to do this to herself? Why?

Answering that simple question—why?—was a massive task. It involved unpacking her substance abuse, her relationship with her mother, with her father, with drugs, with the men in her life, with her job. Underneath all that baggage was her mental health, and her mood disorder. She didn't understand it herself most days: how could she explain it to someone else?

A doctor told her that despite therapy she had a serious mental health issue. A diagnosis of bipolar disorder explained all her actions. Carrie didn't believe him: he was just saying that to make her feel better for being a druggie. That was the rationalization, at least: better a junkie than crazy.

Carrie went to another in a series of drug rehab facility. Back in the 1980s these places were often unregulated, with low success rates, sky-high fees, and no best practices. Addiction isn't curable the way pneumonia is: that most people who enrolled were like Carrie: young people from well-off families who'd be using again in a few years.

Before the overdose Carrie had lined up a prime movie role: she had been days away from filming an ensemble murder mystery based on the board game of *Clue*. She would have been the biggest name in the cast, and her vamp role—as Miss Scarlet, a Washington DC madam—was also the secret killer. (At least in one of the film's multiple endings.)

Carrie was the sort of person who snuck junk food to a health spa retreat, so wasn't going to let a little thing like drug rehab stop her from a part. This was the '80s; she could multitask. "She said, 'Oh yes, they'll let me out during the day and I'll just come back at night,'" *Clue's* writer-director, Jonathan Lynn, said. "And I thought, 'Really?' …The insurance company got involved and said 'Absolutely not. What are you thinking?'" Her part went to Lesley Ann Warren.

The rehab worked, at least in the short term. One day at a time, she earned a week, a month, and finally a year of sobriety. But the actions most people would attribute to a relapse—bursts of energy, followed by nasty or sorrowful moods—were still part of her sober life. Like addiction, mental illness was a condition without a cure.

Carrie had been born with every advantage a person could want, yet her mental illness reduced all that to marginalia. Fame and fortune didn't matter to the bats in the belfry. No matter her roles on screen or in life, at heart she was uncontrolled, uncontrollable. "Roy" and "Pam," her two personified moods, would never leave Carrie. Just like Leia.

There was another *Star Wars* parallel: in "Pam" she had her own personal Jedi Knight, humble and virtuous and pacifistic. And right besides that knight was "Roy," the Dark Side, the ego-boosting id, the cold hyper shadow. George always talked about not good winning over evil but a balance between light and dark. Carrie's whole life was unbalanced.

Single again, Carrie stayed in a new house she bought near Mulholland Drive. Todd was her roommate: his marriage had ended as well. They had become very different people—he was now a recording engineer and a born-again Christian—but they were still each other's siblings, and thus best friends. Her round-the-world trips now were with her brother in tow: Singapore, the Orient Express, Israel. In China, she wrote to friends saying she was "sending you a postcard from the edge of the world," and tucked that phrase away for later.

She was set up on dates with senators, movie stars, and musicians. Like the doctor who pumped her stomach, they were willing to overlook red flags in order to win a date with a princess. She was more concerned with her internal life than her love life. When it came to therapy, Carrie was a hedonist. Her first therapist was an older man, who she traded for a young man, then a woman. Each held up a different mirror, reflecting different facets of her personality.

One of her fist jobs after rehab was an action comedy called *Hollywood Vice Squad*: she played a young officer who tried to impress veteran detectives by making a big porn bust. She brought a tagalong little-sister energy to the project, but it was a seedy film—half the time she was undercover as a prostitute. She also made a *Disney Channel* TV movie, which was demoralizing on the other end of the spectrum.

The roles weren't getting better: maybe Paul was right. Maybe she should walk away.

In 1986 her grandfather, who she was very close to, passed away. At his memorial service, Carrie stood up and read a poem she had written. It was in the form of a recipe, the ingredients you needed to add to get her grandpa. It was sweet and funny, the words well chosen and closely observed.

Maybe writing was what she should be doing. She signed a contract to write a book of funny essays, called *Money Dearest*. The offer came to her while she was in rehab: a publisher had read a witty interview with her, and saw potential in her as a writer.

She was assigned a ghost writer, Paul Slansky, who if things went badly would do most of the actual writing. Carrie began a series of in-character rambles, some on yellow legal pads, some in person to Paul. He recorded them, and often stood agog watching her. She would almost physically transform into the character she was portraying, male and female, old and young, straight or strung out. It was the best acting he'd ever seen her do.

These character sketches could be very funny at times, but they weren't essays that could be typed up. It was definitely something, though. The book evolved from nonfiction to fiction. Paul's job because figuring out ways to slice and dice the monologues into a sequential story.

Some fiction falls under the category of *roman à clef*. A *roman à clef* fictionalizes the author's life, sometimes wholly, sometimes just enough to call it fiction. Everyone from Kerouac to Proust to Plath summered on the clefs of Roma, tempting the read to wonder how much of each story was real, and how much imagined. Carrie nicknamed it "faction."

Her factional book's main character would be Suzanne Vale, who was Carrie by any other name. Same addictions, same experiences, same movie star mom and absent dad. Same giant brown eyes and petite frame, same rock-solid grandparents, same childhood insomnia. The only difference was Suzanne had never starred in the world's biggest movie.

As Suzanne, Carrie could write about her life without having to align it with the actual facts. Facts were unfunny, repetitive, dull: facts often missed the point. Suzanne was Carrie's diplomatic immunity: she could make up whatever she wanted one minute, and describe the minutiae of her real life the next.

But there are downside to playing fast and loose with the truth. Carrie lost one friend when John Belushi died, and lost another—John's wife Judy—when she gave an interview to Bob Woodward about it. Judy claimed Carrie exaggerated her late husband's drug use, which he then quoted verbatim. His book *Wired* barely touched on John's humor, kindness, or talent, instead painting him as little more than a sentient drug vacuum. That might have been how Carrie remembered it, but her memory was not to be trusted.

Carrie's novel had a whipping razorblade of a title, *Postcards From the Edge*, dreamed up during her China trip with Todd. The book begins with dual first-person narratives of Susanne and Alex, both in rehab. Suzanne is quiet and snide and yearning. Alex is a rageful egotist. They describe the bad food, the boredom, the nuthouse atmosphere, the denials. From there the book changes form, into a conversation between two people identified only by pronouns. Then it becomes a third-person narrative of Suzanne's post-rehab days, and then correspondence from her.

The format shifts were distancing: readers kept having the rug pulled out from under them. But the crazy quilt of styles, each from a different backyard pacing session, worked if the book was thought of not as a novel but as a short story collection. Each story was different in tone and tempo and content, but part of a whole, with overlapping characters.

Carrie's book was a concept album about how getting clean isn't the last step but the first.

Carrie fought back against the "this-is-your-brain-on-drugs" imagery of addiction: Suzanne's fried brain *was* her "before" picture. She was a recovering drug addict, yes, but also a crazy person, actress, love interest, and daughter. Most of all, she was unmoored. "Portraying reality had become her way of experiencing it," she wrote. "[Suzanne] knew how to act like a regular person. She was self-consciously unselfconscious."

Postcards lacked traditional conflicts. The closest thing to a narrative was Suzanne being unsure if her new boyfriend actually liked her. "It was as though she doubted her own judgement, which in fact she did. For years her judgment had told her to take drugs. Why should she think her logic had improved that much in just two years?"

Here was the walking tour of the inside of her head: a mixture of bon mots and gutpunches. She could follow a light trilling about fame with a blood-draining realization that she now expected to die because she wasn't trying to kill herself anymore. For people who thought she would play coy due to fictionalizing, buckle up. "[T]o avoid being coy," Carrie joked, "I ended up being explicit."

Good blurbs—Steve Martin said it was "savagely funny and savagely revealing"—turned into good reviews. *The New York Times* called it "at one harrowing and hilarious," and the *LA Times Book Review* said it was "a serious piece of work." Anyone who knew an addict knew the voice Carrie was writing in, with humor so dark it emitted Hawking radiation. As with AA itself, qualification led to identification. The more she told her story, the more others recognized themselves in her failings.

It also unleashed the first bumper crop of Carrie Fisher Sentences upon the world.

"[i]n the beginning our main activity is a nonactivity in that you simply don't do drugs. That's what we're all doing here: Not Drugs."

"Was I celebrating, or drowning my sorrows? Or celebrating my sorrows?"

"It's like an Alanon jumps out the window and someone else's life flashes in front of their eyes."

"It's like I've got a visa for happiness, but for sadness I've got a lifetime pass."

"I think that's what maturity is: a stoic response to endless reality."

"The junkie of the seventies is the athlete of the eighties."

"Sometimes I don't think I was made with reality in mind."

The book hit the bestseller list—not surprising, given the rubberneck factor—but few were expecting it to be so meaningful. Goodbye actress, hello novelist!

But some things can't be rebranded. Despite the book's success, despite her prowess, people still thought of her as *Star Wars* first. Look, Princess Leia wrote a novel!

Those buns must be held on with Crazy Glue.

Chapter 18: "Instant Gratification Takes Too Long"

Carrie had written *Postcards* in an ersatz, one-woman-show style. She thought maybe she could take the stage and continue monologuing, a mix of performance and storytelling. But then the film rights to the novel were snapped up, and greenlit by Columbia Pictures. That didn't happen everyday: someone with power wanted this movie to be made.

That someone was an ex-boyfriend of her named Mike Nichols. Mike Nichols of *The Graduate*! *Catch 22*! *Who's Afraid of [One of Carrie's Former Stepmoms]*! He'd just completed *Working Girl*, where he directed an insecure actress with substance issues who came from a Hollywood family. That became his next film's theme: a story about addiction, recovery, acting, fame, money, sex, love, power, and romance. (Are those enough themes?)

One standard way of adapting a novel into a screenplay is by "stuffing the pages into the camera"—that is, transcribing each novel scene into screenplay form. The screenwriter's job became trimming and condensing the story to under two hours.

That worked for books already written like screenplays. *Postcards from the Edge* was not like that. The first third is devoted to a character who never recurs, the storytelling style keeps changing, and there's no real ending. Luckily, film had a genre just for this type of story—the character study. Building a story around the volcanic character of Suzanne was one reason Nichols was drawn to the project.

Another reason was that Carrie had gone public about her drug abuse and mental illnesses. Mike Nichols was an intensely private person, and two things he was most private about were his drug use and his mental illness. Her semi-autobiography life story was also his. Carrie ran into him once and immediately knew he was using: she told Meryl Streep, who wrote Carrie off as thinking everyone was on drugs.

Turning *Postcards* into a movie required building a new story from scratch: the screenplay would have the book's flavor, but few of its scenes or dialogue. And who better to perform this magic act than Carrie herself? She knew Suzanne inside and out, after all, and could refocus the story cinematically. Carrie had a less creative term for the process: "throwing the book into the backyard and setting fire to it." She wanted to call this new sorta-sequel story *Hollywood & Vine*, but Nichols insisted the title stay the same: people knew the book's title, if not the contents. She would receive a BAFTA nomination for her transformative work.

Perhaps in the spirit of cutting and shaping, Carrie got a dramatically short new haircut. A 60-and-loving-it haircut, a I-kicked-cancer's-butt haircut. Carrie gave the main character of her in-the-works second novel that same severe haircut. "But as soon as it was gone," she wrote, "it haunted her—phantom split ends, dry day-by-night, never-to-be-seen-again hair. She looked at herself like a feminine boy, a sick pixie, someone bad at sports, introverted, androgynous, shy, a renegade choir boy." Yes, there's of course more: "She wanted her hair back. She looked like an elfin peach, a bewildered thug, an aging tomboy for peace."

Just as Nichols worked with actors to discover the underlying truth of each performance, he worked with Carrie to find the underlying truth of her life story. One of Nichols' storytelling maxims was there were only three types of scenes: negotiations, seductions, and fights. Suzanne negotiated with herself plenty about sobriety, and her on-screen love interest took care of seductions. That left fights: who could Suzanne fight with?

"Hello, Suzanne? It's your mother, Doris."

In the book, Doris was a minor character. Nichols pressed Carrie to make the mother-daughter relationship the crux of the story: everything would now revolve not around Suzanne's sobriety but Suzanne moving back in with her aging film-star mother. This was very close to setting up a tripod in front of a mirror. The film's plot became a mother-daughter rivalry, with mom the antagonist. "My mother and I get along fine," Carrie said in an interview, "but who's going to go see a movie about two woman that get along fine, and by the end of the picture they get along better?"

It's all too easy to turn a Hollywood mother into a monster: all together now, "No… wire… hangers… *EVER!*" But just as Suzanne was and wasn't Carrie, "Doris Mann" was and wasn't Debbie Reynolds. Doris was every bad act of Debbie's minus any redeeming one, a person as described by their worst enemy. Carrie/Suzanne loved and respected Debbie/Doris, while still feeling dominated and stymied by her.

Creating the screenplay took months, not weeks, since both parties were busy with other creative endeavors. When they found the time to discuss a scene, Carrie would madly write up a pass on a legal pad, and show it to Mike. Sometimes they'd work on the phone, her in LA, he in New York. Scene by scene the narrative cohered.

Mike noticed Carrie's acting gigs post- *Postcards* had gotten notably better. Watch her delightful performance throughout *When Harry Met Sally*, especially a technically demanding phone scene done in one take on three sets. Or her frustration as being the only adult in a roomful of manchilds in *The 'Burbs*. Or what became for a while her stock in trade: the shrew, the manhater, the chilly executive with a skintight décolletaged power suit. (Male-written stories abounded with boardroom women of this stripe: wonder why?) "[It] was among her best work because it was no longer the only thing she did," Mike said. "Writing gave her an authority beyond acting."

Carrie and Martin Short presented the two short-subject awards at the 1989 Academy Awards: it was someone's idea of a joke to have two vertically challenged actors presenting, one with the actual last name of Short. Carrie and Martin decided on a better joke: she walked on stage wearing a black dress with a stylish jacket coverup... and then Martin walked out dressed identically.

Eventually the *Postcards* script was finished, and casting begin. Suzanne would be played by Nichols' muse, Meryl Streep, who first met Carrie when she was briefly dating Nichols. Streep auditioned for the director while Carrie was "curled at his feet like a cat... he stroked her hair and she just sat there purring." That small ball of fur was Streep's new screenwriter. "Out-of-control actor" was any actor's dream role—plus, she got to sing, and to be funny!

For Doris, Nichols chose Shirley MacLaine, a rival to Debbie Reynolds from back in the day: Shirley swore Debbie stole the title role of *Unsinkable Molly Brown* from her. Debbie had wanted to play Doris, of course, which did nothing to dissuade people from thinking she *was* Doris. Dennis Quaid, Richard Dreyfuss, Gene Hackman, and Annette Bening rounded out the cast. (Carrie opted out of cameoing in the film: "There were too many celebrities. It would have looked like *Love Boat*.")

As Mike Nichols' biographer Mark Harris noted, Mike Nichols and Meryl Streep had made *Heartburn* a few years before this, another *roman-à-clef* novel about a famous woman (Nora Ephron) going through comedic trauma. This was a de facto sequel. And, it turns out, *Postcards* was the film that made Meryl Streep into *Meryl Streep*, the woman who could do anything.

Meryl Streep started to become more Carrie-like: Carrie picked at her thumb, so Meryl had Suzanne pick at her thumb. In a later tribute to Meryl, Carrie joked that people would start mixing up the two of them, and that Carrie always ended up feeling worse for it. "After *Postcards* premiered, I began daily to see the pain and disappointment in the eyes of my family and friends every time I wasn't Meryl." She called this " *Merylnoma Streeptococcus.*"

At some point they became friends, and seriously discussed cowriting a film together. Meryl would become godmother to Carrie's daughter. Carrie was always the crasser one of the two: she would listen in on Meryl in the bathroom at a party, and then announce the play-by-play to the crowd when she reappeared.

Location scouters for *Postcards* needed to find a mansion suitable for filming interior scenes, with architecture that told a story. They thought they found a perfect house—it was available for rent, and had a beautiful grand spiral staircase. Then they found out who owned the house: Connie Stevens, Carrie's dad's third wife. So Carrie's fake mother's house would be her former stepmother's actual house.

The film reopened the can of worms about how much of the story was real. Doris wasn't Debbie, Carrie said, in an *Entertainment Weekly* cover story—whose cover featured the actor-turned-novelist-turned-screenwriter in a shimmering silver gown. Debbie was "better than the mother I deserve," Carrie said. Debbie of course agreed—in her second memoir she said that due to "a fair amount of improvising on set" the movie contained "exaggerations… that weren't in Carrie's book."

You didn't have to be a Page Six reader to know that many big and little details about Doris rang true. The fictionalization came more from the editing: highlighting someone's negatives while ignoring their positives can be just as mean as lying. (The movie's drug-fueled Hollywood was also no exaggeration; Dennis Quaid checked into rehab immediately after making a drug-rehab movie.)

Todd saw the film of *Postcards* as both true and not. This was Carrie's perspective on things, but her perspective was flawed. "The truth is, [Carrie] couldn't have been more wrong," he said. "She was perpetually trying to compete with Mom, which created a lot of resentment and, for many years, put Carrie in the sad position of running hard to win a race that she didn't even realize she was running all by herself." This was bolstered by Debbie's continual rooting for her daughter's success. She fully supported Carrie, even if it meant supporting a book and now a movie that seems to slander her as a drunk-driving narcissist.

Audiences laughed, and tried to play Sherlock Holmes, deducing who was based on who. Critics were less kind: Roger Ebert said the film focused more on gossip than hard truths.

Were those Carrie's memories of her mom? A combination of mental illness and self-medicating had done a real number to her hippocampus. She didn't remember much of her childhood: the photos of her growing up were like seeing some other girl, not herself. And what she did remember, her version of things, did not always hang plumb with reality.

As she was working on the screenplay and acting, Carrie was also writing her second novel. *Surrender the Pink* was about soap opera writer Dinah Kaufman, perhaps inspired by Carrie's role in a soap opera film, *Soapdish*. Dinah, like Suzanne before her, was Carrie: same age, same build, same background, same mom. Carrie bequeathed "Roy" and "Pam" onto Dinah. "One mood is the meal, the next mood is the check," she said. It was safer to be "Pam," but it felt better to be "Roy." Dinah even had trouble sleeping, picked at her thumb, and took a cooking class to impress her man, as Carrie did for Paul.

Paul had worried that Carrie would portray him negatively in *Postcards*: she did not portray him *at all*. This was her biggest fictionalization: she excluded. To keep the focus on Suzanne's rehab, recovery, and ribaldry, she excluded her solid relationship with Todd, her role as Leia, her mental illness… and Paul Simon. "So I'll be in the second book," he predicted, a bit wounded.

Yes he was: in the second book, Paul became successful playwright Rudy Genzler. Dinah and Rudy's rocky relationship mirrored Carrie and Paul's like a stencil. Even more meta, Dinah ends up writing a character based on Rudy into her soap opera, using him as inspiration. It really goes off the deep end when Dinah falls in love with the fictional version of Rudy she wrote!

Dinah's relationship problems stemmed from her insecurities. "The men [Dinah] was drawn to were somewhat formidable, intellectual, artistic," she wrote. "So Dinah basically did not think that she was

133

intellectual, artistic, mature, or respectable. She combed the earth in search of her better half. Once she found him, she thought 'Who does he think he is?'"

The writing was better than *Postcards*, with fewer epigrams, and more humor that worked in context, instead of as birthday-card one-liners. Carrie's time with Mike Nichols had opened up the world of story structure: her characters were now in constant conflict. And she showed not told: a woman sneaking around her ex's closet lets the reader know that she's not over him in an evocative way.

Paul and Carrie's relationship had been on hold for the making of *Graceland*, his triumphal album, and for her first two books. After a year of absence, they rejoined each other's lives but still lived separately. She once again doted on Harper, and helped Paul pick out clothes to give to Art Garfunkel as a birthday present.

It was drugs that finally split them apart for good—a drug that, wonder of wonders, Carrie had never tried. For a follow-up to *Graceland*, Paul had been visiting Brazil to record with local musicians. Carrie went with him one time, and they took a trip down the Amazon. A local faith healer—a *bruja*, literally "witch"—was said to help people heal from spiritual woes via an ayahuasca ceremony. Ayahuasca was a hallucinogenic substance.

After seeing a day's worth of patients, the *bruja* brewed them a pot of special tea. As they drank it, they were warned that any snakes they saw were probably just visions. Probably. Soon, the *bruja* said, they'd be able to see their own souls, including any damages, and maybe see how it could be fixed.

What Carrie learned about herself during the ceremony she kept private. But it was what Paul learned that shocked her: he said his only problem in life was an elbow that was a bit sore. The *bruja* all but rolled his eyes; you come all this way to pretend you're perfect? To keep your guard up?

They held each other during their mental voyage, his head in her lap, she imagining his enormous brain was crushing her. They talked and talked, sitting in the jungle. Nothing she did for him was right: even when she tried to compliment him, he'd get upset that it wasn't the *right* compliment. "It was like debate club," she said. He could only feel good, it seemed, when he was winning the argument.

Paul, in turn, felt like she was part of him, and he could only be whole in her presence. But it would never be a relationship of equals.

Simon and Garfunkel would never quite stop—reunion tours, threats of a new album, appearances in each other's lives. But Simon and Fisher were now done. That last journey had proven they were different people on different paths. "It was usually me who would go back to him," she said, "but he finally said we just couldn't see each other anymore, which meant I couldn't keep trying to get back into his life."

Having finally said goodbye—finding "the strength to let you go," as Paul memorably put it in the song "Further to Fly"—they were both ready for new loves. Carrie was not just ready; in 1990 she had a new bestselling book hitting stands in *Surrender the Pink*, and the #1 movie in America in *Postcards From the Edge*. Due to her status, her book/movie tour included spots on *The Arsenio Hall Show*. She joked that her whole drug problem was just "research" to make her books more realistic.

Chapter 19: Young Turks

We've never seen Leia doing her job.

Leia, for all her rebel leadership, is a politician. Her job begins only when all parties put down their weapons, shake hands, and negotiate. But we don't see that part of the *Star Wars* world, because backroom deal-making doesn't move many action figures.

Every movie that's ever been made, though, had happened due to men and women with Leia's skillset. They arrange the bank financing, the location permits, the profit-share agreements, even whose name comes first in the credits. Much of this negotiating is among friends and colleagues, and few people want to fleece their collaborators. It's why there's so much power in a handshake deal: the promise is to treat the other fairly.

One of the major themes of *Star Wars* was the power of friendship: together, the heroes do what they couldn't do alone. It's a theme as old as storytelling itself, and reflects Hollywood's history of powerful friendships underpinning the film world. George Lucas was in one of those groups: the 1970s film school brats. Carrie was in a separate one of actresses doing their best in a man's world.

Behind the studio glitz was the world of talent agencies. Friendships ruled the roost there, too. Five friends from the staid William Morris Agency had broken off to found the Creative Artists Agency, or CAA. CAA often acted more like producers than agents: they matched script with stars, stars with directors, assembling "packages" ready to greenlight. Both Irvin Kershner and Richard Marquand had been CAA members.

Agents may have been the new rock stars, but they still weren't, you know, *movie stars*. "As far as agents dating or sleeping with clients," said Ron Meyers, one of CAA's founders, "the first rule of thumb is: don't." But many did: absolute power seduces absolutely.

Bryan Lourd's life exemplified the maxim that the harder you work the luckier you get. He had started as a gofer for CBS, coming in early and staying late. He became unofficial assistant to the network's president, who recommended he join a talent agency, where his nonstop energy and people skills would be more justly rewarded. Six months later, he started in the mailroom at the William Morris Agency. Two *days* after that—after a secretary unexpectedly quit—he was manning a key agent's desk, right as the agent was helping create *The Cosby Show*.

Soon Bryan was representing Madonna.

Bryan rolled with a group of fellow CAA agents, who got nicknamed the Young Turks. "All of us in the mailroom looked up to him and wanted to curry favor with him," one future agent remembered of Lourd. With stylishly long blond hair and stockbroker glasses, he looked every bit the Gordon Gecko type.

Bryan didn't represent Carrie, so their dating was aboveboard. In Bryan, Carrie found an even-tempered partner. He was used to dealing with temperamental stars, liking and respecting them not despite but because of their quirks. And he wasn't starstruck: he was always in the room with Carrie, never Leia. They soon moved in together into her place near Mulholland.

"Sometimes I'm with a guy and I think 'I love this person. This is it.'" Carrie wrote in *Postcards*. "But who I love is who I am when I'm with him, and it has almost nothing to do with him. It's me having an excuse to just do myself one more time, proving once again I'm bright and I'm funny and I'm powerful and that I can. That I still know how to pour blood in their shark pools." She wrote that before meeting Bryan, but it's a universal sentiment.

Bryan chose to be kind, but he was capable of steeliness. Carrie knew that to be a good agent, sometimes the gloves had to come off. She told Michael Wimer, one of Bryan's agent friends, that Michael wasn't like the other agents. She didn't mean he was bad at his job—he was among the best of the best—but that he had moral lines he wouldn't cross. One agent (not Michael or Bryan) notoriously called a bomb threat to an airline, just so an important person wouldn't miss their flight. Others plied their clients with their contraband of choice, covered up their indiscretions, or got their relatives on payrolls.

That was the job: part butler, part enabler. Part Jewish mother, part mob enforcer. For people who already were all those things, like Bryan, agenting was like a seven-footer with great aim discovering the sport of basketball. For people who weren't of that particular ENFP Meyer-Briggs personality type, the job could be an ill fit. "Carrie has always been one of the smartest, most prescient people in this town," Michael Wimer said. Wimer took her advice and left CAA, becoming a successful producer.

Bryan never left CAA: he was a big fish in a big pond. He became one of the agency's biggest stars, which had the camaraderie of a sports team and the ruthlessness of a gladiator pit. Later, Bryan would be described as "a little bit of Mother Teresa and a little bit of Tony Soprano": not many people fit *that* bill.

That was who Carrie needed: the eye of her hurricane. Someone who she could tell would be a good father one day. "Carrie definitely picked the right person with whom to co-parent," her sister Joely said, "almost as if she knew what was coming for her, and that she wasn't going to be able to get up and make the sandwiches."

Carrie had been married before, and it didn't take, so she didn't want to make the same mistake twice. She and Bryan decided they wanted to start a family, and to stay committed to each other, but not to sign on any dotted lines. Together, but unmarried. In industry parlance, their relationship was a deal memo. A handshake: do right by me, and I'll do right by you.

Before *Surrender the Pink* hit bookstores, Steven Spielberg had snapped up the movie rights for a seven-figure fee. But the film would become one of the subjects trapped in what's called development hell. Development hell was where film projects went to die. For each one film that hit theaters, an insane multiplier of scripts, treatments, and options lingered in the seventh level. Sometimes a project's champion moved onto other pastures. Sometimes the star lost heat, or a similar project was in the works elsewhere. There often wasn't a reason why a project didn't get made: mere anarchy would do.

The million-dollar option was great for Carrie's bank account, but she was at a point where she'd rather the movie be made. Welcome to being a professional screenwriter: most make their money from stories that never get filmed.

If only she knew a high-powered agent to grease some wheels…? But Bryan was not *that* sort of agent. And Carrie was no producer's mistress looking for a part in a movie. She was at the grown-up's table now, and up here people accepted how little control they ultimately had.

She had gotten extraordinarily lucky to have her debut novel filmed, and to have it be a commercial and critical success. But the first time the words "Screenplay by Carrie Fisher" graced the screen would also be the last. *Postcards from the Edge* would be her only writing credit.

Postcards, now in postproduction, gained a Carly Simon score. Then the president of Columbia Pictures—the only female studio head in Hollywood—resigned. If you've ever thrown away someone else's half-eaten sandwich, you know the fate of movies made under one regime and released under another. It's a power-game movie: better to let the films die on the vine than to release them to great fanfare, and have the fanfare directed at your predecessor.

That seemed to be *Postcards'* fate, a female-focused film with not an explosion in sight. But when it opened in September of 1990, it unseated the summer hit *Ghost* to be #1 at the box office. It would eventually make almost $40 million, and be the first film of the yearly Oscar race.

Carrie's heralded screenplay received awards and nominations, but not from the Academy of Motion Pictures Arts and Sciences. Meryl Streep got nominated, though, and as was Shel Silverstein, for writing a honky-tonk song for Meryl to belt.

Carrie had a harder time of it. She took a stab at the small screen, writing a sitcom pilot called *Esme's Little Nap.* The premise was that a comatose mother (Andrea Martin) would narrate her family's life dealing with a missing mom, after grandma movies in to care for the kids. Carrie got Debbie to play the grandmother. CBS shot a pilot in 1991, but it was one of a crowd of supernatural shows, all considered to be knockoffs of *Ghost. Esme* never aired.

Carrie was a proven screenwriter, and a name talent, but those two didn't gel together.

That didn't mean she was done writing for the movies, though.

Chapter 20: Off the Hook

More than the stars need to align to get a studio to greenlight a movie: the director and producer need to as well. If such a syzygy happens, no one wants to spoil the mood by pointing out, say, that the screenplay is set in wintertime and you're set to film in August. Or that the romantic two leads have the chemistry of a hubcap and a turkey sub.

A film's screenplay is more than just dialogue. Most of the screenwriter's work is creating the invisible structure that allows 100 short conversations to turn into a complicated drama. *Do we need scene 78, or is it implied by scene 79? If we switched scenes 65 and 66 around, could we create more suspense? Combining scene 5 and scene 80 into scene 26 could alter the lead's motivations.* Once that is done, the actual writing of dialogue begins. But even then the structure is pliable. It's an old screenwriting joke that the problem with the third act is the first and second act.

Then the actors come in. Many act like Carrie did on the set of the first *Star Wars*: treat the words as inviable as Shakespeare. Others— especially leads—realize the words are there to serve the actors, not vice versa. Just as costumes are tailored to fit and flatter, dialogue needs to be personalized as well.

When given an inch, some actors will take a mile. Some count their lines, to ensure they have as many as their costars. Others throw out the script and make up their lines in the heat of the bounce lightning. It's the screenwriter's job to fix any plot holes this causes, by rearranging everyone else's lines. The script is both the foundation of the plot, and also the first thing to be cast aside as filmmakers discover and uncover what the real story is.

Steven Spielberg had technically been in a movie with Carrie: he had a cameo as a clerk in *The Blues Brothers*. He loved how she told a story, the voice and verve she brought to the page. And now he needed her help.

He was working on the biggest-budgeted film of his career, a tale of Peter Pan all grown up called *Hook*. Robin Williams was Peter and Dustin Hoffman was Hook: both actors were well known for ad-libbing on set. He didn't want the female lead, Julia Roberts' Tinkerbell, to feel staid by comparison: she had to be a pint-size quip factory equal to Peter and Hook, always funny but also insightful and wounded.

At least that's how she came off after Carrie rewrote her scenes. Lines like "If less is more, there's no end to me, Peter Pan" are vintage Carrie, as is Peter calling her a "firefly from hell." Some bleed with her particular pathos. "You know that place between sleep and awake? That place where you still remember dreaming? That's where I'll always love you, Peter Pan. That's where I'll be waiting."

To capture Tink and Peter's interactions, Spielberg put Carrie in a room with Robin Williams. "Robin was astonishing," Carrie remembered: he was what she called "anti-selfish," always trying to delight everyone else in the room. He was an unconscious mimic. He'd start imitating how people walked and moved not from malice but from empathy: he was literally walking in their footsteps.

Ten years ago Carrie would've been a shoo-in to be cast as Tink. But now her words and ideas were going to be given to a younger, thinner, prettier actress. Only Peter Pan never grows up.

Carrie does show up in *Hook*: blink and you'll miss her. For one effects scene, Tinkerbell flies over the distinctive triple lantern lights of Westminster Bridge, dangling Peter like a load of laundry. Tink sheds so much fairy dust that a kissing couple starts floating in air. Carrie was the floating woman in question. And the man, her paramour? George Lucas.

If multiple screenwriters work on a film project, the Writers Guild of America decides how they'll share the credit. Who gets "Story by" vs who gets "Screenplay by"—there's a difference. There's also a difference between pairs of writers joined by an "and" and pairs joined by an "&". The more credit you get, the bigger your royalty checks are, so it's worth fighting for.

The screenplay to *Hook* was the result of three screenwriters. The WGA adjudicators decided two of them—the two who weren't Carrie—would share cowriting credit. Her work on the Tink scenes wasn't enough to merit a credit: no "and," no "&". This also meant no royalties for the film, since only credited screenwriters got those.

Carrie had another avenue left: arbitration. She could have fought

WGA over its decision, maybe get one of those ampersands, which could net her hundreds of thousands in royalties. But she had done the work as a favor to a friend; the film was practically shooting when she was "writing" it. And due to her station in life, she didn't need to fight over a check, even a six-figure one.

Crucially, she also knew what the impact to her reputation would be if she fought and won credit: nothing. A #1 bestseller that became a #1 movie changed nothing: she was still the artist formerly known as Leia. Nothing would change that, so why sweat the small stuff?

Going uncredited, ironically, was a publicity masterstroke. This was an era of last-minute saves. *Saturday Night Live* has found success after its original cast left by cycling new actors in and out. Recent TV hits *The Simpsons, The Wonder Years,* and *Twin Peaks* all began airing as mid-season replacements. Big projects routinely needed nimble-fingered eleventh-hour help.

It was an open secret that Carrie helped write *Hook*, a commercial hit. Word got out that she could jujitsu a poor script into workable shape, and do it mid-production. Just like that, without so much as hanging up a shingle, Carrie was now in the "script doctor" business. Script doctors could get in the neighborhood of $100,000 for their services *each week*. In exchange, they waived WGA credit and royalties.

A-list writers from Quentin Tarantino to Elaine May to Aaron Sorkin all did such work: it's appealing for artists to be mere craftsmen, fixing someone else's story instead of weaving their own. Such jobs were nicknamed "firemen," and it could be demoralizing work—as one script doc griped, you turned terrible movies into merely bad ones, and in front of people who did not want you there.

What, specifically, did script doctors do? They "[b]ring out the character," Carrie said in her third novel, "make them more defined, insightful, funny, compelling—in a word, make their conflict worth attending to for up to, but God forbid not beyond, two big-budget hours." It could also just mean adding extra jokes, which Carrie could do as well.

Much of script doctoring was "personality management," which is a lower-stakes version of hostage negotiation. Just like the "I love you"/"I know" *Empire Strikes Back* scene, every actor wants to contribute, and none wants to feel left out. Carrie found herself performing shuttle diplomacy via golf cart, from trailer to director's chair to producer's bungalow, to get all parties to agree to film a key scene a certain way. It was difficult to get half a dozen creative types to all feel like they'd won an argument. Her lifetime of party hosting must have come in handy: she already knew how to keep volatile egos separated, how to ensure no one flew off the handle or harshed the buzz.

One day Carrie got a call: a nun was in trouble. The nun was Sister Mary Clarence, a lounge singer hiding out from the Mob. The film *Sister Act* had cycled through screenwriters, directors, stars, and costars. No one knew if—to use a joke about the production—they were remaking Debbie's film *The Singing Nun* or parodying it.

Carrie was to be the handler of the new lead, Whoopi Goldberg: they'd costarred in *Soapdish* together. Goldberg couldn't sing the way original star Bette Midler could, but she was funny, and a box office star. The role had been rewritten to suit her: one change was that her love interest was now Black. Goldberg objected: she wanted a white actor. This sort of racial issue was a third rail in Hollywood: Black actors couldn't have nonblack love interests, otherwise "middle America" might not see the movie, or even allow it to play in theaters. Right or wrong, it fell to Carrie to get Whoopi to agree to a Black actor.

Carrie, driving around the studio neighborhood in her black Mercedes coupe, at one point saw Whoopi's Jeep pull up next to hers at a stop light. They made eye contact. In lieu of rolling the windows down, Whoopi picked up her car phone and called Carrie's car phone: two cans and a string, LA style.

"I don't particularly advise people to take my advice," Carrie began, then said despite Whoopi being morally in the right, she should avoid fighting with the film's producers. "Send [the producer] a hatchet and say 'Please bury this on both our behalfs.'" To Carrie, the right present solved any dispute. Whoopi sent the hatchet, and a compromise was reached. A Black actor was cast in the role, but he was now no longer a love interest.

This was Carrie's new job: still on the set, but now writing the lines for other actresses to say. Sometimes she'd commute to a studio lot; occasionally she'd get flown out to a location.

She was one of a sea of script doctors who tried to save *The Last Action Hero*, a high-concept action comedy about a movie character who escapes into the real world. She teamed up with Whoopi Goldberg again for *Made in America*, a romantic comedy about—watch out, middle America—an interracial romance. And she worked with Warren Beatty again on *Love Affair*.

The best screenwriting often didn't involve dialogue. In the cartoon *Anastasia*, Anya sings the heartfelt song "Journey to the Past" while traveling to Paris. But the proposed visual, of her riding a bike, wasn't clicking. Carrie pitched that Anya instead should be slowly walking through a snowy path, leaving footsteps behind her. The change created a moment still cherished by fans of animation.

Actors sometimes perform differently each take, to give the director choices in the editing room. Carrie brought this skill to script doctoring. *Anastasia's* director Don Bluth said she'd come up with not one line of dialogue but three or four alternates, and a branching series of responses for other characters to say in response. This sort of work helped the director make their own choices for scenes, and feel more ownership.

Some of Carrie's time on set was as advice giver to younger stars. She'd tell actors—and actresses in particular—not to "betray your archetype." If people see you as a certain type, in other words, don't chomp at the bit to play its polar opposite just to show off your range. The greater your steps away from the roles that put you in the limelight, the father from the limelight you went. Bolt too far away, and you'd be in the dark.

The love of an audience is a gift, a temporary gift. If you want that love to remain, you have to earn it by acting correctly onscreen—and off. Carrie knew from experience no one wanted to cast a big-screen cutie pie who didn't also act like that when the cameras stopped rolling. Personas outweigh talent. It wasn't fair, it wasn't right, but it was true.

There's no Internet Movie Database listing any of Dr. Carrie Fisher's punch-up work, but the whispernet of gossip remembers. Films she's rumored to have worked on include *Coyote Ugly*, *Kate and Leopold*, *Lethal Weapon 3*, *Outbreak*, *Milk Money*, *The Mirror Has Two Faces*, *My Girl 2*, *The River Wild*, *Scream 3*, *So I Married an Axe Murderer*, and *The Wedding Singer*. Those were just the movies that got made: others were tinkered with but failed to get filmed. All were undertaken as secret diplomatic missions, her work escaping undetected.

One of Carrie's specialties was movies with female leads. In fact, many of the characters she wrote for were roles she might have been offered just a few years ago. "The fact that she made these young beauties sound smarter and funnier than they were was a fate she didn't wish to consider at just that moment," she wrote in her third book.

With all this regular income rolling in—paid weekly no less, like a regular office job—Carrie could up her spending lifestyle. When a friend of hers with HIV developed AIDS and couldn't pay for his care, she covered the bills. "I make a lot of money for what I do," she told him, "and if I don't share that money with anyone, I will go to hell." She also began working with AIDS charities, donating money and attending galas with Bryan. Wasn't that how other doctors lived?

Chapter 21: Us Spring Chickens

In the 1956 film *Bundle of Joy*, two department store workers take care of an abandoned baby. The comedy was rushed into production, actively disliked by cast and crew as it was being made, and then disliked by critics when it came out. The "No Bundle of Joy" headlines were inevitable.

This was Carrie Fisher's second film: she was negative four months old. Debbie Reynolds, fittingly, was pregnant when filming. Carrie's first film was *Tammy and the Bachelor*, made just a few months before *Bundle of Joy*. That would be a big hit for her mom, thanks to a popular song: people called Debbie "Tammy" the way they'd later call her daughter "Leia".

Carrie was born on October 21, 1956, in Burbank: a picture of her ran in tabloids that week. She was famous from birth. "I was in *Modern Screen* at two hours old," she joked on *The Tonight Show*, "and it wasn't even a good picture."

Carrie Fisher Sentence: "I was born into big celebrity. It could only diminish."

Her parents' marriage lasted all of four years, the last two hanging on by splintering fingernails, read about by the same supermarket checkout line tabloid readers who gobbled up her birth photos. Debbie's second marriage had somehow fared even worse. Carrie's marriage to Paul lasted just over a year. Thus, the lack of trust in her mom's third husband, a man who Carrie hadn't even met. But she gave him a chance. For a film where she gets married, she had him cameo as her character's dad, walking her down the aisle.

Carrie Fisher Sentence: "I was born imagining myself with an apron on, with pies cooling on the window sill and babies crying upstairs. I thought all that stuff would somehow anchor me to the planet, that it was the weight I needed to keep from just flying off into space." *Surrender the Pink* was flooded with sentiment like that: it was Carrie's underlying desire for maternal normalcy. She wanted to be a mother.

Despite the ectopic pregnancy—which came with worries of postsurgical infertility—Carrie was able to conceive again, with Bryan. She went off her antidepressants, to ensure her daughter's development was as healthy as possible. Billie Catherine Lourd was born on July 17, 1992.

Debbie had never been a phone-it-in mother: Carrie felt Debbie was trying to win Mother of the Year awards every single day. It had been exhausting. But guess who you turn into when you become a mother. Carrie realized with horror she now wanted to do that exact same thing for Billie.

Her twin worries were becoming a bad mother and becoming her *own* mother. "[Y]ou may have found that I was deficient in demonstrativeness," she would write in her third book, which was about motherhood, "although perhaps they've come up with a vitamin supplement for it." For Carrie, there was maybe a pill for everything.

She had a more specific concern, as well, about her mental status. If she fell down and couldn't get back up, Billie would be left motherless. She had never had the strength to stay sober for too long: now she had someone relying on her. Would caring for another person give her that strength? Or just make her stumble sooner?

It turned out Billie unlocked in Carrie a reservoir of determination she didn't know she had. "Billie came to her, to us," Aunt Joely said, "proof that there was light in the darkness of celebrity mishaps and mismarriages." Uncle Todd agreed: "You're the reason we had Carrie for so many extra innings," he said.

Suicidal ideation can be incredibly potent: the certainty and clarity that no one would miss you if you were gone. Billie obliterated that: someone would absolutely miss her, someone who needed her every day. There was now a force of light stronger than the darkness. "I've had depressions that are very, very, very bad," she said a few years later. "You pretty much know what that means. But I have a daughter, and those are just not viable options."

Carrie's new life experiences informed her third book, with the dad-joke title of *Delusions of Grandma*, released in 1993. *Delusions* was all about birth and its opposite, what Carrie called the "reverse labor" of death. She created a third pseudonym—Cora the script doctor—and gave her a plateful of worries. Cora dealt with forgetfulness, insomnia, fear of marriage, fear of aging, and helping a friend dying of AIDS.

Bryan the agent became Ray the entertainment lawyer: both kind, Southern, with hair "gold and thinning," who could pat her to sleep when she was restless. Cora treats Ray like a pile of free bird seed: she's wary at his supposed decency. Aren't all the good men supposed to be gay or married? Ray breaks up with her... and then she discovers she's pregnant. She starts writing her unborn daughter letters, in case she dies. (One is signed "Your motel, Mom.")

Like the previous two books, *Delusions* was a regular State of the Carrie address: here's who she was, what she was thinking and worrying about. It took longer for her to write: she was a new mother now, and her days were claimed by other writing gigs, and with caring for baby Billie. *Delusions* lacked the focus of her second book—again possibly due to the baby.

She had written a book every three years, so if things kept on schedule, her fourth book would be in 1996 or so. But schedules go out the window when you have a child. And the script doctor work, while less rewarding, was quick and lucrative. Plus she had a new writing partner, *Seinfeld* and *Murphy Brown* veteran Elaine Pope: together they were pitching ideas for movies and TV shows. She had more and more reasons not to throw her kimono open to the world.

She almost didn't notice that her acting career was sunsetting. After appearing in her friend Nora Ephron's directorial debut *This Is My Life*, in 1992, there was nothing else on the horizon. As far as she knew, that would be her final film. She was a writer and a mother now, both roles that didn't require people to comment on her appearance.

"I don't like my looks," she said in a 1998 interview. In an industry where 50-year-olds routinely looked like 30-year-olds, she was a 40-year-old mom who dared to actually look like a 40-year-old mom. "Did you know," she wrote in *Delusions*, "that women have extra fat cells, to protect their unborn children? That is why men get craggy good looks that give them character as they get older, while we get the bleary, melted, overage-broad option."

One downside of the "if you got it, flaunt it" Cool Girl philosophy is that one day you won't "got it" anymore. What then, hide in a cave? Devote your days to dieting and exercise and cosmetic surgery and hour-long makeup regimens, all to please the people who require all women to look like pin-up models? Carrie began to realize she had spent years trying to appease these slimeballs, who undressed her with their eyes whenever she entered a room. They had moved onto a new crop of 19-year-olds. She was now invisible to them.

What to do when you were a woman who has had, as Lynda Barry put it, a lot of birthdays? One of Carrie's friends, Penny Marshall, had smartly pivoted into directing once her sitcom *Laverne & Shirley* was off the air. In a five-year span she made the box office smashes *Big, Awakenings*, and *A League of Their Own*—her comic knowledge and killer timing made her a great director.

Carrie had found her own niche, as wordsmith to the stars. Two former actresses, in a business where if you were over 25 you were an old hag, and they both were in control of their careers.

Old hags? Nobody here but us spring chickens.

Carrie Fisher Sentence: "What doesn't kill you makes you look really, really bad."

For all they spent time together, they only collaborated once, on a Revlon commercial. What was hanging out with them like? Carrie gave us a fictionalized clue. In *Postcards*, Suzanne is best friends with "Lucy," a fellow actress. Suzanne feeds Lucy lines to use on an upcoming talk show appearance, but Lucy can't remember if she used them on a previous talk show a few years ago. They agree on talk show etiquette: the host is allowed to flirt with you on air, but never off.

"Why do I feel like the practical one of the two of us?" Suzanne wonders. "I'm like a ditz in my own life, but as soon as I'm in yours, I have something to do. Cleaning up the mess as you go."

"I don't know, I think I'm good for you that way," Lucy replied. "I make you feel like you're stable, when you're completely not."

In Penny's memoir, she said that Carrie "thought everyone was smarter than she was... in reality, she was smarter than everyone. She was brilliant... Carrie read voraciously." Both women had huge friend circles, so sometimes when Carrie stopped over at Penny's she would be the odd one. To Penny's friends, some of Carrie's innuendos and jokes didn't make much sense. She was broadcasting every thought as she had it, thoughts often delivered as jokes. Everyone laughed, but on reflection, the comments didn't made sense.

She would rummage through her purse, call it "Pol Pot," then say "in reference to my first husband." That was a jet-black joke, yeah, and not really funny. And was she actually comparing Paul Simon to a genocidal dictator? Because they had similar-sounding first names? Was this the same Carrie, who for years never said a bad word about Paul for fear it might leak to the press? Didn't she know how such a jab might come across?

Strike that: she always knew how she came across. "Don't think I don't know how this looks," she'd say, head buried halfway through her bag, rear end sticking out like it was waiting for a KICK ME sign. "And moreover, don't think I don't know what you're thinking."

Carrie and Penny had October birthdays, and threw legendary joint parties. They switched whose house it would be at every year. There were no invitations: everything was done via phone calls. As the parties got better, Carrie's assistant would start fielding calls from people who weren't invited, trying to wrangle a plus-one.

The word "birthday party" suggests candles, a cake, and people crowded around a single table. This was not that. This was a social gathering, and Carrie the second-generation socialite was right at home. One year Penny carried around a silent alarm: she'd been robbed recently, and didn't want anyone pretending to be a guest pulling a B&E. Another year they actually caught an uninvited guest: they let him stay, since the partycrasher was David Bowie.

Carrie gave everyone odd nicknames—odd in that it was simply a different name, like Joseph. You knew you were in with her when she called you "Howard," assuming you were not actually a Howard. Since she understood "Pam" and "Roy" better once she named them, and she understood her friends better if she could rebrand them as well.

Eventually the fêtes had to stop: they kept getting bigger, and there was only so big you could go without both draining the bank account and inviting complete strangers. Then it wasn't your party: you were just the checkbook. The year they saw the odd couple of Salman Rushdie and Shaquille O'Neal standing next to each other, waiting for their cars to be valeted, they realized their creation had grown too large. October 2001 was their last year of dual birthday parties.

"Our crazy lives have meshed perfectly," Penny wrote, thanking Carrie. "We've always said it's because we never liked the same drugs or men, but I know there's more to it." The "more to it than that" angle prompted rumors that they were gay, a rumor Carrie loved so much she kept a *National Enquirer* story about it on her refrigerator door, near her

"When mama ain't happy, ain't nobody happy" magnet. "We're not lesbians," she said in 2002, "we're loonies!"

Eventually Penny relocated to New York, while Carrie remained on the West Coast. They had to buy plane tickets for a face-to-face now. The remove is one of the truest tests of friendship. Neighbors, roommates, coworkers can all becomes friends, but how many last when distance enters the picture? Carrie and Penny would rub shoulders at art auctions, AIDS benefits, and other fancy fare, but lost a step between them.

To be Carrie's friend was to be her best friend. She didn't do anything in half measures. She developed close friendship with enough actresses to fill a Rexall drugstore: besides Penny Marshall, there were Beverly D'Angelo, Meryl Streep, Meg Ryan, her half-sister Joely Fisher, etc. All of them could be the Lucy to Carrie's Suzanne. All of them were, at one point.

Chapter 22: Recognition

Two months before Billie was born, vice president Dan Quayle criticized the sitcom character Murphy Brown for being a single mother. Carrie was also an unwed mother, except not fictional.

Families were not their paperwork. Families were not always homogenous husband/wife/baby trios. Loving relationships and strong bonds could exist in with almost any configuration of parental figure and child. Single parents, unmarried couples, divorced couples, gay couples: all could provide warm and loving homes for children.

Bryan's career was on the rise. The last of the five original founders of CAA had just left, and Bryan and his friends were poised to become the new unofficial heads of the agency, with power to outvote the other partners. They could and they would: it was eat or be eaten. Soon one of the Young Turks was CAA's official president, and Bryan was a managing partner. They had the power.

Bryan's specialty was diplomacy. "Bryan," departing head Michael Ovitz said, "could act as ombudsman, which would be needed to fuel and oil the massive number of key relationships that would touch the agency." The Turks agreed to remain friends, to not let money or power drive a wedge between them, as had just happened with the departing CAA founders.

In an era where agents were on the covers of newspapers, Bryan relished staying behind the curtain. A 2016 book about CAA featured interviews with all major and minor players—all except Bryan. His years with the outspoken Carrie never led to him to the habit of, as Carrie put it, wearing his underwear on the outside. On the contrary; it made him value privacy all the more.

Carrie, with a now-three-year-old Billie, headed out to Las Vegas to visit her mother. Debbie joked that Billie should be known not as "Carrie Fisher's daughter" but as "Debbie Reynolds' granddaughter." Carrie was briefly playing agent herself: her friend Albert Brooks had written a script called *Mother* about a man with a passive-aggressive mom. This film could be the Debbie Reynolds Comeback, Carrie knew.

Once in Vegas, she arrived at the new Debbie Reynolds Casino. Yes, her mom now owned a casino. It was Carrie's first time there, and she was rendered speechless by what was inside. All those old movie props and costumes her Mom bought decades ago were now on display. The outfits Debbie and her friends had worn on the big screen in the 1950s were hanging up as if in a museum. Even the lighting was vintage: the chandeliers were from *Gone With the Wind*.

It should have been the crowning moment of Debbie's career. But alas, Debbie's third husband had run off, after thoroughly robbing her of her assets over a period of years. The hotel and casino were thus in dire financial straits, and she was putting on shows every night just to keep the lights on.

If Debbie's first divorce has been a tragedy, and her second divorce a mystery—teenage Carrie had flown to Spain with her mom to learn about Harry's affairs from a family friend—this third divorce was a war. Carrie had waited anxiously by the phone for news, young Billie, by her side, as Debbie broke into her ex-husband's house. She carted off a truckload of her own possessions he had stolen, made copies of reams of tax documents, and discovered proof of a possible second family. The documents proved he'd been stealing from her since the beginning.

Indefatigable, Debbie now spent her days in meetings about debt lawsuits, and her nights dancing up a storm. On nights she had off, she took one-night gigs anyplace that would book her. It was a brutal workload for anyone, much less a woman in her 60s who had been recently hospitalized with a bleeding ulcer.

Carrie got Debbie to do the Albert Brooks movie. It was her first lead film role since the 1960s. The return to the big screen earned Debbie critical praise, a Golden Globe nomination, and a new career. From then on, she received steady work as goofy grandmas in cartoon voiceovers, TV movies, and sitcoms. She acted more than Carrie did, in fact, who was done with it save for playing herself in her sister Joely's sitcom. (Even then, she was more writer than actress, and rewrote her own lines.)

As a writer for the 1997 Academy Awards, Carrie scripted Debbie's onstage banter. Debbie hadn't been nominated for an Oscar for *Mother*, and presenting was thus considered a consolation prize. She joked about an AA-style meeting for actors who didn't get nominated. At one point she stops reading her cue cards and says "Who wrote this drivel?" That prompted Carrie to walk on, to exchange scripted insults for a minute.

Carrie and Bryan bought a ranch house together in 1994, near Coldwater Canyon. It was a Spanish-style mansion, owned by a series of movie stars, including Bette Davis. Carrie swore she saw the ghost of another former resident, costume designer Edith Head, walking the halls at night. She was surprised, not at seeing a ghost, but that the fashion maven was dressed so shabbily.

They renovated, and Carrie decided to personalize the kitchen. In lieu of picking out a backsplash, she had floor tile cut to allow room for an 18-inch-long Prozac pill illustration, half avocado and half Creamsicle. Much of her décor, Carrie joked, looked like "something that ought to be left to a miniature golf course." It'd look trashy in a mobile home, but in a mansion, it became trashy's nouveau-riche cousin eccentric.

Carrie was in a new house she had made her own, making new memories, with good money coming in, Billie safe by her side. She was as stable and content as she would ever be. Bryan arranged this; he wanted her and Billie as secure and safe as they could be. A safety net.

After they'd settled in, Bryan told her that he was leaving Carrie. Leaving her for a man.

Bryan was… gay? Carrie must have flashed back to all those years as a teenage chorus girl kissing gay men. Maybe that was what drew her to him: men behind glass were her type. Maybe she always knew.

Hollywood was full of gay people, but most were closeted, to a degree. Bryan was one of the first to go public, opening the door for many others in front and behind the cameras. If he could live his life honestly, so could they. Something you're not ashamed of shouldn't be a secret.

Carrie never processed this properly. She would make snide jokes about her superpower to "turn men gay." If another LA-area woman found herself in the same situation, Carrie would become a one-woman welcome-wagon. Join the club, she'd joke, decoder rings were on the way.

As an autobiographical novelist, this life event that dropped into her lap had everything: love, sex, power, betrayal, humor. But she was busy with other projects, and with Billie. More importantly, writing a book about Bryan in her scorched-earth style would be a real act of aggression. It was not a good move for someone trying to co-parent and share custody and be pleasant around each other. And Bryan was a very private person who'd done a very brave public thing: why thrash him for it? Carrie borrowed a page from Bryan's life handbook, and held her tongue.

Harrison, Dan, Paul, now Bryan: maybe she just wasn't fated to be in a relationship. From now on, like a proper older Jewish lady, she would play matchmaker instead. Sure, if some young movie star wanted a smooch from good ol' Princess Leia, she was up for it. But she stopped looking for anything beyond that. That particular happy ending would stay in development hell.

When it works well, parents who live apart go from offering one happy home for their kids to offering two. Carrie and Bryan acted civilly in front of Billie, and soon it wasn't an act. Bryan, true to form, was a stable grounding presence. "He will be a great and dedicated parent," she wrote in *Delusions*, "and I will toil meekly in his shadow by comparison. But I will toil all the same."

When the caretaker's cottage next door to her ranch house was put up for sale in 1999, Carrie knew who she wanted as her new neighbor. Debbie moved in as her daughter's next-door neighbor. They kept separate lives—they might go a week without seeing each other—but Debbie's presence was calming. Someone was nearby to take the wheel if Carrie ever had another episode.

Growing up, Carrie had been raised with the help of a parade of nannies. She swore if she ever had kids she'd be their actual mother, not just the help's supervisor. Now that she had a child—a very overscheduled child at that—she found she also had job responsibilities that kept her at her desk or away on the set. As a result, enter the parade of nannies, who took Billie from ice skating to swimming to French lessons.

"The nannies were still the arrangers of things, the organizers of all the activities that make up a child of Hollywood's life," she wrote in her eventual fourth book. Carrie could afford the help, and needed it, but still felt the sting that she wasn't mothering Billie right.

Chapter 23: The Empire Line

Pop quiz: which *Star Wars* actor worked with George Lucas on *Indiana Jones*? The answer is usually Harrison Ford… but one time, it was Carrie Fisher.

George's new project was a TV series, *The Young Indiana Jones Chronicles*, which started airing in 1992. Each episode showed either grade school Henry Jones, Jr going on a trip around the world with his philosopher dad, or two-fisted tales of teenage Indy in the Great War. It was intended as educational programming, but edutainment might be the better word. You'd learn more if there wasn't so much action, and you might be more entertained more if there weren't so many historical figures shoehorned in. The show featured big-budget action setpieces, location shooting around the world, and casts of hundreds.

George needed a lot of scripts: they were making two years' worth of hourlong episodes, at much higher cost than a regular show, but cheap compared with making a movie. One of George's ideas was teen Indy falling in love with Mata Hari in Paris in 1916. He knew Carrie could deliver whipsmart romantic dialogue. Plus, she would get to have Indy attack tabloid muckrakers.

The episode began in modern day, with eye-patched Old Indy—yes, a third Indiana Jones—in a checkout lane. After seeing a ridiculous story in a gossip magazine (a Jane Fonda/Mikhail Gorbachev romance!), he begins to tell the checkout clerk about a story from his past. Cue the episode-long flashback.

After Carrie handed in her draft, George had notes. Usually his people would deal with it, but for Carrie's script George was hands-on. She found herself in a particular nightmare: George was crossing out all her dialogue, which she felt was authentic and real to the characters… and was replacing it with *George Lucas dialogue*. Flowery sentimental dreck! Without a hint of irony! No one but George talked like that.

"We couldn't disagree more, in any world, about love scenes," she said. "I mean hours of it, hours of 'why wouldn't you say that? I talk like that.'" Carrie felt people didn't push back on George: "they let him get away with it because he's Lucas." George eventually agreed to Carrie's version of the draft changes, after a faux-serious duel where they held up toys that cursed when you pressed a button. An argument via swear droids.

Then the shooting script arrived on Carrie's doorstep. Gone was Carrie's dialogue, replaced by George's corny sincerity. "He let me win the draft, then he went off and shot it and he changed it. I went crazy! I didn't want the shimmering-arm, hair-in-the-moonlight stuff." But what could she do? It's hard to win a fight against the guy who owns the studio.

The episode, "Paris, October 1916," aired in 1993, and was repackaged a number of ways, including being recut with another episode into a feature film subtitled *Demons of Deception*. The DVD release included a Mata Hari documentary along with the episode, meant to be shown in schools.

Young Indiana Jones Chronicles was educational in another way. It taught George how to be a producer, how to manage a set without being on it every day. And it was film school for a new group of Lucasfilm employees, who bonded while filming in far-flung locations. They learned how to inexpensively add CGI extensions to shots, how to communicate with the home office, and how to bring in a film shoot on time and under budget.

That trained film crew of George's was going to come in handy.

* * *

In 1991, a sci-fi novel by author Timothy Zahn called *Heir to the Empire* hypersped its way to the *New York Times* bestseller list. This was unexpected, since it was a *Star Wars* novel.

There is a word for a movie series that no longer cranks out new installments: that word is "dead." After 1983 toymakers tried putting out new *Star Wars* toys, but without a corresponding movie few bought them. The Marvel comic continued for a few more years, and Lucasfilm had briefly aired cartoons about *Ewoks* and *Droids*. In 1987 the Disney theme parks opened a *Star Tours* ride. The franchise had been mothballed ever since. Even the *Star Wars* fan club was disbanded.

Zahn had been tapped by Lucasfilm as a test for signs of life. He would write another chapter in the *Star Wars* mythos. Not just any old space yarn would do: he had to write about what happened to Han, Luke, and Leia after *Return of the Jedi*. "The readers had to hear Mark Hamill's and Carrie Fisher's and Harrison Ford's voices inside my quotation marks," he wrote in an introduction to an anniversary edition of the book.

The hardcover was priced cheap, at 15 bucks, which helped it sell. Zahn went to work on second and third novels: it was *Star Wars*, of course this would be a trilogy. This led to understandable confusion that Zahn was novelizing George's screenplays for the unfilmed sequel trilogy. He wasn't: new characters like reluctant assassin Mada Jade and the cunning Grand Admiral Thrawn were original to Zahn. As was his overarching story, about a pocket of the Empire that refused to concede, and was trying to overthrow the New Republic.

Leia Organa Solo—she was now married to Han, and in a very 1990s decision combined her and Han's last names—was leading the post-Imperial government from the city-planet of Coruscant. She was pregnant with twins, and discovering her new Force abilities. Zahn wrote Leia as a bit uncomfortable with pageantry: she's ill at ease in cocktail parties. She has the new trilogy's toughest job: drafting a constitution for the New Republic that all planets will sign. Winning is easy, governing's harder.

Luke is Leia's Jedi teacher, and Leia—for maybe the first time in her life—is not a quick study. She wonders if her time isn't better spent trying to run the provisional government. In a telling lack of confidence, she can't even ask Luke to build her a lightsaber. Bringing twins into the world while hammering out a peace accord fills her day: she can't do all that and also train.

Zahn's books include dozens of clever ideas: animals who hunt with Jedi powers, an alien race who call Leia "Lady Vader," and a lost fleet of abandoned Destroyers up for grabs to whoever finds them first. At one point Threepio is reprogrammed to sound like Leia so she can radio from two places at once. Thrawn, who has a Holmesian intellect, sees through the charade: he knows the real Leia would never break radio silence.

The plot has Han and Luke gallivant around the galaxy, searching out foes who mean to kidnap Leia—to steal her unborn Force-sensitive kids. Leia hides out on Chewbacca's home planet, which she hadn't been to since Life Day, 1978. "Though I tried to give each of the three main movie characters a fair share of the action," Zahn said, "it was in the nature of this part of the story that Leia was a bit shortchanged."

There was no reason why a tie-in novel to a decade-old movie franchise should have smelled the bestseller list, much less sat atop it. And yet it did. How? George's theory of the franchise's popularity invoked another Holy Trinity: he described himself as the Father of the franchise, the trilogy's cast and crew as the Son, and the fans as the Holy Ghost. Fans were eager for more *Star Wars* stories, in any medium they could get it.

The following year, in addition to Zahn's second book *Dark Force Rising*, Lucasfilm released a trilogy of books aimed at young readers: in one, Jabba's father Zorba the Hutt seeks revenge against Leia. The next year Zahn finished his trilogy with *The Last Command*, where Leia gives birth to Jaina and Jacen, and snoops out a spy on Coruscant, while Luke and Han have to deal with Thrawn's newfound fleet of spaceships and the army of clones piloting them.

In 1994, six *Star Wars* books came out, including the bestselling *Courtship of Princess Leia*, explaining how Han put a ring on it. *Star Wars* adopted a number line theory: instead of every book taking place sequentially, each book took place between two others. *Courtship*, for instance, was after *Return of the Jedi* but before *Heir to the Empire*.

Dark Horse Comics then started releasing new *Star Wars* comics, beginning with the handpainted *Dark Empire*. In it, a clone of Emperor Palpatine wreaks havoc, and according to a thousand-year-old prophecy Leia needs to be the one to defeat him.

LucasArts, the game division, got into the holy spirit of things as well. It released a pair of *Star Wars* games in 1991, and made a custom game for each new gaming system as they hit the marketplace. Like couture clothing, each game reflected the strengths of its system: the PC's speed for *X-Wing*, or the Super Nintendo's graphical oomph for *Super Star Wars*.

In 1995, 10 *Star Wars* books came out: the number went up every year from there. Most every story either built off the movies or the Timothy Zahn books: those became the Old and New Testament. The tone, the humor, the creativity, the focus on adventure, and Manichean battles between good and evil were all reflective of these foundational texts.

This was how George had always imagined and designed *Star Wars* to work: a fully stocked sandbox for storytellers to be able to spin any tale they wanted. Back when he lived and breathed film, he could only imagine these stories as films. But films were expensive. Imagination was cheap, though, and writers had an unlimited budget.

Zahn's new take on Leia predominated: here was the diplomat, the politician, the mind that stood up to torture and didn't break, who withstood the death of her planet. In other parts of the genre world, tough capable women began to dominate—Captain Kathryn Janeway from *Star Trek: Voyager*, Judi Dench's M from the James Bond films, Trinity from *The Matrix*, Cortana from the *Halo* video games, and a certain warrior princess named *Xena*. All done the Leia way.

Chapter 24: Memory Palaces

So *Star Wars* was now back—in every form the 1990s had to offer but movies.

Adults who rewatch the formative movies of their childhood find that the films are different. Like wine and cheese, childhood films ripen while on the shelf, gathering the plummy taste of nostalgia.

Nostalgia, not the Force, is the most seductive power in the universe. Nostalgia—a mix of pleasure and sadness when remembering the past—made things from yesteryear seem better than things today. *Star Wars* was a good film, but thanks to nostalgia, many people believed no film could ever hold a candle to it. Nostalgia makes people believe this about everything of their childhood, from candy to sports to music to children's behavior.

Nostalgia is a lie, of course, a lie that makes the world seem in permanent decline. William Faulkner boiled it down to five words: "Memory believes," he wrote in *Light in August*, "before knowing remembers." We remember what we *felt*, in other words, not what we *thought*.

Our plastic brains are constantly editing our memory, updating reality to reflect what we're currently experiencing. An experience can become better and better each time it's remembered. Our locked-away memories change: we change them, in fact, each time we revisit them.

What was different for the nostalgia of "Generation X"—the children of the Baby Boomer generation—was Gen X's focus on media. Movies and books and magazines and music and theater and cartoons and newspapers and radio and TV and cable and video games and the Internet: Gen X life was often just a cornucopia of story installments.

And the best story of all time, Gen Xers knew, was *Star Wars*. This was an economically true statement. Dollars don't lie, and *Star Wars* stood atop the global office all these years later like a colossus, its "intellectual property" unequalled. There hadn't been any more since 1983: the dream was over. This disappointment gibed with '90s kids' own stymied dreams. Gen Xers rewatched the films of their youth on VHS, BetaMax, and LaserDisc, just as their Boomer parents listened to golden oldies on AM radio.

Star Wars had well and truly left the realm of mere entertainment to become modern mythology. And Leia, way more than Luke or Han, was the biggest benefactor of this godhood. Partly this was gender-line vote-splitting. Partly it was Leia's improved storyline when the trilogy's overarching story was considered. Partly it was that Leia kept popping up in pop culture: Vespa in *Spaceballs*, the Transformer Arcee, and dozens of fictional warrior women.

And then there was Jennifer Aniston.

In the third-season premiere of the sitcom *Friends*, airing in September of 1996, Aniston's Rachel dresses in Leia's *Return of the Jedi* gold bikini—and her *New Hope* twin-bun hairstyle to boot. This was because she heard her boyfriend Ross had a crush on Carrie Fisher. The onslaught of imagery was almost Jungian in terms of awakening Ross' libido. "Is the hair wrong?" she asks him: he's too flabbergasted to answer.

Ross wasn't the only one.

"I'm an S&M joke on *Friends*!" Carrie would protest, years later. But Ross was not the only one to have "The One With the Princess Leia Fantasy," as the episode was called. For a post-Vietnam America, *Star Wars* was the only war people knew. Princess Leia was their Rosie the Riveter, their Hanoi Jane, their Molly Pitcher.

The coiner of the phrase "Generation X" was Canadian novelist Douglas Coupland: in what he called the "life after God," secular figures took the place of the saints and martyrs of previous generations. So Leia also became the Gen X Virgin Mary, Joan of Arc, and Our Lady of Guadalupe.

Leia was a hero for cynics who saw the world as a rigged game with corrupt authorities. For those who didn't want to sell anything, buy anything, or process anything, Leia was their hard-bitten ideal, the princess of their memory palaces.

The underground river of *Star Wars'* continued popularity sprang up in surprising places. Kevin Smith's 1994 slacker film *Clerks* featured a hilariously profane conversation about how many innocents were on board the Death Star when it blew up. A year later, a Darth Vader action figure would come alive in *The Indian in the Cupboard*—directed by Frank "Yoda" Oz. Two years after that, *The Fifth Element* featured a character with an unmistakable Princess Leia coif.

In people's heads, Leia Organa was a real living person. She possessed the clarity of purpose of *A New Hope*, the complexity of *Empire Strikes Back*, and the certainty of *Return of the Jedi*. This Leia was a far better character than George ever wrote, or indeed that Carrie ever get to play.

It's this Leia that fans read about via the Expanded Universe—the nickname for the ever-growing series of stories brachiating out from the *Star Wars* films. In one such story, a Stormtrooper who witnesses her tête-a-tête with Grand Moff Tarkin joins her side, because he so admires her bravery under duress. In another, the captain of her blockade runner sacrifices himself because of brave words she told him. A third tells of Leia's parents, who ironically wish they'd kept her on Alderaan, not knowing the irony that her dangerous mission will keep her alive. The ghost of Obi-Wan wishes that he had trained the mature Leia, not the brash Luke. The garbage monster grabs Luke because in the monster's world females are the fighters, and it was scared to grab Leia.

Instead of Leia changing, these stories were about how Leia changed everyone she came in contact with. Each act of hers, no matter how small, would become codified and lionized and sanctified. Princess Leia stories were now nothing less than hagiography.

* * *

Hollywood realized that instead of being on-call during production, script doctors should work on a screenplay in preproduction. Rewriting a script cost a fraction of fixing it on set. Producers then started commissioning multiple concurrent rewrites, then grabbing the choicest bits from each treatment. Both of these were smart financial decisions, but to script doctors like Carrie they were ruinous.

Her final script-doctored film was *Intolerable Cruelty*, a divorce-lawyer comedy, which would sit around for a decade before being filmed. That was that: Carrie hung up her stethoscope. The doctor was no longer in.

"It was a long, very lucrative episode on my life. But it's complicated to do that," she said to *Newsweek* in 2008. "Now it's all changed, actually. Now in order to get a rewrite job, you have to submit your notes for your ideas on how to fix the script. So they can get all the notes from all the different writers, keep the notes and not hire you. That's free work, and that's what I always call life-wasting events."

Free was not a word Carrie used much. As Hollywood royalty, she never had the relationship to money that most people did. Even the nouveau riche appreciated it in ways she did not. She was generous to friends, and to strangers—she sent flowers to Marcia Clark after a particular tough day on the OJ Simpson murder trial. To charities her presence was often more valuable than a check. Regardless of her cash inflow, she spent lavishly, flew first class around the world, drove the newest Mercedes models, vacationed almost every season at five-star resorts.

Most people who are bad with money end up broke, or buried in debt. But being bad with money is psychological issue at heart, not a fiscal one. The same people who don't want to go to the doctor also don't want to know how much they owe to Visa. Carrie hired someone to take care of her business expenses. So long as her card wasn't declined, she didn't need to know what she had in the bank.

She grew up wanting nothing, was rich before she could legally drink, and had moved onto a series of absurdly well-paying writing gigs. Not many socialites spent their days earning the money they used to pay the caterers at night. But now the script doctor work was gone. And she just did not have the time or perhaps the ability to put together a fourth book.

Other script doctors had leveraged their secret success to aboveboard writer/director deals. Joss Whedon pivoted from clandestine work on *Waterworld* and *Speed* to staking his reputation on *Buffy the Vampire Slayer*. The writer of *Stuart Little* and teen comedies became, in a surprising twist, *The Sixth Sense*'s M. Night Shyamalan.

But Carrie's success rate at pitching her own projects was low. She could put words in other people's mouths, but original premises were never a strength. It was as if a life other than the one she was living was unimaginable, unrealistic.

"The habit of expression," Henry James wrote, "leads to the search for something to express." Carrie had expressed her story, via fiction, in three books and one screenplay. Just as she didn't feel the need as a teenager to sing and dance on stage, and then lost the desire to act, now she felt little compulsion to write. So what was next?

She wanted to be a person she couldn't imagine writing about: a regular person. Someone who could walk down the street unnoticed, shop in peace, be there for her daughter when school was let out. Have a meal without being asked for a photo by a stranger. Go to a movie and not see someone she slept with on screen.

Some people who found movie success left LA when it was time to have a family, back to a quiet town where movies were a distraction from life, not life itself. Others retired but stayed local, just in case an opportunity popped up. Some stayed as long as they could, fighting against the undertow that pulled them out of the spotlight to make way for new talent.

Carrie couldn't leave: showbiz was the small town she was born into. To leave it would be to quit her Mom, who when cut bled tinsel. And to quit Bryan, who was becoming one of the most powerful people in entertainment.

There was another reason why she so coveted a normal life: her ongoing mental health. The National Institute of Mental Health estimates that only 5% of people with mental health issues have "severe mental illness." That is, illness that "resulted in functional impairment which substantially interferes with or limits one or more major life activities."

Carrie was one of that unlucky 5%. Both as an addict and as someone diagnosed with bipolar disorder, she knew disaster could strike at any time. There were days where an unkind word would make her break into tears for three hours straight. Or lead her into road rages where, to prevent causing an accident, she smashed her phone into the steering wheel, over and over. Or talk to her friend nonstop for up to eight hours. Even if she left LA, she'd still be living on a fault line.

She was invited to write for the final season of the sitcom *Roseanne*: Roseanne Barr was a friend. She wrote a story where John Goodman's mother, who for this episode was recast as Debbie Reynolds, went off her meds and was trying to kill her son. Roseanne's TV son had a line where he was excited to rewatch *Return of the Jedi* because of "Princess Leia in a bikini." Debbie Reynolds smacks her fake grandson for saying this, about her real daughter.

There's a joke in Hollywood that you go from "Who's Jane Doe" to "Get me Jane Doe" to "get me a young Jane Doe" back to "Who's Jane Doe?" Carrie had lost the fight to be seen as a versatile actress, but she refused to slide into anonymity. The woman who used to grin and bear it when Leia came up now did little *but* bring up Princess Leia. She even

Jeff Ryan

showed up at the MTV Movie Awards, to bequeath a 20-year-belated award to Chewbacca.

Around this time she got a call from the *Los Angeles Times*. It was for a profile on George Lucas, who was rereleasing the *Star Wars* trilogy with augmented special effects. The films would all become #1 box office hits upon release, but George didn't want to talk to the press. Carrie did, though: she gave the reporter better quotes than a used car dealer.

She received the usual question about making *Star Wars*, but the reporter focused on George's post-*Star Wars* life. In lieu of making films himself, he had been spending the last 15 years up in Marin County, turning "Skywalker Ranch" into his own studio.

"Skywalker is where George gets to make the rules," she said. He was, in fact, remaking reality. Each new building came with a fictional backstory. A visitor would think this brand-new facility was actually a hundred years old.

George could do that because he was rich beyond compare. The sort of rich where he walked around in ballcaps and worn jeans, with nothing to prove to anyone. He'd built his utopia, and now got to live there rent-free.

Carrie was stuck living in reality. In this way, she had achieved her goal: she was just like everyone else.

Chapter 25: Younger Now by Far

In spring of 1998, when *Titanic* passed *Star Wars* to be America's all-time #1 box office film, George took out a congratulatory full-page color ad, with all the trilogy's characters stuck on the sinking ship. Chewie was cannonballing off the deck, Threepio was blaming Artoo for the disaster, Jabba was having a last cocktail, and the Emperor had commandeered a rowboat full of Jawas. Han and Leia were at the stern of the ship, acting out the "King of the World" pose.

This ad was a wonderful tradition, going back to 1977, when *Star Wars* overtook *Jaws* as the most profitable film of all time. Each time a baton was passed—by *E.T., Empire Strikes Back, Jurassic Park*, etc.—a full-page ad would celebrate the box office victory, as one director toasted another.

The records were getting broken more easily. Partly this was due to multiplexes and inflation and an expanding nation. But it was also the result of the movie world learning its lesson from *Star Wars.* Every summer was now filled with pricey "event" movies. A hit movie in the early 1980s could make at most about $100 million: Hollywood couldn't imagine a number bigger than that. But in the marketplace of the late 1990s, the right film could conceivably gross ten times that amount. Think of it: a billion dollars, from one movie.

That was what had caused George Lucas, after 15 years in a cave, to see his shadow and return to moviemaking. In 1994 he announced he was going to finally make three more *Star Wars* films he'd been promising since 1977. Not sequels, though: prequels. The world would finally see what caused Jedi Knight Anakin Skywalker to become Sith Lord Darth Vader.

Young Indy had given him a lean, mean film crew. Industrial Light and Magic had recently added lots of VFX critters to the original trilogy using computer imagery. Hiding in plain sight, he also had them working

169

on preproduction work for the prequels: people assumed it was for the rerelease. He'd even financing an inexpensive 1940s mystery, *Radioland Murders*, to test out how digital sets could work.

A month after *Radioland Murders* came and went from theaters, George went to work on the script for *Episode I: The Phantom Menace*, on the same door desk he used when that was all he could afford. He still wrote with a pencil and a pad: everyone is part Luddite. And he called all his A-list director friends to direct the picture. They all said he should direct it himself.

Well, if he was going to be stuck in the director's chair, he was going to finally direct a movie his way. For the prequel George created a new method of filmmaking, based on all his frustrations the last time he was in the saddle. Why build expensive sets, rip them down, only to rebuild them for a reshoot? Why devote so little time to editing? Why have an expensive crew standing around purposelessly most of the day?

Ironically, it took his multimillionaire clout to set up cheap ways to make a film. Digital sets allowed actors to stay on location while appearing in far-flung locales. Physical sets were built in warehouses, not expensive soundstages, so they could stand for months. Actor's contracts included reshoot times. Effects-wise, George had ILM do much of the postproduction work in preproduction, saving time and budget. He filmed in 1997, giving himself an unheard-of 2 years of editing time for a 1999 release. And he hired new film-school graduates: they were cheap, worked hard, and never picked up what George considered the bad habits of mainstream moviemaking.

One of George's boldest ideas would fly under the radar. Every director had a Sophie's choice to make when one actor nails take 2, and their scene partner nails take 3. Now, thanks to digital split screen editing, he could combine take 2 and take 3 into a single collaged shot. He stopped looking for great shots, and started looking for great *bits* inside each shot. This became a challenge to actors—in lieu of acting on a set with fellow actors, they now recited lines to a tennis ball on a stick in a green room.

George brought on board a mix of new and experienced actors. For Luke and Leia's mom, Queen Amidala, he hired Natalie Portman, an old soul who at 16 already had five films under her belt. "Natalie is very strong and mature for her age," George said, "and like Carrie Fisher she has the personality to carry the role of a leader." Playing l'il Anakin Skywalker—

maybe Vader someday later, now he's just a small fry—was Jake Lloyd, a towheaded seven-year old. Ewan McGregor was young Obi-Wan Kenobi, complete with very credible Alec Guinness impression. He was apprentice to a Jedi master played by stoic Liam Neeson.

Before George started rolling, he wanted the opinion of a certain retired script doctor. Carrie had recently saved George from a drunk indie director who accosted him at a party, saying that George had single-handedly ruined serious filmmaking. She read George's script and gave him feedback. This turned out to be a rare privilege: most of the actors were only given their lines on the day of filming, and at day's end had to hand them back.

Carrie was one of a handful who actually knew what the film was going to be. What did she think? She told a reporter "I've read it, and I can't wait to see it, 'cause I know George does better than what's on the page, if that's possible." Leia herself couldn't have more diplomatically said "it stinks."

Not a shy person with feedback, Carrie did more than give George advice; she may have given the script a free treatment. The two leads were supposed to be Leia's parents, so who better than the princess herself to ensure the dialogue and plot beats felt in rhythm with the first installments?

Roger Christian, who worked on all three previous films in various capacities, was a second unit director for the fourth film. He credits Carrie for penning a comical scene where Threepio, minus his gold plating, is chastised by Artoo. "I beg your pardon," Threepio says to a beeping Artoo, "but what do you mean, 'naked'?" Artoo elaborates. "'My *parts* are showing?' My goodness, oh!"

George, a liberal guy, had named an evil alien Nute Gunray—pulling from Newt Gingrich and Ronald Reagan's names. Carrie may have given Nute a sidekick named Lott Dod. The Lott was after a third Republican politician, Trent Lott. The Dod was after Democratic senator Chris Dodd. Why a Democrat? Carrie went on a date with Dodd in the 1980s, and he acted beyond boorishly. Revenge: a dish best served with hot buttered popcorn in 3000 theaters.

As with her other ghosting duties, Carrie's *Phantom Menace* work went unacknowledged. George would get all the credit for *Phantom Menace*…

…or all the blame.

Perhaps no film with such anticipation could live up to the hype, or please multiple generations of fans. Perhaps a film so dedicated to its world-building only draws attention to areas without as much care. George's new filmmaking tricks had created wonders, but sterilized, sanitized wonders. In that way, it was as chilly as his dystopian film *THX-1138*.

George had been worried about Anakin's youth: would audiences believe such a young boy could fly a spaceship, as he does in the finale? Audiences were fine with that: hey, he was a Jedi. What they were put off by were things like the offensive characterizations, the tonal shifts, Anakin retconned into being Threepio's creator, and 90 solid minutes of Jar-Jar Binks.

One new idea was especially criticized: midi-chlorians. Midi-chlorians were the mitochondria-like bacteria that allowed certain people to tap into the Force. Being a Jedi wasn't a mystical journey, or even a genetic heritage. You could Jedi yourself up with a booster shot. George's idea about the Force—and he was *George Lucas*, mind you—was that everyone had the Force within them. Anyone could be a Jedi, not just clan Skywalker.

It used to be that fans loved but critics disliked George's films. Now his oldest fans had become the critics. Ten-year-olds, though, gobbled it up like 10-year-olds did back in 1977: they vastly preferred this shiny action-packed adventure to the boring, staid original trilogy. To quote another car-loving Californian, "Guess you guys aren't ready for that yet... but your kids are gonna love it."

The Phantom Menace was the #1 box office hit of 1999. It earned over a billion dollars in worldwide box office, the first time the global box office outgrossed the US. Hollywood decided to start rebooting many of its older movie franchises, everything from *Planet of the Apes* to *Terminator* and *Superman*.

The new generation of *Star Wars* fans snapped up more *Star Wars* merchandise than the GDP of a midsize country. Lego alone moved $2 billion worth of *Star Wars*-branded toys during the *Phantom Menace* launch. (The toymaker also invented a clever wordless comic of stylized Jedi and Sith minifigures going on adventures, which would prompt a whole new series of Lego games, comics, cartoons, and film franchises. There are now two dozen Leia Lego minifigs.)

Despite not appearing in *Phantom Menace*, Princess Leia once again because a hot commodity. Toy stories that ordered bulk quantities of other *Star Wars* figures were given a free Princess Leia figure, a bit like a baker's dozen bonus. Smart shoppers realized the Leias were a steal, worth way more than market value. Some even went on road trips, clearing out toy stores of Leias to resell on eBay.

Carrie joked about how jealous she was that her on-screen mother, Queen Amidala—or "Queen Armadillo" as she put it—got so many costume changes. Portman was complimentary of her on-screen relative: "It definitely did come into play how strong and smart a character Carrie Fisher portrayed, because I think that a lot of that is passed on from parent to child," Portman said in an interview. "I think George wrote Amidala as a strong, smart character, but it helped to know that I had this great woman before me who had portrayed her character as a fiery woman."

Portman's career would blossom with seeming ease: she went from prestige pictures to indie hits to blockbuster fare. Oscar nominations and leading roles abounded. She even did *SNL*, where she rapped: all this and she was funny, too! George has once again cast his royalty well. Portman's success meant Queen Amidala would be just one of a series of memorable roles for her.

Carrie, on the other hand, returned to acting but usually as stunt casting. She was a double entendre-spouting nun in *Jay and Silent Bob Strike Back*, Dr. Katz's ex-wife in *Dr. Katz, Professional Therapist*, and a therapist in the first *Austin Powers* film. For better or for worse, she was no longer an actress: she was Carrie "Princess Leia" Fisher playing an actress.

Leia was tattooed on society's brain. Around this time, Carrie decided on some ink of her own. With Billie in tow, she drove to Tattoo Mania, on the Sunset Strip. On her right ankle, Carrie got a handful of moons, stars, and planets etched in blue. (Technically, this violated her no-needles rule.) She'd now bring the stars with her wherever she went.

Or maybe the Turkish flag. "All in all, it somehow had the overall effect of a patriotic solar bruise, but patriotic to a country in the Middle East," she wrote in her fourth book. It didn't look galactic enough, so she returned to the tattooist's chair and got a teal and purple nebula added to the celestial scene. Teal and purple are bruise colors, though. For the rest of her life, if Carrie wore a skirt or capri pants, she looked like she'd been recently kicked by a horse.

The garish tattoo was in its own way a perfect metaphor. A woman who was public with so many of her injuries was now sporting one for the world to see. Only up close could you see that the injury was in fact art. A fake injury. A phantom menace.

Chapter 26: Oh, My Papa

In 1998, Debbie, Carrie, and Todd Fisher were jointly awarded the Platinum Circle Award, given out by the American Film Institute for a family's collective contribution to the world of cinema. But there was someone missing from the award. Not on stage was the scoundrel ex-husband who gave his name and little else to Carrie and Todd.

Eddie Fisher, once again, was defined by his conspicuous absences.

One of Todd's very first memories of Carrie was her, around age four, standing on a couch, looking out the window. Her dad was supposed to come pick her up; he had promised he would come. So she stood, and waited, and looked out the window. Eddie Fisher never showed up that day.

What may be worse than an absent father is one who shows up at staggered intervals, makes promises of being around forever, and then disappears. Carrie guessed her father had a kind of "emotional ADD": he routinely made heartfelt promises, which were forgotten once the person he pledged undying love to was out of his eyeline. Eddie's self-destructive habits and lothario ways took him to extremes.

Carrie joked that she was the product of a broken mansion: the broken part was real enough. Growing up, everyone around her knew the one thing she didn't: Eddie had abandoned her. He had some more kids, and then abandoned them as well. The formerly good boy singer with the back-row baritone was a deadbeat dad.

In *Postcards,* she described this as "the Oedipal thing... my father leaving when I was very young so I knew how to pine for men, but not how to love them." She extrapolates in *Surrender*: "My father loved me and I never saw him. He might as well not have loved me. So, I guess I confuse love with absence."

Eddie Fisher was a fixture of 1950s tabloids. He and Debbie were an item, married on Rosh Hashanah. Four years later, he left her for Elizabeth Taylor, who was recently widowed. After Liz in turn left him for Richard Burton, he shacked up with Connie Stevens, pretending to be married. After a hard word from Frank Sinatra, he flew a pregnant Connie to Puerto Rico to actually officially wed. A year later, that was over as well. You need a flow chart to understand it all.

"I was always drawn to woman who didn't want me," Carrie had her father figure in *Surrender* say. "I don't know, it just seems like my wiring in this area was crossed." In his memoir, the real Eddie concurs: "The right woman for me was always the next one. The more unavailable a woman was, the more attractive she was to me." Carrie, desperate for her father's love, was therefore repellant.

Eddie Fisher stories: He bought the same suit in one hundred different hues. He spelled multiple family members' names wrong in his memoir. He married Liz Taylor three and a half hours after divorcing Debbie Reynolds. He repeatedly asked to see every female in his life in the nude, including his kids. He drove drunk with his kids in the car, and shot up heroin with them watching. He traded girlfriends with fellow crooners like they were baseball cards. He swallowed his incredibly expensive hearing aids, since they looked like pills. He buddied up to his kids only when they became famous, or were dating famous people. He would brag about being the world's worst father, brag because they still loved him nonetheless.

In Carrie's fourth book she described her dad's middle-aged cosmetic surgery: "He gets facelifts. Can you believe that? He's had so many, he looks Chinese. Which is handy, 'cause he likes to go out with Asian women." (Eddie's fifth and final wife was Chinese American.)

Carrie bought into a New York co-op in the early 1980s, and stayed there when she was in town. Eddie asked if he could visit her. Carrie said yes… and Eddie moved in for a year. Sometimes they did drugs together, father and daughter. This debauchery became too much even for her. She started booking hotel rooms rather than staying in her own place. When Debbie heard about this, she flew cross-country and kicked him out the only way she knew would work: she wrote him a check. In his memoir, Eddie joked that he'd abandoned his kids for free, but now was getting paid for it.

Using the prescription lenses of retrospect, it's easy to see he was an addict. Addicted to sex, addicted to drugs, addicted to spending, addicted to gambling. His 1950s TV show was even called *Coke Time*—after a sponsor, but still.

Eddie became the archetypical male addict—risk-taking, lacking self-control, delusional. It's not who he had been—the prototypical Nice

175

Jewish Boy™—but it's who he became. His life revolved around the next girl, the next fix, the next charge card, the next bet. Combined with his I Gotta Be Me personality, he was a five-foot-five bull in a china shop. (There's a female archetype for an addict as well. This person is shy, cautious, suffering from mental illness, and using drugs to self-medicate. That fit Carrie, with her chicken-and-egg mood disorder and addictions.)

Father and daughter would share addictions, trips to rehab, and personal lives that resembled demilitarized zones. For all Carrie's closeness with her mom over the decades, she was just as much her father's daughter. Good fathers give their daughter strong role models to emulate, but so do bad fathers. Eddie was not a good father, but he became a prime example of a way some people go about living their life. Not even Darth Vader could have been a worse role model.

In her 20s, Carrie realized Eddie would never step up, never be anything like a parent to her. (This was after she married another short, prodigiously talented Jewish singer in Paul Simon.) If she wanted a relationship with her dad, *she'd* have to be the parent figure to *him*. "After all these years of not being part of my life, she forced me into her life," Eddie said.

This failed: Eddie would not stop being Eddie. He bailed on appointments, bedded random women, and mounted up huge debts. She tried again when she was seeing Paul, but that failed, too. Third strike time: "I'm going to give you a chance to be a grandfather," she said when Billie was born: he failed there as well. Eddie Fisher was a rock in Carrie's life, but only to the extent that it made her Sisyphus.

Like a coach who unites a team by their hatred of him, Eddie left strong families in his wake. In 1999, Carrie, Debbie, and Billie went on a Hawaiian vacation. Along for the ride were Connie Stevens, and her daughters Joely and Tricia. The three sisters were like triplets, Carrie felt: Eddie had sired and abandoned the same little girl three times in a row. The triplets decided to dance naked in the sand with Billie, a dance of female empowerment: we are more than the man who ruined us. We are bonded, stronger together.

Carrie Fisher Sentence: "That's it, I'm having my DNA fumigated."

Some families talk: the Fisher clan wrote. Debbie had written a memoir the year after *Postcards* came out, and in 1999 Eddie published a book-length rebuttal. Eddie bragged about the women he slept with, how great his voice was, and how Debbie was a relative nobody when he met her. She was a phony, her good-girl thing just a facade: she was worse than him. You can almost smell the alcohol seeping through the pages.

There is one undeniably true fact in the book, though: Eddie had been gifted with a truly wonderful voice. But his hard living abused his million-dollar pipes: he now sounded like a slumming lounge singer instead of a booming baritone. In this Carrie was her father's daughter. Her decades of smoking also had begun to turn her pipes raspy: as of her early 40s, she now sounded like a salty diner waitress.

With acting and now screenwriting in Carrie's rearview mirror, most of her on-camera appearances were as herself, on talk shows. People had become familiar with her over the last 10 years this way: chatting on the couch with Jay Leno, presenting an award along with a wry joke or two. Sometimes she was soft-spoken, other times outrageous. She was a regular guest of a British chat show by Ruby Wax, and that experience perhaps sold her on trying out the other side of the desk.

Conversations from the Edge with Carrie Fisher would air on Oxygen, Oprah Winfrey's new feel-good female-centered channel. Most cable subscribers didn't even get the channel: there would be no #1 show to match the #1 movie and #1 book.

Conversations aimed to be a different type of talk show. For one thing, there was no desk, and no audience: it was filmed in Carrie's living room. (She had wanted the bedroom at first: she often entertained guests while watching TV in bed.) It would be a true conversation: no blue notecards from a pre-interview, just soft flattering lighting and an unhurried pace. The unspoken promise was that each guest would be as pull-no-punches honest as Carrie about acting, fame, romance, and life.

Way back in *Postcards*, a friend of Suzanne's said she'd be good at hosting a talk show. "That's what I'm afraid of," Suzanne replied. "I'm afraid I'd be good, and I'd end up the Joanne Worley of my generation." (Joanne Worley was a boisterous comedic actress who ended up spending more time in the 1970s on panel shows like *Match Game* than acting.)

Cut to 20 years later, and Carrie now saw herself as, as she put it, "Hamburger Helper next to the juicy porterhouse of 'currently starring in'". A "not-quite-has-been", but no longer fresh. So maybe it was time for her to be the slightly famous person talking to really famous people. She was self-aware enough to both rue and appreciate that her current position was maybe a step down for her, but a huge opportunity for most anyone else. Joanne Worley it was.

Booking guests—the "get"—is usually the hardest part of a talk show. The bigger the name, the better they played the exposure game, and the less they'd be willing to grant an interview off in the three-digit hinterlands of a new cable channel. Stars knew how to play the interview game—serving up finely tuned anecdotes while keeping their true lives private.

This was where Carrie's lifetime of royal treatment came in handy. Most interviews were improv-ved camaraderie, not an actual conversation. Carrie had had real conversations with everyone who'd ever been filmed, and stars were used to letting their hair down in front of her. This was their chance to have a real conversation. So after decades of public exposure, people like Robin Williams and Diane Keaton jumped at the chance.

Not everyone jumped. Those carefully built celebrity facades are carefully built for a reason. Some superb actors have the personality of blank notebooks. Some comedians are dour when they're not "on," and some sparkling wits are very dark under the razzmatazz. (At least one showbiz wife told her husband to never speak in public, lest he lose his macho mystique and be revealed as a himbo.)

Carrie knew Sharon Stone was more than sexy, and that Lisa Kudrow more than weird. And that it would be a great role reversal for Carrie to interview someone like Diane Sawyer. And that Jude Law and Ben Affleck were more than just pretty faces.

Each star would drive up to Carrie's house, and she'd invite them in, cameras rolling for the opening of the door. She'd apologize for the show starting off with a literal entrance. They'd sit in chairs in front of a grand fireplace. They held their tongues during make-up: both parties knew to save it for when cameras were rolling.

If Carrie was good she'd remember to pause the talk for commercial breaks. If she wasn't, it'd be up to the editors to find the breaks. The conversations weren't polished for TV; she'd ask their opinions about 9/11, about fame, addiction, parents, everything. Sometimes she'd go to her subjects, as with George Lucas, which was filmed at Skywalker Ranch. If need be, the producers would add explanatory chyrons saying that their friend "Steve" was Steven Spielberg.

She razzed George for blowing off a get-together with her to attend a fundraising party at the Playboy Mansion— *sure*, George was only there for the love of cinema, *sure*. She commiserated with Courtney Love about drug abuse, and with Melanie Griffith about growing up with famous parents.

Carrie had a hard time doing the invisible work of "presenting" a conversation to the audience: actual conversation can be a mess of crosstalk, unpulled threads of story, and commiserations with guests for personal-life problems the viewers at home might not relate to. At its best and worst, it felt like listening in on a post-awards show chat between two old friends letting their guards down.

The show lasted 20 episodes, spread over two years. The long-form interview was a tough sell on TV: it would find a more natural home on podcasts. Carrie did get some nice outfits from the show's wardrobe budget. And she wrote in her fourth novel if anyone swore on "set" and her daughter was around, they had to put a dollar in a swear jar. The book daughter was purposefully lingering, to save up for a Game Boy via the crew's cursing.

Carrie's alter ego "had fallen into doing the cable talk show 'thing' like she's fallen into acting and then just as easily fallen out of it—though it felt to her as though the tumble was a little slower going out than it was been crashing in." She had done the show she wanted to, and found a new way to be herself in public. But television wasn't a big fan of new ideas: it preferred old standbys, like the seven-minute celebrity interview.

It also liked reunions. For the last decade, beloved shows ranging from *The Brady Bunch* to *The Waltons* all filmed specials that reunited the casts for another romp. Despite their subsequent endeavors, the actors were shackled in people's memories to a hit role from the past: wonder what that's like.

Film critic Gene Siskel said that a movie with big stars had a challenge: it had to be more interesting that watching those actors eating lunch together. Who would be nice, who'd be mean, who'd be vain? That was what Carrie saw growing up when Debbie's friends came over: a bunch of past-their-prime diva actresses gabbing over the craft services table.

She wrote a TV film to bolster her mom's resurgent acting career, *These Old Broads*, about such aging actresses. Debbie Reynolds would be one of the four leads, naturally. But what about the other three? Adding Shirley MacLaine into the mix would be tempestuous, since she kindasorta played Debbie in *Postcards*. Lauren Bacall, on no one's shortlist of the nicest people in Hollywood, would be great as an ice queen still disliked by all. And dare to dream, maybe Carrie could write a role for Elizabeth Taylor—like Liz Taylor would ever do TV.

Bacall ended up replaced by Joan Collins before filming, but everyone else, somehow, agreed to their parts. Liz Taylor did it to make up for Debbie and Carrie for the Eddie thing. The film shot on set at MGM, where the Fisher family had grown up. Carrie gave herself a small role as a prostitute, a somewhat damning bit of self-criticism. This script was full of takedowns and putdowns, and unless viewers were conversant in 1960s scandals much of the humor would go over their head.

The film was a joy to make, despite being about how much everyone hated the sight of each other. The cast truly bonded, enjoying every day together. Unfortunately, the finished product failed the Gene Siskel test: watching these old rivals become friends over a lunch would have been more interesting than seeing their characters take scripted pot shots at each other. It was a big hit when it aired, with over 15 million primetime viewers—numbers Carrie would have loved for her talk show.

Chapter 27: Next to Normal

There was too much Leia in the world to keep straight. New *Star Wars* stories kept showing up on the daily via coloring books, comics, chapter books, stickers, and video games. How to keep it all straight?

Answer: a database started in the year 2000, nicknamed the Holocron after a Jedi data storage cube. The Holocron listed every action and appearance of every character in every single media form, from cereal boxes to action figures to, yes, the *Star Wars Holiday Special*.

At the apex of the Holocron was the G-level, reserved for the theatrical films. G-level content overshadowed everything else. G stood not for *God* but *George*. Below the G level were seeded all the PlayStation games, TV movies, comics, and paperbacks, so they didn't conflict. George forbid two stories about Admiral Ackbar's watery home planet of Mon Calamari portrayed it differently.

But such conflicts happened—they were bound to. This was where the Holocron's leveling system helped decide things. As the Synod of Coruscant, it decided whose story got to "count," and whose was deemed imaginary. So that 11-page comic about Princess Leia's youthful pranks when on Alderaan, called *The Princess Leia Diaries*, published in *Star Wars Tales* #11 in 2002? That's what actually happened in young Leia's life… that is, until a show like *Obi-Wan Kenobi* comes about and says that Leia was kidnapped as a child.

* * *

Going public as someone with a severe mental illness was the act of a crazy woman.

In an interview with Diane Sawyer on ABC's *Primetime Thursday*, on December 21, 2000, Carrie said what very few public figures had ever said. "I'm manic depressive… I am mentally ill," she said. No jokes about Princess Leia being nuttier than squirrel poop, just a declarative sentence.

Copping to having a mental illness was not a personal failing; if anything, it was an admission that some of her failings were beyond her control. Millions of people hid this truth: the special aired a home video of Carrie joking "I haven't lost my mind, it's lost me." They hide it because everyone else hides it, because of the stigma from within and without.

Carrie couldn't control all her thoughts, or all her actions, but she could control letting people know why. Stigma be damned: you wouldn't treat someone with a diagnosis of breast cancer or Parkinson's disease this way. Yet everyone did, her included. No more. Time to come out of the closet.

"I'm manic depressive... I can say that. I'm not ashamed of that. I survived that, I'm still surviving that, but bring it on. Better you than me." To a nation of people secretly filling scripts for antidepressants, it was an act of bravery. They weren't alone. To those who were too afraid to even go to a doctor or therapist, they weren't alone either.

Going public is not a one-time announcement. It's a permanent commitment, a promise to never hide that part of yourself again. For the rest of Carrie's life, her mental health would be part of her daily conversation with others, just as much as "How's Debbie doing?" and "How's Luke doing?" She also became a magnet for the sort of people just like her, who'd had a lifetime of troubles and needed help taking the first step to wellness.

For years after being officially diagnosed as bipolar, Carrie lived in denial. She thought it silly that her pill problem hid a deeper problem, which in turn could be treated with... different pills? For too long she treated her prescription medication as optional, replacing them with the sort of meds not covered by insurance copays.

But then came a manic episode from hell, followed by a depressive period *in* hell. For six sleepless days her decisions ranged from bad to worse. "The world of manic depression is a world of bad judgement calls... 'cause it all seems like a good idea at the time! A great idea!" Then a stay in a psychiatric ward, where she was so sluggish she struggled to perform basic activities. When asked to sign her name, she put a pen in her left hand, and very slowly and deliberately wrote the word "SHAME."

During a relatively brief moment of lucidity, Bryan was visiting her, his remaining hair graying and neatly clipped. She imagined her evil side as just for a moment distracted, sitting in a chair on the opposite side of the room. She begged Bryan to take care of Billie, since she no longer could.

After that, there was no denying that she needed her meds to stay normal. Or at least next to normal.

For Carrie, going public was one more bit of oversharing, one more skeleton from her walk-in closet. But it was a crucial moment in the world of mental health. Mental illnesses are sometimes called the invisible illnesses, and not just because they don't present with external signs. The people who have them can hide it. Seeing someone known for on-screen heroism admitting to it—and not just garden-variety depression or anxiety but full-blown bipolar disorder—made a difference.

Carrie had always been able to afford the best care. And she had an understanding mother, who for decades had worked with metal health charities. Even those advantages weren't always enough: Carrie had trouble balancing the right meds, just like everyone else with a medicine cabinet of little orange bottles.

What would Carrie's life have been without her advantages? Carrie began to find out. She began to meet women who'd walked the same path she did, but without her privileges. Some were living on disability, others were dealing with addiction, or just trying to keep a lid on the day. She met them at AA meetings, while shopping, at events: they were everywhere. Invisible, but no longer. And they saw themselves in her. If she could go public about needing help, so could they.

Carrie frankly admitted that when people said they loved her, it meant they loved "Roy"—the life of the party, the Ups. But here were people who said they loved Carrie for "Pam," the Downs. Who, in fact, loved all of her, light and dark, Jedi and Sith. There are few more welcoming and empowering moments that when you realize you're not alone out there.

* * *

In 2002 Carrie appeared in a TV show (*The Nero Wolfe Mysteries*) and a movie (*Charlie's Angels: Full Throttle*). But the big event of her year was a film she was not in: the new *Star Wars* movie *Episode II: Attack of the Clones.*

Carrie reportedly helped out on the script again, but it was still

George's film, for better or worse. Once again no one got to read the script until the day of shooting—but now the secrecy extended to the preproduction crew. This meant sets and costumes were built without knowing what scenes they would be featured in. The upside-down filmmaking created more problems and reshoots—but it also allowed George to postpone writing for as long as humanly possible.

Carrie got invited to *Star Wars*-related event after event, since the film's plot was about how Princess Leia's parents fell in love. As a connection to the original trilogy, Natalie Portman's Padmé for one scene sports a complicated double-bunned hairstyle, which looked like a brown lacquered modern art museum. The elaborate 'do was meant to suggest that Leia's hairstyle was actually a toned-down tribute to her late mom. "I never met Carrie Fisher before I did the film," Natalie said. "I recently met her for the first time. We were at an event together, and she introduced me as her mother!"

* * *

In 2004, Joely called her sister late at night. Joely was in New York, and had been drinking for days. She had a husband and three-year-old daughter back in California, who didn't know where she was. This was her rock bottom, maybe the worst moment in her life.

"Don't worry," Carrie responded, almost blithely. "You're a periodic." This came off as a bit dismissive: Joely could have died! But to Carrie, a three-day alcohol bender was like a thin person complaining they'd gained five pounds. What Joely considered her nadir had been Carrie's day-to-day life for a decade.

Joely returned to her family in Los Angeles—Carrie was right, she sobered up quickly—and she and Carrie turned an AA meeting into a Fisher family reunion. "At least you're not bipolar," she told her sister later. "Eddie's bipolar. I'm bipolar." A dab of alcoholism was nothing, comparatively, with the serious problems that fueled her and her father.

Many of Carrie's days during the first decade of the 21st century were spent self-confined in bed. With her pillows and mattress as a *locus amoenus*, she would watch TV ultramarathons, unable to either leave the bed or go to sleep. In *Postcards* she described the television as a "liquid scrapbook." Flipping channels took less physical and mental effort than flipping pages.

In the past she'd been a movie star, screenwriter, and princess. That was then. Now she was "simply a shadow cast by the giant of her former self," as she'd put in one of her books. Current binge-watcher, current chainsmoker, current basket case. Some days Billie took care of her.

Going public after her episode, being able to accept and talk about that part of herself, seemed to have broken her writer's block. No more hiding behind alter egos: this time around, she'd finally write a proper this-actually-happened memoir.

But the period she wanted to write about was so subjective, and her memory of it was so unreliable. Once again, her life had to become a true story best told by fiction. The result was 2004's *The Best Awful There Is*, whose title was later shortened to *The Best Awful*.

For *The Best Awful*, Carrie returned to her *Postcards From the Edge* alter ego, Suzanne Vale, now even more deliberately Carrie. How deliberate? Suzanne at once point tells her daughter, "Your father is gay, your mother is a drug addict/manic-depressive, your grandmother tap dances for a living, and your grandfather shot speed." The daughter also has the same eyelid freckle as Billie did. Any resemblance is purely coincidental, huh?

The Best Awful begins with short scenes that got the reader up to speed on Suzanne's life: the parties, the gay ex-lover who was frustratingly perfect, the hilarious friends, the feeling that bad decisions were the only ones left to make. At times it feels more like descriptions of unwritten novels than chapters of an actual novel.

It also produced a bumper crop of new Carrie Fisher Sentences.

"'The other day, I actually forgot the term *senior moment*.'"

"'I hate lying. I'm no good at it, which is why I was such a mediocre actress.'"

"Suzanne's inner riches and eccentricities were kept hidden under the watchful eye of the little pills she took to medicate the colorful version of herself back to a drabber, whiter shade of pale."

"Death: Coming soon! Sooner that you'd care to think!"

The plot kicks in when Suzanne decides to stop taking some of her mediations, to be a better lover. Then she stops taking all of them: a reverse relapse. Her writing's at its best when describing way-out-of-control desires—she describes it as "an avalanche ever gathering force". Every action seems to make things more dire—going off some meds, trying new meds, a "medication vacation"—she was a walking worst-case scenario. She ends up wanting to die but not to commit suicide, so she wishes for a fatal disease or accident—an end of pain without guilt.

Little mentions ring true—paparazzi cameras "recording her battle to accept a life so often seeming so inexplicably unacceptable," for instance, or her scoring drugs despite being clean and sober just so a man who used would go to bed with her. With each page she reflected on her life as a woman, mother, daughter, addict. She dug deeper, challenging her own motivations and opinions, while also detailing the joys and damages a sustained manic episode can do to herself and the people around her. At heart, deep down there, under all the mistake, was a little girl who couldn't sleep. If you want to know Carrie, this is by far her best book.

Suzanne worried about the consequences of her mental illness on her daughter. She wrote that she "felt as if she were about to free fall over the bad mother cliff where she'd land on the pile populated by such luminaries as Joan [Crawford] and Lana [Turner]—well, Judy [Garland] couldn't have been that good but at least she was funny... they were allowed to be worse as a prize for being so talented, the great artist get-out-of-jail card for this low, low price, while those less blessed paid the full tax for their irresponsible doings."

There would be no more novels after this. Carrie explained why, in the book's final pages: Suzanne's brain had undergone too many abuses. A doctor says "she might never get back all the equipment she'd once had to play with. The familiar toy behind her eyes. The one that gave the world back to her with its own peculiar spin on things... There was no telling what her mind might do now that it wasn't all hers." Control would be harder than ever, madness a permanent resident, doing permanent damage.

Chapter 28: Life After

There's an old joke in Washington that a politician will only lose an election if they get caught with a dead girl or a live boy. Carrie got caught with a dead boy.

Carrie and a new friend, Greg Stevens, spent the Friday night of February 25, 2005, talking, watching *Mrs. Miniver*, smoking her Marlboro Silver Kings, and getting high snorting cocaine and crushed OxyContin. Greg was sick: he'd had bronchitis, and he had a history of heart disease. The 42-year-old fell asleep in Carrie's bed next to her, and never woke up.

Greg was not a Hollywood guy, but a Republican political figure. He was also gay, common in Hollywood but rare in the GOP. He was in town for Bryan Lourd's yearly Oscar party, and was staying the night with Carrie. What may have bonded them was drugs: you party with who's holding, not with who you'd want to party with. A publicly sober woman can only get good and wrecked with someone who can keep it secret. A gay Republican, by definition, can keep secrets. Now Greg was dead, presumably of an overdose… and he had done nothing that Carrie hadn't done right there next to him.

Opioids like OxyContin rewrite the brain in dangerous ways: addicts' lives become dedicated to scoring the next fix the way a drowning person's body tries to breathe. If Carrie tried to detox cold turkey, the process might kill her. Extreme measures would be taken, at a clinic in England, to keep her alive. By the time she had returned to California she was down to a quarter of an Oxy pill a day.

Todd was a war movie buff, and realized that Carrie's guilt was no different than soldiers dealing with post-traumatic stress. The siblings watched war movies together, to see how the military members dealt with survivor's guilt. Carrie was so taken by a line in Clint Eastwood's *Heartbreak Ridge*—"Adapt! Overcome! Persevere!"—she painted the words over her bed. It reflected her acceptance of the past, and her ability to change the present. All she had to do was never give up.

Carrie Fisher Sentence: "You know, if you live long enough you're a survivor."

Friends and family corralled around her, to keep her spirits up. She got a travel assignment for the *New York Times Magazine*, and brought along Billie, Paul Simon's son Harper, three assistants—and for good luck, Meg Ryan. All this to visit Canadian towns with double-entendre names, like Spread Eagle, Newfoundland. "We're juvenile. I'm sorry," she wrote. Billie, now 13, spent much of the trip in silent embarrassment as her mom and her friends spent all day making sex jokes.

She took these travel assignments for another reason: money. Like her mother before her, like half of Hollywood it seemed, Carrie had trusted the wrong someone with her finances. One day she found out she'd been systematically cleaned out. She didn't even own her home anymore. Her seven-digit lifestyle—the spending sprees, the five-star holidays, the new cars—now had to be paid for somehow.

Rehab didn't stick: her Oxy usage went back up. Her weight went up as well, which made her depressed, which then brought on more pills. She'd now been in more rehabs than she'd been in sci-fi movies: why wasn't she dead yet? She should have perished a half-dozen times by now, like so many of her friends. The alligator when she was little, choking on a Brussel sprout, so many overdoses—death's aim was apparently worse than a Stormtrooper's.

She acted sober, or as sober as she could while relapsing. One day Carrie drove Billie and some of her friends to the mall for a shopping trip, while she was heavily altered. No one was injured, but Carrie could have killed everyone in the car. Bryan heard about it, and realized the sad truth: Carrie was no longer a fit mother. He called a lawyer, to arrange for sole custody over Billie.

If life were a movie, the threat of killing your daughter, or of losing her to the courts, would do the trick and kick Carrie sober. But addiction can't be won over by love any more than it can be by willpower. Bryan's act drove a wedge between him and Carrie's family, who defended her even when her actions were indefensible. (They would later reconcile: "For one of the busiest men on Earth you've been a rock and stable life raft for Billie," Todd wrote later.) Carrie also knew what Bryan was doing was right. Her current mental state *did* made her an unfit mother. Even if she could hold onto shared custody, had she lost her daughter forever?

Another addiction movie scene would be a heartfelt plea from the addict to a family court judge. But years of Carrie being Carrie had shredded her impulse control. If she spoke in her defense, she'd be her own worst champion, and probably set a land speed record for self-incriminating comments.

In engineering terms, the filter between her brain and her mouth had catastrophically failed. She could never control her thoughts, but now each thought was *voiced*. Her words became a firehose, delivered to one and all without any inhibitions. She'd talk to her daughter about sex, to her mother about drugs, to total strangers about her most intimate habits. It made every social interaction a challenge: if you asked Carrie how she was feeling, if she liked an outfit, or how she felt about an old friend, you'd get a double-barreled response.

That began making Carrie a bit of a hero, in the eyes of the masses who knew her diagnosis. They saw in her banter a voice that couldn't help but speak truth to power. Carrie had all her life been a great listener: now in her place was an interrupter, an insulter, a self-denigrator, a dispenser of snark, all via a voice that was no longer whiskey and honey but a cured-meat rasp.

Carrie treated her past the way a monk with a cat-o-nine tails treats his back skin. Her verbal tirades were like backyard fireworks, and she always stood too close, receiving a facefull of damage. She had always been funny, but now she was a regular Don Rickles.

The third of the prequels, *Star Wars: Episode III—Revenge of the Sith*, hit theaters in 2005: by a comfortable margin it was the biggest film of the year. And many felt the best of the new trilogy to boot, culminating in the injurious lava duel that forces Anakin to Vader up. The principal cast recreated a behind-the-scene shot from *Empire Strikes Back*: Natalie Portman stands in her faux-daughter's place, while Hayden Christiansen sits to the left in the Mark Hamill spot, and Ewan MacGregor is slumped on the right in the Harrison Ford pose. George Lucas is in the same spot both times, happier this time around, and with grayer hair.

The final prequel ends with the birth of Luke and Leia, played by lifelike dolls ginned up by the creature department, and then a real baby. This scene seems to contradict what Leia said in Jedi about remembering her mom, since baby Leia sees her mother Padmé for all of three seconds before Padmé dies. (Holocron to the rescue: later stories clarified that Leia was remembering *pictures* of her birth mother.)

Three years after *Sith* hit theaters, the cartoon *Star Wars: The Clone*

Wars began airing on TV. It was set between *Episodes II* and *III*, and the first few episodes were released in theaters, technically making it a fourth *Star Wars* prequel film. But George had finished the origin story he'd wanted to tell. Time to take a victory lap or two.

The American Film Institute's tribute to George Lucas was one of those victory laps. Or at least it was supposed to be... before they invited Carrie. She strode out on stage wearing a slimming black jacket over a black sparking dress, and lips puffy enough to look like she was having an allergic reaction to shellfish. ("Were they meant to look younger?" Carrie wrote two years earlier, about such augmentation. "Sexier by virtue of this pouty, bee-stung mouth?")

It was what the lips said that drew everyone's attention. "Hello, I'm Mrs. Han Solo, and I'm an alcoholic," she began, followed by a testy inhalation and cough, perfectly timed for comedic impact. It was triple-axel opening that referred to her most recent troubles, her film history, and (if you squinted) Leia's ongoing role in the Expanded Universe.

The camera cut to George, on a dais surrounded by Steven Spielberg and his daughters. He smiles politely and claps the way a person with a stroke would clap: raising one hand and dropping it on the other. It was the look of someone who realized they're about to be roasted.

"I'm an alcoholic because... George Lucas ruined my life," Carrie said. George chuckled. "I mean that in the nicest possible way," she added.

"Fifty-seven years ago," she said, "I did his little *Star Wars* film, a cult film that then went on to redefine what they laughingly refer to as 'the face of cinema.'" The one sentence has an exaggeration about her age, a faux denigration of *Star Wars*, another faux denigration, and then a slap across the brow of the filmmaking industry as a whole for its low standards. It's an exhausting amount of contempt, and the audience is stunned: Are we supposed to laugh? If so, at which part?

After this comes a good-natured joke about George's stoicism, a less good-natured joke about George as a director—"but like any abused child wearing a metal bikini chained to a giant slug about to die, I keep coming back for more"—and a joke about how the cast all had stalkers now thanks to the trilogy's success. "It's lovely," Carrie ad-libbed.

She takes her time with each word, adding pauses and stops to maximize her timing, hitting unusual words that make each joke feel funnier, truer, more her. On George owning Leia's likeness: "Every time I look in a mirror I have to send you a check for a couple of bucks!" She even buffaloes through a Pez-dispenser joke that Mark Hamill had previously made.

It's the comedy equivalent of a polished dance routine: she is trying her very hardest. When she pivots to praise, it's not so much heartfelt as spat out. This may be because, as she says, "I now spent the latter half of my Leia-laden life helping to hurl [compliments] your way!"

For the four minutes she was on stage, the focus on the night was not George, not Leia, but Carrie. Even her housewrecking last line—"I *hope* I slept with you to get the job, because if not, who the hell was that guy?"—is a shot at herself, not at him.

George, of course, didn't need four more minutes of applause. At that point in her life, though, Carrie did. She'd soon grab a recurring role on the cartoon *Family Guy* as Angela, Peter's domineering boss, as well as other roles where a harridan was needed. And she showed up for other roasts, where her full-auto takedowns were welcome.

Carrie also turned to a treatment seemingly discontinued with leeches and bloodletting: electroconvulsive therapy. Modern ECT, though, was precise and clinical: the patient was asleep when it happened, and thanks to muscle relaxants and general anesthesia, there was no pain or discomfort. The shock produced a brain seizure, which was akin to turning a computer off and on, so it would reboot with fewer bugs.

Despite being an outpatient procedure, it wasn't for garden-variety takers of antidepressants. For most people, medication and therapy kept them on an even keel. But Carrie was the poster child for a behavioral illness so profound and uncontrollable that it destroyed her life with regularity. If something wasn't done, if would kill her. "[W]hen weighing the choice between ECT and DOA," she wrote, "the decision is easy to make."

Carrie was driven to a clinic, and had stickers with electrodes placed bitemporally on either side of her forehead. She was put under sedation. Then 400 volts of energy were ported into her gray matter. Her brain seized, like an epileptic shock. This *was* epilepsy, prescription epilepsy. She went back every few weeks, each time for another medically induced reboot.

ECT worked for her, in that it pulled her out of a deep depression. For the first time in years, she experienced the clarity and control she has previously only found with drugs. But the drug addict side of her was still there. Just as when she was clean and sober she still had to deal with her mood disorder, now when she was clear-headed she had to deal with her constant need to score a fix.

The lines and actions of a sober addict are identical to one who is using. All addicts are actors, and each show is the same. You must set your family at ease that your days of lying and using are in the past, that you're now at peace. You don't win an Oscar for this performance: you win another chance to proclaim your hard-fought sobriety the next day.

In Al-Anon meetings around the world are posters with the three Cs: you didn't cause it, you can't cure it, and you can't control it. Addiction is a disease, one someone else has, and they are the ones living their life. Those posters read very differently for the addicts themselves, though. "You can't control it" can be a useful reminder for someone tempted to crack open just one beer. But for someone whose clean days are measured in weeks instead of decades, it's discouraging.

* * *

The more people in Carrie's orbit around her to monitor her, the better. Harper Simon had moved in with Carrie, while recording his first album. (Harper had had his own share of drug issues over the years.) He was big into collaborating, even with his other stepmom Edie Brickell. Since he was living with Carrie, Rhymin' Simon the younger thought he'd work with her to cowrite a song.

For all her years of writing, all her years of singing, and all her years with Paul, Carrie had never once written a song. Never even considered it: the Fishers and Reynolds *interpreted* songs. But with her stepson's guidance, she began to free-associate words. Certain ideas clicked with certain others, and themes started to shine through the chaos. Harper provided melody to match the lyrical content, and a song was born.

The song was called "Shine." Its lyrics appears to be standard lost-love material: "Where do you think we went wrong/ Can we go back and watch it again?" But it's a song from a mother to a child, Carrie wishing she was there more for Harper. "Maybe I didn't love you the way that you wanted/But I've never loved anyone more." (Paul helped shine up the lyrics to "Shine:" it wouldn't be a Carrie/Paul collaboration unless both tried to get the last word.)

The experience seemed to free her up: when another musician stayed over—Sean Lennon this time, another son of greatness—she improvised lines while he tinkled on a piano. They cowrote what they called "Bird Song," based on Carrie's only-she-would-think this realization that birds are hateful, and bird singing is nasty. And years later she'd work with yet another musical son—Rufus Wainwright—reading a Shakespeare sonnet in a soft Atlantic accent for a concept album of his.

* * *

A show on Channel 4 on the BBC called *Bring Back...* attempted to reunite the casts of past hits. For 2008's *Bring Back... Star Wars*, host Justin Lee Collins gamely used his beer gut and a couch to pose as Jabba the Hutt, with a shackled model wearing Leia's harem outfit.

After striking out with Mark Hamill and Harrison Ford, Justin said he was "going after the sexiest woman in the galaxy," while showing a clip of his fingers feeling up a photo of Carrie. "We're heard she's bored of talking about *Star Wars*, so we've lied to her agent and said we're making a show about something else... so I'm off to her house, unannounced, and uninvited." It's queasy to watch such an invasion of privacy, especially one done in the name of fun. Welcome to every day of Carrie Fisher's life.

She eventually agreed to an interview, but in her current mental state, she was like a prisoner on truth serum. Decades-long secrets she'd kept started to crumble.

"I went on the film saying 'I'm going to have an affair!'" Carrie announced to the interviewer. "Like it was a kiwi, an exotic fruit—because I'd never had one." There were a few married people on the set of *Star Wars*: she hadn't been specific about who. Then: "I had a crush on Harrison for sure," she said. "Harrison is *great* fun when he's had a few drinks."

She was aiming for subtle, but Carrie circa 2008 was as subtle as gas leak in a steel mill. She'd all but blurted out her and Harrison's 30-year-old secret. It would have been damaging for him: he had one of the biggest films of his spectacular career coming out , *Indiana Jones and the Kingdom of the Crystal Skull*. Carrie, on the other hand, had a bit role in a low-budget horror movie. (And to film *that* she missed the funeral for Todd's wife; the show must go on.) Revealing their secret affair now could be seen as an act of spite, and jealousy.

But it was so much yelling in the wind. Her comments were taken as standard Carrie Fisher blabber. Better remembered was that she recorded a hologram-style greeting in lieu of attending the "reunion."

She'd let the cat out of the bag, and it had slunk back in. No one listens to a has-been.

Carrie would change that. Her newest iteration of being herself was a one-woman show, called *Wishful Drinking*. The poster image was of Leia face down drunk on a bar, martini glass tipping over from one hand. The show stitched together lots of stories of her life—life with Paul Simon, Bryan leaving her for another man, Greg Stevens overdosing next to her—all interlaced with slideshow imagery. The anything-for-a-laugh ethos even made her put on a Leia wig. To help younger audience members, she included a flow chart to understand all the Debbie Reynolds/Eddie Fisher stuff. (Joely, after watching the show, complained that Carrie had been mean to Connie Stevens, her mom. She had been, but like radioactivity, Carrie was mean to everyone.)

Like AA-meeting drunkalogues, it sometimes came off as braggy: look how much wilder my life has been than yours! Many of the jokes and stories were familiar from her books, but were now being presented as nonfiction. "Carrie," her sister Joely said, "found a way to make her flaws Louvre caliber." She sang, her voice a staringly strong surprise. But was this how Carrie wanted to be remembered, narrating a flow chart of parental infidelity? Maybe this was all she was capable of now, with her brain pumping on fewer pistons than before.

The one-woman show moved from LA's Geffen Playhouse to the Bay Area's Berkeley Repertory Theatre, after swapping directors. Then it arrived in New York, Washington DC, Seattle, and various one-night-only venues. It was taped for HBO, and earned an Emmy nomination. Carrie was her mother's daughter, packing them in night after night.

Part of the show were regular meet-and-greets with fans, waiting with *Playbills* to be signed. One man had a tattoo of harem Leia on his left arm: he wanted her to sign it, so he could get the signature inked as well. She signed as Carrie, not as Leia.

(Carrie's signature starts off neat, both Rs in CARRIE like toppling skyscrapers. The FISHER is a wonderful mess: the letters all overlap, like transparency layers too close together. The final R extends its tail out like a tripod leg, a flying buttress of support for the collapsing heap.)

After *Wishful Drinking*, Carrie tried for another one-woman show. It was a different stripe of autobiographical, called *A Spy in the House of Me*. She booked an expensive theater in Phoenix for a week of engagements in April 2008, with the expectations to go to tour. The second show would be part story of who she might have been with different parents, part obligatory jokes about Ewoks. But *Wishful Drinking* delivered bridges burned and scathing truths. Following it up with essentially fiction wasn't what her audiences expected, or frankly wanted. When a raconteur runs of out stories, she should be kind enough to cease talking. Her follow-up show closed after a week.

(While she was away on tour, an actor friend, Craig Bierko, used her bathroom. He used it to film an internet talk show where he interviewed people while they were both in a bathtub. "The bathroom itself is enormous: it's like the size of a studio apartment. [She] has a piano in it, of course. Naturally. She's Carrie Fisher: she has a piano in her bathroom.")

It was during her touring that Carrie, trying to stay away from hard substances, fell into soft drinks, junk food, and anything with ingredients that sounds like sci-fi energy sources. She would consume "anything that floated by" as she went about her day. "I don't eat a lot, but anything I ate was awful. Coca-Cola, Balance bars… those are fine in moderation, but I'm not someone who understands the notion of moderation. I would have six a day."

By the end of the tour, Carrie was approaching 180 pounds, double her younger size. Some of this was due to her meds: weight gain was a common problem in recovery, where eating a feeling or two seemed the least bad way to feel better. She never saw herself as pretty, even back in the salad days of Leia—and of salads. "I think I sort of thought I was passable, but I'm a business where people are gorgeous and my mother was gorgeous, so I grew up thinking 'well, I don't look like that.'"

Speaking of not looking like herself, "Mike and Carrie Fisher" were featured in at 2010 *People Magazine* issue, which ran pictures of their wedding. The Carrie in this case was country singer Carrie Underwood, who'd married hockey player Mike Fisher. To avoid understandable confusion, this Carrie kept her last name.

* * *

Eddie Fisher was dying.

Around 2010, he had been diagnosed with Parkinson's disease, arthritis, and prostate cancer. He was incapable of taking care of himself, and after his most recent wife died he had floundered. He mixed up his daughter with his granddaughters.

Eddie has had a bad relationship with his own abusive father, and all his life was desperate for approval he never got from the old man. This was the cycle: the grandfather was toxic to the father, the father was toxic to the daughter. As his most famous song said, Oh, my Papa.

Another one of Eddie's songs was "If I Loved You"; young Carrie would sometimes duet with him on it, if he was in town and remembered that she existed. Now pushing 50, Carrie still didn't know the answer to the question: did her father love her? She knelt by his bedside, showering him with praise, every bit of her aching to just be told "I love you" in return.

Eddie never did. He couldn't say it. For all his vocal prowess, that was one note he could never hit. Not even if it was a lie.

On Wednesday, September 22, 2010, a nurse called Carrie, saying that Eddie didn't have long. She and her sisters decided to fly out the next morning, but he died an hour after the phone call. Their goodbye to their father, then, happened in the minutes before his cremation. The short old man with a big gut lying in a box didn't look much like her dad. He wasn't even dressed well: he was in a hospital gown. Carrie prepared her sisters for what their dad looked like. Then they all serenaded him with an Irving Berlin tune, and tucked some joints into his coffin. "We love you, Oh My Papa," she said, escorting her sisters out of the crematorium. Then she boarded a plane to do a gig.

In 2011, Carrie was by Debbie's side as she at long last auctioned off some of her movie memorabilia. To draw publicity for the auction they appeared on *The Oprah Winfrey Show* together, and sang. For Debbie this was a defeat: she had spent decades trying to build a museum to house these relics. In an O Henry twist, she had to sell the props and costumes to cover a loan for when the *third* attempt to build the museum foundered.

The day started out as heartbreak. Debbie was hiding it well, upbeat and chipper, gladhanding bidders in person, on the phone, and online. Then the sales figures started to come in: each item went for many times its asking price. The *Monkey Business* car Carrie once drove went for over $200 grand. The ruby slippers? $510,000. Marilyn Monroe's subway dress? $4.6 million, not including a 20% auction house fee. The day ended with Debbie richer by $22.8 million.

And this was just a *portion* of the collection! The following year she auctioned off what turned into the single most valuable prop from a science fiction movie ever. It was never once seen on camera... because it *was* the camera, a Panasonic PSR35 mm. It was used to film a certain 1977 sci-fi film of Carrie's.

Carrie Fisher Sentence: "I have anorexic thinking, but I can't seem to muster the behavior." After *Wishful Drinking* finished touring, Carrie joined the weight-loss program Jenny Craig as a spokesperson. This was more than vanity: she had a BMI of 34, which wasn't healthy for anyone, much less someone with her history with drugs

She got down to 130 pounds, no longer overweight. Lumpy Space Princess was back to being Princess Bubblegum: she looked healthier than she had in years. Penny Marshall called her for advice: soon they were microwaving prepackaged dinners together. Many conversations about her weight loss led to comments about swimsuit season, and one particular metal bikini. She would not go to the beach with the outfit, she said, but "Maybe I'd wear it for myself."

That was a rare sentence of hers without profanity. In full truth-hurts mode, Carrie had gone from X-Wings to f-bombs: decorum was for suckers. At Todd's wedding to a new love, Carrie vaped throughout, and then dropped the wedding rings. Oops.

In the *Star Wars Expanded Universe* books, Leia has a white-haired assistant named Winter Celchu. Winter was Leia's childhood friend on Alderaan, a combination lady's maid and spymaster. She never left Leia's side. Carrie, on the other hand, couldn't seem to keep an assistant: each new one lasted for less time than the previous one. Like the seasons, every year brought a new Winter.

Wishful Drinking was transcribed into a short memoir: it was Carrie's first book of actual nonfiction. It sold well enough so that a second short memoir followed, this one titled *Shockaholic*. The Leia picture on this one was of a poseable Leia doll covered her eyes in embarrassment.

Shockaholic's premise was that ECT was bettering Carrie's life, but at the expense of whiting out huge chunks of her memory. So she was presenting stories she wanted to share before they were gone. (That was also the premise of *Wishful Drinking*, but *shh*.) Among the memories were being sexually harassed at a dinner by Ted Kennedy, Michael Jackson trying to get pictures of Billie from her, struggles with losing weight, and how she lost her father. There was no one-woman show for *Shockaholic*: Carrie probably couldn't handle the touring necessary to bring it to theaters, much less being cogent on stage two hours a night.

Jeff Ryan

"Bad news," one review spat about the book, "for anyone who thought Carrie Fisher had finally stopped talking about herself. Sorry, but after all of her seemingly endless blathering on about her nose-bleed high-class problems, it appears she has yet another brand-new problem to overshare about (though don't expect to relate to it)." This poisoned-pen piece, believe it or not, was the publisher's own description of the book.

Shockaholic was scattered and minor-league: assorted celebrity run-ins do not a memoir make. And both books suffered from Carrie's new rudderless style, which worked better when spoken. Without her inflection and tone as guardrails, the words were of someone going through a dark patch, not someone who'd exited it.

The second memoir concludes with a story of her singing on stage with her father, as a round of applause makes a weak dying man rise to his feet one more time. Ending the book with praise for her dad was puzzling: why expect readers to cheer for Eddie Fisher? "She is due," *The Guardian* wrote, with the sizzle of a hot iron on flesh, "for another spot of self-appraisal in rehab. You can detoxify the body, but it's harder to rid an addled head of its false virtues."

Fame was yet another addiction, one Carrie had sometimes tried to escape but couldn't. It was literally her family history: before she was an addict, before she was a basket case, she was famous. So was everyone around her. And fame makes people do whatever it takes to stay famous: exposing your secrets over and over, just for another fix of limelight. In this, everyone who read her books, watched her movies, laughed at her jokes, and forwarded her quotes were complicit. Fame is a Class A substance, and her fans were her enablers.

"If it was Hollywood [that was responsible], then we'd all be dope addicts," she said. No, she claimed responsibility for her bad decisions. Her lofty privilege just allowed her the ability to screw up on a grander scale than if she was born to modest means.

Episode III:
Magisterium Or
Yesterday, Today, and Tomorrow

"It struck me today that the people that have had an impact on me are the people who didn't make it. Marilyn Monroe, Judy Garland, Montgomery Clift, Lenny Bruce, Janis Joplin, John Belushi. It's not making it to be Marilyn Monroe, but it is to me.

"In our culture these people are heroes. There's something inside of that—a message that killing yourself like that isn't so bad. All the interesting people do it, the extraordinary ones. A weird, weird message. Most of the people I've admired in show business—comedians, writers, actors—are alcoholics or drug addicts or suicides. It's bizarre. And I get to be in that club now. It's the one thing I cling to in here; Wow, I'm hip now, like the dead people."

—*Carrie Fisher*, Postcards from the Edge

Chapter 29: You Only Leia Twice

In 2011, Lucasfilm needed Carrie to bun up again.

Disney was revamping the *Star Tours* attraction. The ride was now a branching adventure, with each journey beginning with a distress call from a different *Star Wars* character. Imagineers wanted one of these messages to be a hologram of Leia, naturally. They dug up an unused angle of Carrie from her 1976 hologram session: that would be their video.

But video needs audio. So Carrie was in the recording studio, to loop some new dialogue. It ended with the cheesy rewrite of "Help me, *Star Tours*, you're my only hope." She also recorded multiple versions where she said "his," "her," and "them."

This wasn't her first time back doing *Star Wars* voicework. For a *Robot Chicken Star Wars* parody, she voiced a number of characters, including Mon Mothma, who callously orders calamari while having dinner with Admiral Ackbar. She voiced Mon Mothma again for *Family Guy*, where she already had a recurring role. In this episode-long parody, her character Angela played Mon Mothma.

But Leia's career was now largely independent of Carrie. For instance, Carrie had nothing to do with Leia dancing to "Hologram Girl"—a parody of Gwen Stefani's "Hollaback Girl"—in *Kinect Star Wars*. Or with Princess Tator, a *Star Wars*-branded Mrs. Potato Head. Or her *Shadows of the Empire* action figure, where she seems to be wearing one of Jane Fonda's exercise outfits.

Then came 2012.

In August of 2012, Carrie appeared in Orlando, Florida, at *Star Wars Celebration VI*—the fan conventions used Roman numerals, like the films that they worshipped. Mark Hamill was there as well. But the biggest shock came when George Lucas himself casually strolled onto the stage during a panel.

He hadn't come all the way to Florida just for a walk-on: he'd come for lunch with Carrie and Mark. At their meeting he shared a serious of bombshells.

He was stepping down from Lucasfilm.

Amblin Entertainment's Kathleen Kennedy was taking over.

After a decade of rest, the final three films in the *Star Wars* nonet were going to be made: *Episodes VII, VIII,* and *IX.*

And would Mark and Carrie consider suiting up as Luke and Leia again?

George had ideas for a 30-years-later series of stories that would justify bringing back Luke and Leia. They dealt heavily with midi-chlorians, and Luke training a new Jedi. But he was also selling the company to Disney, for $4 billion. They would have ultimate say over the story. Luke and Leia along with everything else would soon be Disney property. Leia would now be a Disney Princess.

The roles of Luke and Leia had been lodestones and millstones, burdens and privileges, guardian angels and bête noires. A lifetime of work separated Carrie and Mark from their 1983 selves. They were veterans of the *Star Wars...* and now they were being drafted.

Mark wasn't sure if he wanted Luke to return: he was not a trim, clean-shaven youth anymore. Carrie, on the other hand, said yes immediately... then started pitching that there could be a role for Billie in the film as well. Billie Lourd was now an adult, and despite her mother's lifelong protests had decided to give the family business of acting a try. This had made Carrie 180 into a stage mother. She saw this multibillion dollar acquisition, and her returning to playing Princess Leia, all as a means to an end: Billie getting a line in a movie.

During this lunch, George may also have, ever so gently, ever so gingerly, brought up that fitness and weight loss would be required if they came back. Luke and Leia had to be in fighting trim.

There was a third member of the band to bring back into the fold: Han. Amazingly, Harrison Ford ended up saying yes. The three would be reunited onscreen. That wizened Delphic oracle "Weird Al" Yankovic was right: they'd be playing these parts till they were old and gray.

With the heroic trio in place, George could officially announce the deal a few months later. The Walt Disney Company did what Darth Vader couldn't: capture the Rebel Alliance. *Star Wars*, like Pixar, *The Muppets*, and Marvel Comics before them, were now under the same roof, held by the same four-fingered Mickey Mouse glove.

With incredible speed, Disney announced that *Star Wars Episodes VII, VII*, and *IX* would be arriving in theaters, starting in 2015, along with multiple standalone films. Disney quickly discarded George's midi-chlorinated ideas for the sequels, which upset him. It would go in a different direction, one that didn't saddle itself with the single most divisive element of the prequels (that George himself kiboshed in later films). It was just as he always feared: after decades of lying in wait, a Hollywood megalith was going to ruin his creations. On the plus side, he was a multibillionaire.

Star Wars' fandom experienced a similar outrage when in 2014, Disney quietly said that all the *Expanded Universe* stories were now to be rebranded *Star Wars Legends*. To give the upcoming movies' storytellers maximum freedom, the vast interlaced latticework of novels and comics and video games and cartoons was being torn down. None of that had happened: it was all a dream, or if you preferred an alternate reality. The last thing that could definitively be said to happen in the *Star Wars* universe was the Ewoks' Yub-Nub dance. (And even *that* had been changed by the 1997 special edition, which replaced the song.)

Just like that, Grand Admiral Thrawn was Death Starred into oblivion. So were Leia and Han's children, their marriage, and 30 years of character development. Leia had recently managed to stop the galactic threat of the Yuuzhan Vong, and was about the become the oldest Jedi trainee ever. Those stories would now never continue. It was as if millions of voices cried out in terror, and were suddenly silenced.

The new story of what happened to the rebel heroes after they defeated the Empire would inform the backstory of *Episode VII*. The now Lucas-less Lucasfilm planned on introducing a new group of 20-something heroes as leads, and find key places for the original trilogy's original trinity.

Harrison had, since 1983, gone on to become arguably the world's biggest and most consistent box office draw. He wasn't just Han Solo; he was Indiana Jones, Richard Kimble, Jack Ryan, and Rick Deckard. In the last decade he'd gone for roles that suited his gruffer persona. An *Entertainment Weekly* review of one of these films said, "Ford looks like he barely wants to be in the *movie*." Call it altitude sickness: being on the top for too long changes your personality.

Mark had rarely been seen since 1983, but often heard. His face was Luke's, but behind the microphone he could become anyone. The beyond-maniacal laugh he developed as *Amadeus* on stage, for instance, he put to use as the Joker on *Batman: The Animated Series*. Since them he'd been in more cartoons that a red stick of dynamite, often voicing characters just as explosive.

And Carrie, compared with Harrison the Hero and Mark the Mimic? Her biggest event in 2012 was the new love of her life, Gary. Gary was a French bulldog puppy, a black-and-tan brindle. Gary's tongue stuck out of that side of his mouth like he was always carrying a slice of prime rib. Gary was also walleyed: like Carrie, it was impossible for him to keep both eyes on any given subject. He was too big to be carried in a purse, too small to walk, and too heavy to be carried. He could lick his own eyeballs, though.

Gary—she loved people names for dogs—was Carrie's therapy dog. When she was low, Gary cheered her up. When she was anxious, Gary calmed her down. "Gary is like my heart," she said. "He's anxious when he's away from me." When she went, he went: planes, stage, talk shows, movie sets—even her new part-time job as a lap dancer.

"Celebrity lap dancing" was what Carrie called the autograph circuit. Actors of every stripe of fame, from the who's who to the who's that?, sold vintage headshots to collectors, or to hawkers who flipped them on eBay. Despite past financial woes, she'd never needed money so badly as to sell her autograph.

But now, puzzlingly, the biggest stars in the world were doing it. The name actor would only appear for a few hours at a stretch, charging up to $250 a signature, or more. Doing this put their name and face on promotional materials for big conventions, raised visibility for their upcoming projects, and let them meet fans from across the country. That was the real reason: stars needed "fan cred." If you did a con, it meant that you were a real person.

So Carrie, despite her landed-gentry life, started doing shows. She had a dozen Leia pictures, and sold them autographed for $70 a pop. She always wore her purple glasses, which she joked made her at least *appear* smart. (If Leia was ever made a Jedi, she wanted a purple lightsaber.) She would add a "PLO" after some signatures, which fans took to mean "Palestinian Liberation Organization" before realizing it was "Princess Leia Organa."

In a special "room"—really just a curtained section of the exhibit hall—she would pose with people, and chat for a few minutes. They'd put the photos from their meet-and-greet on their walls, on their Christmas cards, and their Facebook profiles. Many of them wore a "space bun" hairstyle, in honor of her. She posed with women who showed off life-size tattoos of Leia's face. She was hugged by strangers who would cry upon seeing her, who'd named their daughters after her, who'd held her as their idol.

Leia meant so much to them, Carrie would say, nodding. She was Leia's caretaker, and the closest thing they would get to meeting the real-life Lady Vader: *Look, kids, it's the Huttslayer!* That was a necessary deflection on Carrie's fault, the same way that a sports star gives credit to the whole team.

But Carrie's fans knew who they were standing in line to meet. Leia was great, sure, but *Carrie* was the one who meant so much to them. The woman who spoke truth to power, shared her struggles about mental illness, and doled out mordant humor about every aspect of her life. The woman who was still fighting the daily battle against the Dark Side. *That* was their hero, not Princess Leia.

Fans learned via the requisite Q&A sessions that behind the character of Leia was an even bigger character in Carrie. One who curled up her legs to sit on a couch, and delivered whip-smart lines with a relaxed, low-energy style familiar to anyone who's ever felt fuzzy-headed from their meds. Who could seduce or slam dunk with a turn of phrase. Who seemed to choose over and over to be kind to all others, and put down only herself.

Some shows she had to cancel, such as Seattle's Emerald City Comic-Con in 2013, due to a "medical emergency." Fans knew what that meant, and they understood. (Carrie overheard one fan saying that the autographs were expensive, yeah, "but when she dies it's really going to be worth a lot." *Gee, thanks.*) Other shows she stayed to chat with everyone afterwards, giving a moment of connection to one and all.

Asking Carrie to re-enter the public spotlight was like asking either of her parents if they would sing a song: but of course! Carrie even got Gary into the action: in 2015 she (or presumably her newest assistant) set up Gary's Instagram page. Gary soon had thousands of followers: he chewed her shoes, so her may as well hold onto her coattails.

To inhabit Leia's body once again, Carrie's body hit the elliptical machine. She joked that Disney had only hired three-quarters of her: "The fourth can't be with me." She sometimes finished a session with a cigarette and a Diet Coke—NutraSweet for the sweet, another joke of hers.

How to mentally reconnect with Leia, after decades of trying to create a galaxy's worth of distance? She decided to write Leia a letter. It doesn't read like a letter to a confidant or old friend so much as a jailhouse letter to the murderer of your spouse. "Dear Princess Leia," she began, "I don't wish to be presumptuous and call you 'Leia,' as it implies a familiarity I don't wish to presume." Carrie's verbiage grew more rococo from there.

"You always act the heroine: I snort the stuff." "At least you look good fighting evil. I look lived in." "Leia plays while I continue to pay and pay and pay." "I fade as you blaze." And, in reference to Leia's eternal youth, "Dorian Organa gives way to Carrie Gray."

"Will it ever end? It probably won't, but I will. I'm pretty sure I will. My sequels will finally, blessedly, stop, while yours will define and absorb an age." Carrie ends with a hope that Leia will "do what I do: make sure you largely enjoy the ride. Skip the hairstyle, but enjoy the ride."

Carrie's movie weight loss got her on the cover of *Good Housekeeping*. "I'm in a business where the only thing that matters is weight and appearance. That is so messed up. They might as well say get younger, because that's how easy it is." Of exercise and dieting, she preferred exercise: "It's easier for me to add an activity than to deny myself something." And regarding her experience as a screenwriter? "My problem is that they talk to me like an actress, but I hear them like a writer."

It's easier to change the character to suit the actor than vice versa. The newly envisioned Leia Organa was no longer called Princess Leia but General Organa. General Organa was a flinty leader, inspiring despite to being beset by personal losses. She and Han were no longer together: they split after their son Ben went to the Dark Side, becoming the Vader-worshipping Kylo Ren. And Luke? No one knew where Luke was.

These changes to Leia's character rejoined the separated psyches of Carrie and Leia. Audiences knew of Carrie's troubles, knew she was much more used-universe than the lipglossed Leia of the original trilogy. Creating a mature Leia who also had her share of heartache and woe would fit Carrie like a glove. The perfect prefect of the Expanded Universe was gone. In her place was Sarah Connor, gripping Madame Defarge's knitting needles.

"This is the Leia that has lost everything," Canadian writer Anne Theriault wrote on Twitter, "her world, her parents, her son to the Dark

Side, her brother to who knows where, her lover. This is the Leia that could easily have broken down or given up. But she was stronger than literally every man in her life. She kept going. Unlike Luke or Han, Leia keeps fighting when things seem impossible. In spite of all the losses she's suffered, in spite of impossible odds."

George had said everything in the millennial-era prequels purposefully "rhymed" with the original trilogy: character relationships, lines, plot developments. There was a rhyme scheme going on with the new cast additions as well. Daisy Ridley's Rey had the gumption and distinct hairstyle of Leia, but Luke's desert wardrobe of burlap. Oscar Isaac's Poe Dameron was a cocky flyer like Han, but lawful good, like Luke. John Boyega's Finn the former stormtrooper was earnest like Luke, but his double-agent story connected him to Leia. And Adam Driver's evil Kylo Ren was practically a Darth Vader cosplayer—but he was really Han and Leia's angry son Ben.

The plot was woven from the same thread George used: robots with secret data, planet-killing weapons, tiny wise aliens, orphans with mysterious parentage, and lowly people who find out they've got a special purpose in the world. Every story beat was as recycled as the parts Rey pulled out of junked spacecraft. (Talk about attack of the clones.)

If Rey, Finn, and Poe were the new teenagers in space, who would be the elders? Han would still be kicking around with Chewbacca, Leia would lead the Resistance (a distinction without much difference from the Rebellion), and Luke… well, Luke was AWOL.

The film's title would be *Star Wars: Episode VII— The Force Awakens*: Carrie joked that it was " *Episode Seven… ty-Two.*" Writing and directing would be wunderkind JJ Abrams, who'd done everything from helping create *Lost* to rebooting *Star Trek*.

The last three times Carrie was in London making *Star Wars* films she threw parties, and the fourth time around was no different. Billie was with her now—she'd succeeded in getting her daughter a background role. She invited the cast and crew to her and Billie's get-togethers, and thanks to new technology could film nastygram video messages to send to anyone too bushed to show up. Most wouldn't miss it for the world.

Actors are told to "break a leg" before a performance. Harrison Ford actually did, due to a sliding-door mishap on set. This delayed filming gave Abrams the time and opportunity to rehash the script, find new bits to bond Finn and Rey together, and reconsider other choices. Kylo Ren's unmasking, for instance, was moved to later in the film: a digital mask was added to his early scenes.

Another vitally important scene was Han's first meeting with Leia. It'd be the characters' first time meeting in years, and for younger viewers the first time in their lifetimes the famed screen couple was on a movie screen. Abrams reconfigured the whole film, in order so Han's first time seeing General Organa would also be moviegoer's first time seeing her. This meant—sigh—that once again the film was halfway over before Carrie arrives: more rhyming. Even more frustratingly, it meant that many scenes she had already filmed had to be left on the cutting room floor. Could be worse: Mark's Luke Skywalker shows up in the film's final minute, and says nothing.

Leia's new story can be seen as one of failure. She fails her son, who succumbs to the Dark Side. She fails her husband: they separate. She fails her responsibilities: her New Alliance has corrupted and becomes the First Order. But you can't struggle without something to struggle against. Leia has no quit in her, no matter how dire things have become. She didn't have Carrie's problems, but they shared an indomitable will, to keep limping along no matter the pain.

Billie's character was called Lieutenant Connix: she and Carrie went to hair and makeup at the same time. As a joke, someone said that Connix's hairstyle should be space buns. "I was going to carry on the family hairstyle," Billie wrote, in a *Time* magazine piece. "[W]e decided to embrace the weird galactic nepotism of it all and went with the mini-Leia buns."

They shared scenes together, with Billie perhaps there as a Carrie wrangler as much as actor. For her sake, Carrie kept checking up on Billie, to see if she was nervous. Billie, like her mom, had grown up around film actors and set visits. But this was her first acting role, and it was in a *Star Wars* film. (This reminded Carrie of the time she had *déjà vu*.) Billie was preternaturally calm. "You know," Carrie told her on the bus ride back to London that night. "Most people aren't as comfortable on sets as you were today."

Billie had gone to college thinking she'd be an event planner. Maybe it was Billie's turn to walk in her mother's footsteps, get the roles her mom couldn't. Fittingly, *The Force Awakens* was a film about new generations taking up the legacy of the old.

And maybe it was Carrie's turn to try acting again as well. She signed up for a recurring role in a British relationship comedy called *Catastrophe*. The show's stars saw her presenting an awards in London, and one whispered "that's your awful mother!" to the other. Carrie played Mia, comedian Rob Delaney's acerbic, shopaholic mother. Her acid-tongued compliments were a perfect fit or the show. It was meticulously scripted, but the stars allowed Carrie to improvise. Sharon Horgan, the other lead, said you could fill hours of DVD extras with them. Carrie even got a role for the other love of her life: Gary played Mia's dog.

Chapter 30: Her True Goddess Self

The media firestorms Carrie had previously experienced with *Star Wars* were the biggest the 1970s had seen. They were downright quaint compared with the modern supersonic digital social media landscape. Nerds had won the eternal nerd/jock conflict, and billions now watched sci-fi, fantasy, and superhero entertainments.

Big movie franchises were living ecological things, biomes, with their own orbits and gravities, price tags as astronomical as their subject matter, and with rituals and customs that had to be obeyed. And like Jedi (and Sith) they had their masters, in this case corporations more focused on the streaming wars than the box office. Of all these attention economies, *Star Wars* was the apex, the original. (It would find a cozy home on Disney+, producing handsome shows not too different from the Expanded Universe books.)

The product sponsorship carpet-bombing for *The Force Awakens* may have single-handedly earned Disney back the $4 billion it paid George for the franchise. Just on the Leia side of things—and she wasn't a lead—the Trix Rabbit sported his ears in Leia buns and wore her white robes, General Organa received multiple action figures, and Cover Girl had a Light Side/Dark Side promotion. When was the last time there was a *cosmetics* cross-promotion for a film?

Star Wars comics returned to Marvel, and true to form issue #1's printing was over a million issues: it'd been years since any comic sold in those numbers. Leia was reimagined for comics—which took place immediately after *A New Hope*—as lithe and muscular, with slick hair so buoyant it was practically tentacles. Actual Carrie back then was alarmingly skinny, but this was the Leia of legend, strong and athletic.

Alan Dean Foster, who wrote the 1976 novelization, was invited back to write the *Force Awakens* novelization. He begins the novel with new scene, of Leia missing Luke: the opening words were "She needed him. And he was nowhere to be found." In the book at least, Leia comes first.

It used to be a joke that some actors spent more time doing press than actually filming: now that was routine. As never-ending as the assembly line of reporters was to Carrie, most reporters could only squeeze in two or three questions. Reporters knew they needed good quotes from their "availability." This meant skipping pleasantries and diving right to intrusive questions about her sobriety, her mental health, her weight, her appearance, her acting ability—no sore point was left unpoked. When *The Today Show* asked what all that was like, she said "Please stop debating about whether or not I've aged well. Unfortunately, it hurts all three of my feelings."

Carrie Fisher Sentence: "Youth and beauty are not accomplishments. They're temporary, happy by-products of time and/or DNA. Don't hold your breath for either."

The Force Awakens' budget was reportedly over $300 million, a big bet from Disney that it would be one of those heralded successes to make one billion dollars. *The Force Awakens* made over *two* billion dollars. Including all the lucrative tie-ins and merchandising, Disney's purchase of Lucasfilm had paid for itself with its very first outing. Fans loved it as well, despite some complaints that this was a Taco Bell requel: the same ingredients, wrapped up in slightly new ways.

George had taken three years between his prequel films, but Disney was a very efficient money-making machine. Carrie was soon back at work on the second film, *Star Wars: Episode VII—The Last Jedi*. A new writer-director, Rian Johnson, was taking over. This was part of the efficiency: having top talent run each film. But not everyone saw *Star Wars* through the same fanboy lenses as JJ Abrams did.

Just as *Force Awakens* contained many purposeful allusions to *A New Hope*, *Last Jedi* was made to echo *Empire Strikes Back*. Rey receiving training from a craggy, bearded Luke Skywalker on a distant planet, just a Luke received it from Yoda. Artoo at one point shows Luke the ancient Leia hologram: to make the audio track sound authentically crummy, ILM staffers rerecorded Carrie's message on audiotape and dragged it through the dirt.

Actual Leia, just like in *Empire*, is stuck in a movie-length chase scene. This time, her flotilla is running out of fuel and shielding, and is being picked off one by one by a First Order battalion. It's a grim way to go, with seemingly no escape.

In one shocking scene, the command bridge explodes, and Leia gets sucked out into the cold vacuum of space. We see her seemingly lifeless body floating, surrounded by debris and corpses, ice crystals forming around her skin. She's unresponsive, drifting. There's no flicker in her eyes, her mouth, her fingers. Carrie had been joking about her own death for decades—now here was Leia, dead on screen.

Then Leia's hand twitches. Her coppery bracelets quiver. Her hand reaches out through the nothingness, a power behind the grasping. A… Force. Leia's unconscious form moves as being pulled by rope, with one arm extended forward. She is steered through the chunks of wreckage, back to the exposed bridge, and is able to reboard the ship before collapsing.

It's a startling scene—Leia as Superman, the Force kicking in like an auxiliary generator. Yet to quote Han Solo, that's not how the Force works! Especially not with someone well into adulthood with no Jedi skills. The movie's novelization makes it clearer: she surfed down a channel of dissipating atmosphere using the power of its floating Force-rich organisms. In order words, midi-chlorians towed her back onto the ship. Her own personal AAA card.

Leia spends the next hour of the film in a hospital room, unconscious. (She does have an affinity for unconsciousness.) She rouses for the finale, where another new Force trick is revealed, by Luke. After training Rey all film, he mysteriously appears in front of the Resistance's salt-planet hideout, and draws the First Order's fire long enough for them to escape. How does he get there, when he's been on another planet all movie? He doesn't; he projects an ethereal image of himself, one that uses so much energy that it kills him. Luke finds a way to save the day without breaking his oath of nonviolence.

Last Jedi was a divisive departure from other *Star Wars* stories. It would have been easy (and expected) to have Luke Rambo it up in a time of need, but harder for him, and the audience, to see him defeated and scared, unwilling to face a problem he felt he caused. Rey and Kylo Ren unceremoniously kill Snoke, who was built up as the new trilogy's big bad. (Good luck to whoever had to make the concluding film: there was no more villain!) Also divisive were scenes in a casino planet full of celebrating war profiteers, who win so long as the fighting continues. These were murky, real-world issues graying up the black and white contrasts. Where would, where *could*, a third film go after this?

During preproduction, Carrie grabbed director Johnson's arm: she had

213

a message of great importance to convey. "We need," she said, "space jewelry." Each piece of jewelry has its own artistic provenance and backstory. The elegant silver-squares necklace she wears at the end of *A New Hope*, for instance, was later revealed as an Organa family heirloom called "chalcendony waves." In a comic, Leia bequeaths it to Lando's copilot Nien Numb after he saved some stranded ex-pat Alderaan citizens.

Kelly Marine Tran's character Rose Tico gained a necklace and a ring, both of which became plot devices. Oscar Isaac's Poe Dameron wore a ring on a necklace. Leia sports a mighty ring on her right ring finger as well, as well as copper bracelets, and a special beacon tracker worn around her other wrist. The gray world became more lived in and realistic than before, plus more fashionable.

Who made each piece of jewelry? What do they mean? Who gave them to each character? Future writers would be able to fill in all of those blanks, in years to come.

* * *

Debbie was in her 80s now. Before she died, Carrie and Todd wanted to make a documentary about her. When the world thought of Debbie Reynolds, they thought of dancing in yellow raincoats. They didn't know what she had lived through: the decades of abuse, mismanagement, and theft. Eddie, she now said, was the *best* of her three ex-husbands—at least he hadn't stolen from her.

They had to act fast: the legends of the Hollywood studio system were on their way out. But when they pitched the documentary to her, she wasn't interested: after 60 years of tap-dancing the bills away, she could finally relax. Her health wasn't great: she had persistent back pain, and she had experienced a TIA. Her time in front of a camera was done, she felt.

The only way to get her on camera for a retrospective, they knew, was for their sake. If they made the documentary about the whole Fisher family, then she'd deign to take part in it. Coincidentally, one of the directors they brought on board was named Fisher Stevens, born Steven Fisher. (He's unrelated to the Fishers, or to Connie Stevens.) He and co-director Alexis Bloom combed through archived footage, movie clips, vintage interviews, photographs, and old magazines, to assemble a feature-length Fisher family tribute.

Carrie was busy during much of the research and production, thanks to *Star Wars'* resurgence making her a hot commodity again. She arranged to be home for a staged scene where she helps Debbie pack for a trip to a casino gig. (In reality, Carrie and Debbie were lifelong travelers, who both had assistants pack for them.)

For a later scene, Carrie agreed to sing a song onstage with her mom, one of her standby songs, "I'll Never Say No." Carrie changed the lyrics: "I'll weep if you want me sad," became "I'll weep because I'm bipolar," and "Today is tomorrow if you want it so" became "Today is tomorrow if you've had too much blow."

She also filmed herself putting the "manic" in "manicurist," when she motormouthed while getting her nails done. The footage is anxiety-inducing to watch: there's no correct way to respond when someone barrages you with words they can't control. This was another brave step for Carrie, showing the unflattering reality of a manic episode. Some viewers were as put off as the manicurists were. But people with mood disorders knew what they were seeing: they were seeing themselves.

The documentary's ending was cemented when Debbie found out that, at age 83, she was going to be given the Screen Actors Guild Life Achievement Award. Great roles may win you an award nomination, but not a career. Great box office may guarantee a career, but not recognition of your peers. Debbie had done that—and she could still act, as a recent de-glammed turn as Liberace's mother in an HBO biopic showed.

Carrie was worried Debbie wouldn't be strong enough to sit for two hours, and then at evening's end make a speech. She and Todd devised a plan: they would escort her to and from the stage, to hide that they were physically propping her up. Kind editing sold the illusion that Debbie could still tap tap tap her way around town.

Carrie began to sour on the documentary, with its necessary focus on the past. Why, when for once the present was exciting? Movies, TV shows, appearances—it was like her party-all-the-time 20s all over again. All of her books were getting rereleased as well, with new covers styled to match the *Wishful Drinking* show's logo, which in turn had copied the *Star Wars* font. For once, having been Leia was for better instead of for worse.

Time to give the people what they want; a book all about her *Star Wars* memories. Too bad she basically didn't have any left. People with no history of substance abuse or electroconvulsive therapy have a hard time remembering 40 years ago. And whatever little Carrie *did* remember might not even be true.

Then Carrie found something she'd forgotten existed; a diary she kept during the making of that first film. In lieu of behind-the-scenes details or anecdotes, it was almost entirely about her long-time-ago, far-far affair with Harrison. Carrie's diary entries were not yet Carrie Fisher Sentences. No, this writer was young, strong, heartfelt, damaged, emotional, unfunny, and wounded. A girl who liked a boy more than he liked her.

Carrie could use this as the spine of a making-of-*Star Wars* memoir. Add to it a bit about her earlier acting, some anecdotes she'd polishing on the tour circuit, profiles of the cast and crew, and a peek into her convention life, and she'd hit a decent page length.

But to write it would be to churn out a book-length tale of infidelity. Young her doesn't come off badly—she was a mentally ill teenager romanced by an older married man. Harrison was the one at fault, and she'd been protecting him for decades with her silence. Harrison, who she still clicked with when they played scenes together.

Harrison, whose reputation could take the hit. Hell, people would probably be impressed! Welcome to yet another difference between men and woman.

Carrie needed a coauthor to combine her current ramblings with her vintage poetry into a coherent book. (Oh the irony of aging: the script doctor now needed a script doctor.) Paul Slansky, who helped edit *Postcards from the Edge* way back when, served as Carrie's ghostwriter role again. She started jotting down lines, ideas, and anecdotes from 1976 in her phone. They'd massage everything into a finished product, called *The Princess Diarist*.

* * *

For those winning honorary Oscars, the ceremony is in November, not February. Debbie was going to be given a second lifetime achievement award, this one the Jean Hersholt Humanitarian Award. It was not given out most years: the last recipient had been Harry Belafonte in 2014. This was a far greater honor than an acting Oscar.

Yet Debbie couldn't be there to get it. On November 14, 2015, during the academy's Governors Awards, Billie Lourd accepted the award for her grandmother; she received it from her godmother, Meryl

Streep. Carrie applauded from the audience. Billie explained how unusual it was for Debbie to not be there for a curtain call, saying "I've never seen her miss a show in her life."

Debbie had suffered a debilitating stroke after back surgery: for entire months, she was touch and go. Some days she didn't know who those around her were, or even who she was. Other days she wanted it all to be over. Carrie's visits to Las Vegas, where her mom was recuperating, ran sweet and sour. Mom, at long last, was the one who needed caring now.

Thinking home would be better, Carrie had Debbie moved back to Coldwater Canyon. Debbie mentioned how beautiful the house was, unaware that she'd lived there for years. Carrie's mama bear instincts made her kick nurses out as soon as she entered her mom's room: she wanted to be the sole conduit for all things Debbie. She'd done it for her dad, and her mom deserved it so much more. "Mom got the incredibly attentive, tender, loving daughter she's always wanted," Todd said, "and Carrie got the mother she didn't have to compete with or risk disappointment anymore." After 60 years of straying, her daughter was finally there for her.

While mid-book, Carrie found a decidedly highbrow use for her pencil. For all her life Debbie never left the bedroom without having a full face of makeup, hair perfectly in place. (Debbie didn't have eyebrows, a detail Carrie meanly snuck into *Postcards from the Edge*.) Had her family ever seen Mom without the war paint? Now she was ignoring it, and thus looked decades older. Carrie made up for her former self, put herself on glam patrol. She drew on her mother's eyebrows each morning.

Chapter 31: Oblivion

The year 2016 began on January 1, 2016. The death curse of 2016 began on January 10, 2016, when David Bowie succumbed to liver cancer. Fans were stunned, not knowing the musician was mortal, much less sick. Four days later, another 69-year-old British titan, the actor Alan Rickman, also died from cancer.

Like a coin coming up tails ten times in a row, it was just coincidence that two beloved figures died in the same week. But when we don't understand something, we make up a mythological story to explains it. A story began to be told to explain the coincidences of celebrity deaths that year, a story bolstered by each subsequent death. The story was this: 2016 itself was killing people.

The year 2016 would strike the *Star Wars* universe: Kenny Baker, who'd been inside the R2D2 can from every film from the original *Star Wars* to *The Force Awakens*, died in August 2016. He was 81, and had been in ill health for a while.

It killed the old: Gene Wilder, age 83; Doris Roberts, age 90. It killed the young: Anton Yelchin, age 27. It killed Abe Vigoda and Zsa Zsa Gabor, stars known for their Methuselah-like longevity. It killed Fidel Castro and Muhammad Ali and Elie Wiesel, all men who had survived the worst the world could serve. It killed directors Garry Marshall and Curtis Hanson. It killed Patty Duke and Florence Henderson, Garry Shandling and Alan Thicke. It killed Leonard Cohen and Arnold Palmer. It killed John Glenn and Nancy Reagan.

It killed Prince.

And it would kill a princess.

* * *

The Fisher family documentary *Bright Lights: Starring Carrie Fisher and Debbie Reynolds* hit the festival circuit in 2016; Cannes in May, and

Telluride in September. It would air on HBO the following year. Carrie was able to attend the Colorado screenings, and answer some questions afterwards. For other screenings the producers would phone up Debbie, or Skype her from her bedroom, to answer audience questions.

One problem with attending the screenings: Carrie had never seen the film. She'd been given a DVD of it for approval, but put off watching it. She claimed she had watched it, though—what could be in there that she hadn't lived through, and talked about ad nauseum? During screenings she would leave the theater, returning for the Q&A.

On one of these screening trips, Todd found out Carrie had run out of her prescription medications. Carrie blamed her assistant, but in truth she'd taken them all already, and maybe some extras. Her life had returned to the globetrotting *Star Wars* days, and so, once again, had her bad habits. Carrie was using again, and covering it up, which as all addicts know is not two crimes but one.

Carrie's first time watching the documentary ended up being in October 2016, in New York. She had no idea one of the scenes in the film, a scene that people had been watching for months, was of Eddie on his deathbed refusing to tell his daughter that he loved her. Audiences stood in awe of her emotional bravery at including that scene, which even for her was taboo-breaking. Carrie stormed out of the screening midway through.

In November, Carrie faced a big birthday—her 60th. The shared birthday parties with Penny Marshall were a thing of the past. She had just finished playing a witch for a movie called *Wonderwell* that filmed in Italy—she was now of an age where she was playing witches. Debbie wanted to throw her daughter a birthday party, and found new energy in planning it. Everyone they could think of was invited, up to and including Carrie's old 1960s Girl Scout Troop. The catering would be the same as when she and Penny had back in the day.

Carrie heard about the party, and refused to go. She wouldn't share a *continent* with her 60th birthday party. Instead, she decided to stay in London, where she had been filming the new season of *Catastrophe*. Her character, Mia, wreaks passive aggressive havoc at a funeral, asking her daughter-in-law during the service to run out and buy her some clothes, and compliments the wife of the deceased that another mourner wants to sleep with her.

Mia is unaware that her son, a recovering alcoholic, has spent the whole season backsliding into drink. He confesses this to her, and Mia uncharacteristically slaps him. What's next is worse: she warns him that if he doesn't stop, he *will* start physically abusing his wife. She finds a way to play this with humor, and understanding, and grief. If she could do all that, perhaps she could survive a cake with enough candles to count as a fire hazard.

But it may not have been the big 6-0 that scared her: joking about growing older was her bread and butter. It may have been that her birthday party was a place she couldn't hide that she was using again. She also may not have wanted to reflect one more time one how little of her 60 years she remembered. She swore to Todd she wasn't coming, but after a talk with Debbie she relented.

Carrie did fly to California for her birthday. She was there in body but not in spirit, since she spent most of her party in bed. Debbie ended up holding court in the living room, covered in a stately cashmere blanket.

* * *

The Princess Diarist came out on November 2016, a month after her 60th birthday. It featured a vintage picture of her, with a pencil added tucked into a bun. Carrie had hoped her book, and its "Carrison" reveal, would lead to good sales. ("Carrison" was the portmanteau she had come up with: she was her own TMZ.) She also gave Harrison a heads-up that she was going to write about their fling. But this was not a simple throwaway mention: the book was framed as a bad-boyfriend book, and Han Solo was the bad boyfriend.

Debbie warned Carrie she shouldn't tell that story. Everyone in Hollywood knew of dozens of stories like that. You weren't supposed to share them with the public until all parties involved were dead. The latter part of Debbie's life has been sharing these salacious crumbs on stage and in memoirs, and every year another dead leading man gave her more material to finally share. Talking truth to power about a living, powerful acting icon was simply not done.

But Carrie was determined to own every aspect of her life, especially her mistakes. There was another reason for the book: "[I]f I didn't write about it, someone else would… Someone who would wait— cowardly—until after my passing to speculate on what happened and make me look bad. No." Again, she felt she might not have too many years left. She wanted to tell her own story.

A book like this with a big reveal can be spoiled by the press: even though reviews were embargoed, gossip sites routinely scoured celeb memoirs in advance for the juicy bits. Carrie, acting as her own scandalmonger, decided to leak it in a *People Magazine* interview that ran on November 15, along with an excerpt of the book. "I was so inexperienced, but I trusted something about him," she told the reporter about Harrison. "He was kind."

Reviews weren't as kind, though: the *Washington Post* said it had "too many cringe-worthy jokes." The *New York Times* said "It may not be great writing, but it's an empathy tractor beam." A *Vogue* reviewer mentions that "cynically, it's not a bad way to sell books."

The book was a mistake, one that wasn't rocketing to the tops of the charts, one that surely damaged her relationship with an old friend, one that made her look desperate and needy. And one that she would have to talk about every night for a month on book tour. "You were right," she told Debbie, after the news hit social media, "I shouldn't have told that story." Carrie had done the seemingly impossible: she'd found a new way to screw up. And she was obliged to dig the hole deeper every single night.

Carrie experienced the modern press juggernaut last year. Now her job was to go up on stage at bookstores every night and present the worst version of herself. Each appearance came with rules, to manage the line and people's expectations. "No posed photos with Carrie will be permitted, only photos from the line," said the rules of New York City's Strand bookstores. "Carrie will not sign memorabilia... the maximum number of books per person is 5."

Most people were not coming out for her book: buying it was the price of admission to see *her*. How few of the hundreds of copies she moved per day would ever be opened to anything other than the page with the autograph? How many people would be in this exact line if she was selling an 8" by 10" glossy from 1977? All these years she thought she was a writer: had she really just been a celebrity lap dancer?

Carrie, the daughter of the unsinkable Debbie Reynolds, would grip-and-grin her way through a month of an embarrassing book tour. Maybe she could make a vacation out of it. She'd seen London plenty, but Belgium was new. So she'd visit Belgium for a few days before her UK book signings.

Debbie, upon hearing this news, was horrified. She had had a premonition about Carrie dying in Belgium, then another one that Carrie's plane returning from Belgium would crash. It was like a dream she'd been trying to grasp but only getting pieces of: Belgium, a plane, death. But her mom had also been seeing ghosts: she received visitors who had been dead for longer than disco. Debbie had had dire premonitions for decades; Carrie included jokes about them in the *Postcards* screenplay.

On November 24, while in a hotel room, Carrie posted to her Twitter account four pictures of herself hugging Gary. In the background were two opened bottles of beer. Belgium is famous for its beer, but Carrie was supposed to be sober. Addicts who relapse are often meticulous with hiding their evidence. Carrie was at the point where she was not remembering to cover up her insobriety. It was a small but crucially telling detail, like Debbie leaving the bedroom sans eyebrows.

The phrase "falling off the wagon" suggests there's only one way to relapse: the nosedive. For many people, though, they elegantly descend into the morass a step at a time. They indulge in a single glass of wine with dinner, like the old days, swearing they won't have a second. And they don't. That makes them comfortable enough to have two glasses the next night. Then a bottle.

Much self-destructive behavior has at its core a need to feel punished, and there's no greater punishment than oblivion. Carrie sometimes referred to suicide as "punctuating [your] sentence before it had run its course." For decades she'd tempted fate with her actions, but the older she got, the less likely she was to survive another relapse. The next Carrie Fisher Sentence would end with a full stop.

* * *

Carrie's book was aided by the release of *Rogue One: A Star Wars Story*. This was Disney's first *Star Wars* spinoff film, just a year after *The Force Awakens*, telling the tale of the rebels (led by a heroic young brunette woman) who stole the Death Star plans that Leia absconded with at the start of *A New Hope*.

Carrie was not in *Rogue One*; Leia, however, was. A young model who shared Carrie's petite build was filmed wearing Leia's buns and white hood. Her face was then digitally altered to better resemble

Carrie's: a similar technology was used to make *Rogue One's* villainous Grand Moff Tarkin look just like Peter Cushing. The Leia stand-in would lip-synch to an archival clip of Carrie saying "hope"—scavenged from a 30-year-old alternate take of "Help me Obi-Wan yadda yadda ya"—which allowed Carrie to still voice the character.

Leia's surprise appearance at *Rogue One's* end, combined with the twist ending that the entire cast dies in the climax, made *Star Wars* once again the talk of the cinema. For the second year in a row, Princess Leia had appeared in the year's #1 box office hit.

Carrie Fisher Sentence: "You know what's funny about death? I mean other than absolutely nothing at all? You'd think we could remember finding out we weren't immortal. Sometimes I see children sobbing at the airports, and I think 'Aww, they've just been told.'"

Her trip home from Belgium was via Heathrow Airport. She texted with Joely, 12 time zones away, whose 20th wedding anniversary was coming up. Carrie weighed in with some hilariously inappropriate comments, and then her phone died. The next morning, phone recharged, she resumed texting, and made plans to meet with Joely's family at Christmastime. Then she, her assistant, and Gary boarded a direct flight to LAX.

Planes can be dangerous places due to the pressurization. Ears pop. The elevation causes radiation exposure. The altitude increases the size of gases in the body, causing discomfort for some. "The effects of reduced cabin air pressure," a World Health Organization report notes, "are usually well tolerated by healthy passengers."

Carrie wasn't a healthy passenger: she was entering her seventh decade of rough life, and she'd been using again. All that rough road left her heart in a weakened condition.

Anyone who's watched a movie knows shortness of breath and stabbing pains in your left arm are the shorthand symptoms of a heart attack. Carrie appeared in one of those movies, in fact: the 2002 con-artist film *Heartbreakers*. But those are the symptoms for *men*. For *women*, the symptoms of a myocardial infarction include nausea and pain in the jaw or neck. This is possibly the most basic health fact that's almost entirely unknown. Women every day have heart attacks and don't even know it, because they've only been taught the *male* signs of heart attack.

If Carrie felt those heart attack symptoms, she may not have recognized them as the alarm bells they were. No shortness of breath, no left-arm stabbing pains, no problem. Movies may have been what caused her to not seek help when it could have saved her life.

* * *

The pilot of Carrie's plane radioed to the Los Angeles International Airport five minutes before landing that they would need medical personal standing by at the gate, as soon as they landed. "We have some, uh, passengers, nurses, assisting the passenger," he says, professionally cool, then adding "we have an unresponsive passenger." "Unresponsive" in pilot jargon often meant "dead."

Minutes after they touched down, an ambulance raced Carrie to Cedars-Sinai Medical Center. Carrie's assistant called Todd, who immediately began driving down from a wine-country trip he was on. While driving, he was contacted by the press, who'd somehow already gotten word. This is what it's like to be famous. A bad connection, a hopeful brother, and an anxious conversation led to a story that circulated in the media that Carrie was in stable condition.

She was not. On the plane ride she'd lost consciousness, and flight attendants couldn't restart her heart. Minutes passed with her brain receiving no oxygen. Once at the hospital, her body temperature was artificially dropped to preserve her. Her heart was restarted, and her body was placed on a slight incline.

Todd used a family code phrase to gain access to the ICU: morbidly, the code was "Trauma Villa." (Guess who picked it.) One by one Carrie's family arrived: Billie, Bryan, Tricia, and Joely, who thought "Trauma Villa" was now a shoo-in as the title of Carrie's next book. Finally Debbie arrived. Her premonitions of Carrie had come true. She was living out every parent's worst nightmare.

Bryan, a problem-solver even in the worst of times, arranged security for the hospital, and for Carrie's house. He knew the media circus would be there, knew and hated it. Sure enough, when the family returned that evening to Carrie's house in Coldwater Canyon, security pushed aside a red carpet's worth of paparazzi, trying to capture pictures of a family in grief. Billie took care of Gary.

One of the few upsides to a loved one on life support is it allows people time to say goodbye. Billie and Bryan stayed together through these days, while Todd stayed with Debbie. One day he even brought

Debbie's Oscar to the ICU, secured in a black box. Maybe *it* could rouse Carrie! But no.

Carrie lay comatose all through Christmas Eve. Like sleepwalkers, everyone stumbled through the festivities, their senses numbed, just waiting. Carrie's presents—among them a new addition to a collection she called "pictures of ugly children"—waited for her, unopened. The evening was capped by the grim news that pop star George Michael, a seemingly healthy 53-year-old, had died on Christmas day. The year 2016 wasn't done.

Debbie, unfathomably, was doing the best of all of them; she even put on novelty reindeer antlers for Christmas dinner. "I can't allow my emotions to take over. This situation is so sad and so dire that if I give in to my emotions, it will kill me, and then I won't be here for her." The parents of addicts wait their whole lives in expectation of this gruesome moment. "It's not natural to outlive your child. This has always been my greatest fear," Debbie wrote. Acting chipper had never been harder, and never been needed more.

Debbie was not preparing to say goodbye, though: she was preparing for Carrie's recovery. "If she comes out of this, she's going to need months of physical and emotional therapy because of her brain being without oxygen for so long," she told Todd. Carrie might have to relearn everything: how to eat, how to walk, even how to speak. "And I'm going to be here for every minute of it."

The days and nights were arranged around one event: the phone call. "When you love someone who suffers from the disease of addiction," comedian and recovering addict Russell Brand wrote, "you await the phone call. There will be a phone call." Every day and every night they waited for the call from the hospital. They knew there was no good news to be had: severe damage had been done. The best they could hope for was no news. The best they could hope was that this purgatory would never end.

Carrie's toxicology report—not even Bryan could stop it from leaking—revealed that her blood had tested positive for alcohol, ecstasy, methadone, opiates, and cocaine. That was a rock concert's worth of drugs, still lingering after a London-to-LA flight. Carrie also had cocaine in her pocket when she boarded the plane, in a small folded paper.

On Tuesday, December 27, doctors decided to gradually increase Carrie's body temperature, to bring her out of her induced coma. Once her inner core warmed up, she suffered another cardiac arrest. She died. Physicians quickly brought her back. The family was alerted, and raced to her side. While they were there, the unthinkable happened three more times: arrest, death, resurrection. What was left on the bed there was a shell, a breathing inert body, nothing more. Carrie joked that her body was her "brain bag." This was an empty bag now, but an empty bag with a will to live.

Daughter, sister, wife, friend, mother: the woman who was all those things was not there anymore. The only thing connecting her to them was a heart that kept falling down, kept being prodded back to its feet. "You have the right to know," one of the doctors told the family, "that the odds of her coming back fully are significantly reduced." In terms of a full recovery? There was no hope.

Carrie's life—or however you thought of a body forced back from death over and over—was minutes away from the end of its journey. The next time her heart stopped beating, doctors did not have to bring her back. It was up to her family to make that call. But who? Todd was her brother, but felt it wasn't his place. Debbie wasn't there: Todd was letting her sleep, giving her the gift of missing this torturous final moments. Bryan was an ex.

It had to be Billie. Billie was the one strong enough, in that moment, to say what had to be said. The next time Carrie died, it would be for good. Doctors would not perform heroic measures: they would let nature take its course. Making that decision for a loved one is an act of a different sort of heroism, one that takes a different sort of strength.

In that final moment, Billie was her mother's hero.

Minutes later, Carrie's heart stopped beating again. The heart that had travelled all around the world. The heart that had inspired generations of women, of movie fans, of people dealing with mental illness. That heart had gotten her into more scrapes than a dozen other women combined, that had survived a lifetime of sins. At the last moment, Carrie was nothing but heart.

A heart that was finally allowed to rest.

Carrie Frances Fisher died a few minutes before 9 a.m. , December 27, 2016.

* * *

In a daze, Todd drove the distance to his mother's house, fought his way through a hundred-meter-crowd of fans and photographers, and then made his longest journey of the day: down the hall to his mother's room. "We lost her," he told Debbie, then cried.

All through that terrible day, Debbie had a clarity and a certainty in her eyes that had been lacking for months. Her whole life was devoted to keeping her family together, keeping the wolves at bay, keeping a legacy for her world. She'd succeeded, on many fronts. Now, though, at what was supposed to be her final years, before her was a loss too big to comprehend.

She had witnessed Todd talking with the hospital, with the doctors, with friends, with the press. He was working through his grief, handling everything like he had for decades. Todd would be okay. Todd didn't need his mother.

Carrie did, though.

The next morning Debbie slept in late, and awoke unusually alert. "I want to be with Carrie," she said. Those were her last words. She then closed her eyes and fell asleep. Her vital signs were normal, but she was unresponsive; it was like her soul had left her body. An ambulance took her to Cedars-Sinai, the same hospital where Carrie had died just the day before. Upon arrival and examination, doctors said she had suffered a massive hemorrhage, and had "maybe an hour" of life left.

Debbie Reynolds died on December 28, 2016, one day after her daughter.

Chapter 32: Posthumous

One voiced was suddenly silenced. And millions cried out.

Jeff Chabotte and his family were playing with their newly adopted kitten, a Christmas present, when they heard. "I didn't cry for any other person who died in 2016, but I cried when Carrie Fisher died," he said. Their new kitten's name was Leia.

The sad news of Carrie's death, Todd said, "hit like a nuclear bomb." 2016's final victims were a mother-daughter act. Daughter dead after a lifetime of demons, mother dead of maternal grief.

Todd didn't buy it. He was there: he felt he knew the truth. Towards the end dying people can hold on, for however long it takes until they feel like their life's work is done. In this case, Debbie realized her life's work had to continue beyond death. There was only one way to be there for Carrie now. Debbie hasn't died of grief: she'd died because she was needed on the other side. The mother and child reunion was only a moment away.

Debbie's final directives changed in the last days of her life. For decades she'd wanted to be cremated, and interred next to her parents. In the hours after Carrie's death, though, that changed. Debbie wanted Carrie put in a big plot, maybe a crypt. "And someday I'll be there, too," she added, meaning her body. Within 24 hours of requesting such an interment, she had died.

So per their wishes, Debbie was not cremated. Per Carrie's wishes, she was. Todd planned a joint service for both women—"his girls," as he always referred to them. To honor Debbie, he ensured that inside the open coffin Debbie looked her absolute best: "beautiful, glowing, and healthy, like Debbie Reynolds getting some well-deserved sleep."

To honor Carrie, Todd put her ashes inside a pill. He and Billie had shopped for cremation urns. Carrie had written a similar urn-shopping scene in one of her novels. In that scene, the urns were too kitschy. Here, though, none were kitschy *enough*. So they decided Carrie would rest inside a giant novelty Prozac capsule. It had been one of her most cherished possessions. When tributing a person of exquisite bad taste, only bad taste will do.

After the service, Carrie—in pill form—was placed inside her mother's coffin. They were buried in Forest Lawn Cemetery: a huge trapezoidal plinth stood over the site, adorned by two white statues holding each other. Mother will cradle daughter forever.

No matter how she actually died, Carrie said, she wanted her obit to record a particular cause of death. This request started backstage at a *Wishful Drinking* performance, when George Lucas tried to explain his reasoning about the whole no-bras-in-space thing. In zero gravity, he said, astronaut bodies swell up, and thus restrictive clothing was a strangulation hazard. Carrie immediately added this to the show, saying that her death had to read "drowned in moonlight, strangled by my own bra."

Mercifully, no newspaper led with that. The *New York Times* called her an "actress, author, and screenwriter." The *Los Angeles Times* called her "an author, actor, activist and personality," since "Fisher eventually became just as famous and beloved for simply being herself." Both mentioned Princess Leia in the first paragraph, as she'd always known they would.

On Thursday, January 5, 2017, the night before the dual funeral, Bryan and Billie held a gathering at Carrie's house. Todd decided it should be "a show," since no one was in the mood to party, but they wanted more of a celebration than a wake. Celebrities mingled and reminisced; Meryl Streep belted out "Happy Days Are Here Again." They promised to make this a yearly event: the #CarrieOn party.

That Saturday, *Bright Lights* premiered on HBO: its airdate had been moved up. A world got to watch two life stories play out, already knowing the end.

2016 cemented how the world of social media chose to mourn. Some people posted their own remembrances. Most retweeted the words of others, whose take seemed to best honor the spirit of the deceased.

Desi Jedeikin, who runs a celebrity podcast called Hollywood Crime Scene, chose dark humor. "Any *Postcards From the Edge* fan has to darkly appreciate the thunder stealing," she wrote on Twitter, referring to Debbie's death so soon after Carrie's. Comedian Patton Oswalt, a recent widower himself, retweeted it to prominence, adding "Carrie would've LOVED this Tweet and, maybe through you, she sent it?" That take became part of their death story: not *just* that they died, not *just* that

Debbie was too heartbroken to live, but that Debbie did it to hog the limelight one last time.

Carrie's death unleashed something in people, a realization that they had always taken her for granted. Carrie was supposed to be unkillable, like Keith Richards. She survived a life no one else would have, and brought joy and understanding and humor to millions. She, not Lady Diana Spencer, was the people's princess.

Many went public with their own history of mental illness, using the hashtag #inhonorofcarrie. What she was being remembered for was not Leia, not even her work as a writer, but her fight against the stigma of mental illness. This was bolstered by her lifetime of not always successfully dealing with it, of in fact dying from complications from it.

A few weeks into 2017, Joely went to an acting audition. She was still grieving, and couldn't nail the part. Afterwards, the casting director asked Joely if she had received the condolence email she had sent. "Yeah," Joely admitted, "I didn't want to lead with the dead Princess."

"She will always be an icon as Leia," costar Kelly Marie Tran said, "but also as Carrie. What an example, you know? I am so fortunate to have met her and I think that she will really live on forever."

As the months went by, Debbie Reynolds' death seemed to fade from memory. She was 84; the death of an old woman is not a tragedy. But Carrie's absence, like *Star Wars*, refused to leave public consciousness. Every day brought more tributes. Joely called her the "intergalactic savior of lost souls." It turned out that while never talking about it, without anyone knowing, she had been helping people her whole life.

Blogger Esther Beadle thanked Carrie for letting herself be filmed in the throes of a manic period. Beadle recognized herself in Carrie's frantic energy. "I play her interview over and over. And each time it feels safer, warmer. Each time more empowering than the last. She knows. I'd found someone." She credited Carrie with making her seek professional mental help.

Singer James Blunt had stayed at Carrie's house during recording of his first album, *Back to Bedlam*. She would taunt him with a life-size Leia cutout she'd put by his bedroom door, to which she'd jokingly added a birth date and death date for Leia. (Her guess was close to the mark, he noted later.) His song "You're Beautiful" was written in her giant bathroom; another song from the album was recording there. And she picked the album's title, *Back to Bedlam*. She was godmother to his son.

In an *LA Magazine* article titled "Carrie Fisher Saved My Life," journalism Mara Shapshay described how she met Carrie in 2005 during a bottoming-out moment. Shapshay was living in her car, unemployed and divorced, with a drug addiction and without access to her bank account. She hadn't showered in two weeks. "Come live with me," Carrie said. Mara did, moving her trash bags of clothes into the guest house. She stayed until she cleaned up, landed a job, and could afford to move out.

A similar article ran on *Vogue.com*: another lost woman had fallen asleep at one of Carrie's parties. Carrie made her breakfast—pancakes and black coffee—talked her through her troubles, let her shower, and said to call if she needed more help. A third article ran on the International Bipolar Foundation's blog: "Carrie Fisher: A Force for Good."

In March, two months after the funeral, Todd organized a full-on show, which was attended by over a thousand people, and streamed around the globe. Attendees watched performances and speeches, interspersed with clips from Carrie's life. During a walk-on—or roll-on—appearance by Artoo, he became stuck, as if he were frozen in grief. Then the tributor became the tribute, as Carrie, from the TV screen, told the audience about Debbie's decades of work with the Thalians, a charity devoted to better understanding mental illness. There were tears, tap dancing, the Gay Men's Chorus of Los Angeles, a Marine Color Guard, copious oversharings regarding sex, all concluded by a standing ovation. And it all happened six feet above the guests of honor.

Billie, one of the show attendees, was the new owner of the Coldwater Canyon house. She grew up here, amid the pleasant chaos, and decided to have it remodeled: no more giant Prozac pill in the kitchen tile. She and Uncle Todd also sorted through many of Carrie's belongings and collectibles: some were auctioned off, while most were put into storage.

Todd was executor for Debbie's estate, which took the better part of a year to settle. He had to decide if he wanted to manage or sell each of the properties his mother owned, and also cover her estate tax bill. During this time he also wrote a memoir about his life, and finished a TV pilot script he had started co-writing with Carrie. It was about growing up the children of celebrities.

Gary the French bulldog would eventually be adopted by one of Carrie's assistants. He lives in Florida now, and he supposedly perks up if he sees Carrie's face on TV.

Princess Leia spent much of the year on signage. The month before Carrie died, Donald Trump had been elected president. Trump had been repeatedly accused of sexual assault, was caught on tape bragging about it, in fact. Then he won the election. Carrie had called him "Jabba the Hutt."

A protest march was set in Washington DC the day after Trump's inauguration. Women wore pink crocheted hat, crudely named after a part of the female anatomy. They held up vulgar signs. They spat with righteous anger at the new White House occupant, and the society that put him there. The march was 200,000 people—and another 5 million around the country—choosing to rebel.

And Leia was their rebel in chief, as the signs made abundantly clear. "A WOMAN'S PLACE IS IN THE RESISTANCE," over an image of *New Hope* Leia holding a blaster. "WE ARE THE RESISTANCE," over another Leia image. "WE ARE THE FORCE." "THE WOMEN STRIKE BACK." "REBEL AGAINST HATE." "CARRIE FISHER SENT ME." "RESISTANCE IS BUILT ON HOPE." "THE 45TH IS A SITH." One protester dressed as Darth Vader, holding a "EVEN I DIDN'T VOTE FOR HIM" sign, on neon pink. Singer Ana Matronic dressed as Leia—even bunned up her red hair—and held a "WE WILL DEFEAT THE DARK SIDE" sign. Carrie had died, but Carrie Nation was alive, kicking, and swinging a hatchet.

One rally spawned many others, and Leia seemed to be at all of them in spirit, and signage. "DON'T LEIA HAND ON MY HEALTH CARE." "ALL ALIENS WELCOME IN THIS REPUBLIC." *Vanity Fair* wrote a whole piece about it; "How Carrie Fisher Became the Surprisingly Face of the Rebellion Against Trump." One image of Rosie the Riveter was altered to give her a red Rebellion tattoo on her mighty bicep—and Carrie Fisher's face. "We Can Do It!"

It wasn't just the left who found strength from Leia. A conservative site, *The Federalist*, ran an article praising Princess Leia as a character who demonstrated emotional strength, and then slammed other movies, and "leftists' views on gender differences," for suggesting women could be as good as men at physical feats. If Carrie read that, her Prozac pill might start revolving.

In July, the 2017 Emmy nominations were released. Carrie received a nomination for her final episode of *Catastrophe*. She'd win other posthumous awards for the performance as well. Her character was written out of the show, with an entire episode given to mourning Mia's death, complete with lots of pitch-black jokes. *Family Guy* gave her character a similar bittersweet sendoff. "I may have lost a boss," Peter Griffith said, for once not joking, "but heaven has gained a Princess."

In January of 2018, Carrie somehow beat out Bruce Springsteen to win a Grammy. The Grammys have a yearly audiobook category, and Carrie's narration of *The Princess Diarist* beat out the Boss, who had narrated his memoir *Born to Run*. One last irony; Carrie won a Grammy despite a lifetime of using her voice via the written word rather than singing.

Billie, during the first year of loss, got a tattoo on her right ankle, above the tibia bulge. It was the same as her mom's—a starfield. While Carrie's was a galactic contusion, Billie's was elegant, stippled linework of geometrically perfect twinkling stars, along with a crescent moon. It has one perfect imperfection: there's a star inside the crescent's embrace. A space fantasy.

As the year went on, Trump's star on the Hollywood Walk of Fame was regularly desecrated. "Good riddance!" Mark Hamill said on Twitter about it, adding "and I know just who they should replace him with. #AStarforCarrie." Carrie, it turned out, had never had a star on the Walk of Fame. In this she was joined by A-listers like Denzel Washington and Julia Roberts—and a retiring fellow named George Lucas—who were famous enough, but didn't want people walking all over them.

There was another reason why, of course; each star requires a $50,000 donation. Most actors do it to help promote an upcoming film. That's what Mark had done: he timed his star ceremony to be a week before *The Last Jedi* was released for streaming. Harrison Ford, who helped induct him, said that "when thinking about today, I was really sorry we don't have the other member of our trio to celebrate with us. But I feel her presence."

Carrie was not the first gone-too-soon celeb to have a posthumous groundswell of star support. The governing board had implemented a five-year waiting period before a deceased person was eligible for a posthumous star. In June of 2021, it happened: Carrie would get her star. "Much love & a very special 1-finger salute to the incomparable, hilarious & irreverent force of nature that was my space sis Carrie Fisher," Mark tweeted. "Her star will blaze from here to eternity."

The Last Jedi hit theaters almost exactly a year after Carrie died. It was troubling as a posthumous film, since it features what appears to be a death scene for Leia, followed by a miracle save. Audience members couldn't help but see not Leia but Carrie was the one who gets sucked out to her doom.

And then the "Leia Poppins" scene came, with Leia floating her way back through the rubble to safety. It evoked tears for some, laughs for others: both coming from the same uncomfortable wellspring. Big emotions need a big release.

The credits give Carrie second billing, and include a note saying "In Loving Memory of our Princess." It would be her final *Star Wars* film, and third film in a row to top the yearly box office.

The Force Awakens had been all about Han, ending in his violent death. *Last Jedi* shifted the focus to Luke, ending with his peaceful death. The final film in this new trilogy was supposed to be Leia's. Would she fulfill her destiny and wield a purple lightsaber? Could she stop the First Order, and her evil son?

Whatever could happen in the ninth film now? Producers announced Carrie would, naturally enough, not be featured in the ninth film. But everything was leading to this denouement: What other story could they tell without Leia?

Chapter 33: End Slate

"I tell my younger friends that one day they'll be at a bar playing pool and they'll look up at the television set and there will be a picture of Princess Leia with two dates underneath, and they'll say 'Aww—she said that would happen.' And then they'll go back to playing pool."

Carrie wrote that in *Wishful Drinking*. She was wrong that no one would care. But she was right that, eventually, life returns to usual. People go back to playing pool.

A Han *Solo* prequel movie came out: it was wildly expensive, thanks partly to Lucasfilm switching directors and scripts halfway through production. *Rogue One* had done something similar, with its own massive reshoots. Releasing a big-budget sci-fi movie every year was proving difficult. Future plans for yearly *Star Wars* movies were quietly shelved.

Billie Lourd's acting career took off: she found a home in horror television shows. First she played a college student on *Scream Queens*, then appeared as multiple characters in the anthology series *American Horror Story*. She also was one of the best parts of the indie comedy *Booksmart*, displaying real comedic chops, and appeared in cheesy Old Navy commercials. She had a big social media following, so much so that Bryan chastised her for her Millennial habit of Instagramming pictures of her food.

Bryan married his longtime partner Bruce Bozzi in October of 2016, adopting Bozzi's daughter. He remains one of the busiest and most successful figures in entertainment, sitting on a half-dozen different boards, all while being a co-chair of CAA. He is one of the leading fundraisers of Democratic candidates on the West Coast. He does not take pictures of his food.

Todd had helped run three auctions of Debbie's memorabilia: he used that experience for a fourth and fifth auction, of some of Debbie's and Carrie's belongings. He decided Debbie's portion of the proceeds would go to the Thalians. Carrie's profits, Billie decided, would go to The Jed Foundation, a suicide prevention charity.

The fourth collection, auctioned in October 2017, went for over $2 million. Auctioned items included Carrie's annotation-filled *Empire Strikes Back* script, her director's chair for *Return of the Jedi*, and a life-size statue of herself as Leia.

Not all of Todd's plans came to fruition. He wanted to recreate Carrie's bedroom on the Debbie Reynolds Dance Studio, which for decades had been a rehearsal space for musicians and dancers. But without the two leading ladies' income streams, the studio couldn't keep running. The lot was sold for over 6 million dollars, and the studio was demolished in February of 2019.

Billie, Bryan, and Todd kept putting one foot in front of another... and so, in various media forms, did Leia. The comics revealed that in trying to steal back frozen Han, Leia had been briefly frozen in carbonite, too. Being successfully unfrozen taught her that she could save Han. In the novels, it's revealed Leia lost her political power when a rival went public that her birth father was Darth Vader. She uses her reduced power to help turn her faction of supporters into the Resistance.

Asking "hey, what about Leia?" after checking in on Carrie's family may feel myopic and childish, like hearing that a postal carrier died and worrying about who will deliver your Thursday Valpak coupons. But most everyone who knew Carrie knew her first as Leia. Leia's heroism was bolstered by Carrie's choices in life, just as Carrie's history rewrote Leia's as a survivor instead of a superstar. It's not disrespectful to wonder about Leia: it's disrespectful not to.

The 2017 book *Leia: Princess of Alderaan* by Claudia Gray gave the first book-length backstory of what it was like to grow up Leia. Her mother's quote of "authority can be given, but leadership must be earned" drives all of Leia's actions, and she tries to do what she can as a royal to stop the Empire without outing herself as a Rebel. A *Star Wars* comic issue featured a grim Leia admitting that she played her cards right when interrogated by Tarkin, and thus would let Alderaan die all over again if she could. She's an unstoppable force, whether using herself as bait to lure an ocean creature to attack, or going undercover as a turncoat royal. (That she got away with because "Stormtroopers think all royals are basically interchangeable.")

Her life and Carrie's grew more intertwined after her death. A storyline set before *The Force Awakens* has General Organa distracting a bank manager by trying to find a home for her mother's collection of gowns. The gowns of her mother Padmé Amidala, that is, not her mother Debbie Reynolds.

In gaming, the newest version of the Kodi media center installation was named Leia: it launched the week after Carrie died. In the island nation of Niue, Leia appeared on a one-ounce silver coin. And thanks to 3D printing, recent Leia action figures now look startlingly realistic. Leia's story via the new Extended Universe, and in our imaginations, will never end.

But *Carrie's* contributions as Leia seemed final. *Star Wars: Episode IX—The Rise of Skywalker* would have to carry on without Carrie-ing on. How to handle it, though?

One answer involved industrial quantities of light and magic. Most actors in modern action films have both stunt doubles and CG ragdoll replicas: the replicas takes the spills not even stunt people could survive. The ragdolls can seamlessly morph into the stunt performers, who then can seamlessly morph into the actor for a close-up. This new breed of movie magic was one way to bring Leia back without Carrie.

George Lucas was one of the first to realize this sort of virtual doppelganger technology was on the horizon, and saw the danger of it. "Tomorrow," he testified before Congress in 1988, "more advanced technology will be able to replace actors with 'fresher faces,' or alter dialogue and change the movement of the actor's lips to match." His testimony was equal parts threat and warning: if we don't do something to ensure otherwise, future generations could alter footage however they liked.

In the era of deepfakes, his point stands. We think of a piece of video as immutable truth, but it's not. With enough money or talent or motivation, you can create any fantastic creature or impossible world you want. A digital replacement of Leia was doable: there already was one in *Rogue One*. So could *Episode IX* go on as scheduled, with a Deepfake Leia? Uh-uh. No matter how photorealistic a fake Leia might look and sound and move, audiences would know it was not Carrie. That would turn them against the movie, rightly so. A purely technological solution seemed out.

Colin Trevorrow, the hit director of *Jurassic World*, was lined up to be the writer/director of the ninth film. He figured that while any "real" version of Leia would be sniffed out as fakery, a "fake" Leia would oddly feel realistic. So he built his movie around a Leia hologram message, a touching callback to the very first film.

His leaked script, called *Duel of the Fates*, has the cast trying to stop blocked communications so that General Organa could go live to the galaxy with a message of rebellion. She convinces old friend Lando Calrissian, now a casino owner, to lend an assist: this would bring Billy Dee Williams back to the franchise.

In this script, Kylo Ren's story arc concludes with him becoming a Force vampire: in a battle with Rey he drains her to near-death. A vision of Luke appears to her, and she recovers enough to keep fighting. She pulls strength to defeat him not from Kylo's dark side, not from the light, but from a balance of light and dark. Leia then uses the Force to reach out to her dying son, who with his final act heals Rey. Leia helps Kylo Ren die redeemed.

Within a year of Carrie's death, Trevorrow left the project. His script wasn't satisfying: but of course it wasn't. Leia's role was limited to some audio messages, psychic whispers, and holograms, all easily fakeable. That wasn't enough Leia, though.

Actors had died mid-film for over a century before the digital age, and low-fidelity workarounds were used to complete filming. How else to add Leia without Carrie?

In a bind, Lucasfilm convinced *The Force Awakens'* writer/director to tackle *Episode IX*. Somehow, JJ Abrams returned. The film, due at end of 2019, had to tie up this trilogy, tie up all *nine* films in fact, deal with Snoke the big bad being killed off in *Last Jedi* and thus leaving the final film with no villain, and also figure out the whole Leia issue. No pressure.

JJ's option 1: simply don't mention Leia, like how the third *Dark Knight* film never mentioned the Joker after Heath Ledger's death. That was ruled out. Leia's character had become the undying soul of the franchise: the prequels culminated in her birth, the original trilogy culminated with her side winning freedom. This trilogy was about her son's battles with the dark side. The filmmakers couldn't show General Organa kicking asteroids and taking names as originally intended, but Leia had to be present in the story. Thematically, she *was* the story.

Onto option 2: Kill Leia before the movie begins. This would let the film open with the remaining characters mourning her, which would reflect the grief of the audience. But this fearful symmetry was also ruled out as wrong for the story. This wasn't any old movie, it was *Star Wars*. Epic, larger-than-life heroes abounded. Such heroes do not die off-stage. Finishing Leia off so ignobly would be a crime the film could never recover from.

A third option, an old standby for everything from Broadway to James Bond, was recasting. ("The role of Princess Leia will now be played by Ellen Barkin.") Again, no: Princess Leia was simply not a recastable role. After all these decades, you'd need an anbaric scalpel to separate Carrie from Leia. They were twinned souls, and a little thing like Carrie's death wasn't enough to cut that bond.

So what was left? How do you give a character a final sendoff when you're so handcuffed? When you can't use another actress, can't *not* include her, can't kill her off, can't shortchange her, and can't digitally replace her? It seemed a no-win situation. One, fittingly, that a character like Leia found herself in over and over. How would *Leia* deal with this, one wonders? What would be the diplomatic solution, that could pivot a glaring weakness into not just a strength, but one of the whole franchise's high points?

* * *

Ever since *Phantom Menace*, George Lucas' remix style of editing had become more evident in filmmaking. Nightly news shows could remove a pause in an interview subject's speech, and inexpensively morph the clip as if the pause was never there. Digital characters would be performed on set by one actor, voiced by a second, and animated by a phalanx. It was commonplace for movies to now feature over a thousand visual effects shots. If a modern director liked a take but dislike the camera angle, it was easier to digitally recreate the entire world of the shot, actors included, and nudge the camera into a better position, rather than ask for another take.

JJ Abrams, like all Generation Xers, had grown up with George as a major influence. He wasn't a remixer, though: he was a reshooter. On his show *Lost*, for instance, his writers would come up with a new theme for an episode (Hurley's a rich lottery winner), and then reshoot bits of dialogue from previous episodes to hint at that theme (Hurley racks up poker losses and says he's "good for it"). Audiences were dazzled at how the show seemed to plan so far ahead. Abrams grew skillful in re-evaluating existing footage to sneak in new plot points.

It was almost uncanny, but those two styles of work, from the past and present helmers of the *Star Wars* world, were exactly what was needed to bring Leia back. Without George's innovations, Hollywood wouldn't have a 20-year track record of transforming the footage you have into the footage you want. And without Abrams' vast experience with reshooting, he wouldn't be able to tackle creating a role for Leia without Carrie Fisher.

There was one more key factor responsible for bringing back Leia: Harrison Ford's broken leg. That injury led to the extra time for the *Force Awakens* script to be polished mid-filming, a decision that cut the General Organa subplot. In other words, there was a larder full of unused scenes of *Carrie Fisher as General Organa*. A movie's worth, perhaps, if doled out the right way.

"It's hard to even talk about it without sounding like I'm being some kind of cosmic spiritual goofball," Abrams said in *Vanity Fair*, "but it felt like we suddenly had found the impossible answer to the impossible question."

Using the footage was its own type of impossible. There was the idealized Leia that Carrie would have played in the ninth movie, full of bold declarations, tough decisions, and weary humor. Then there was a selection of actual Leia scenes, mostly pedestrian conversations without big emotional beats. Somehow Circle A had to fit in square B. "It was a bizarre kind of left-side/right-side of the brain sort of Venn diagram thing," Abrams said of the process.

Once the hard work of writing was done, the "easy" part could begin. "Easy" included all the other tricks available to cover an actor's absence—over-the-shoulder shots, faraway doubles, silhouettes. They were now available, now that Carrie's performance as Leia would be anchor the character. Settings were rewritten: if one scene with Leia dialogue happened at night, the scene drawing from it would as well, to explain the lighting. Another Leia scene had been filmed outdoors in dappled sunshine, so the new rebel base was now on a forest planet, to explain the leafy shadows on her face.

What else did "easy" entail? In this case it meant new scenes would have to be very carefully lit to match the extant Leia footage from *The Force Awakens* and *The Last Jedi*. Components from old and new scenes would be blended together, along with snippets of dialogue. New costumes and hairstyles would be digitally added, otherwise it'd be apparent Leia hadn't changed her clothes in four years. All-new backgrounds and foregrounds were added. Carrie's face was often the only "real" thing floating in the shot, one small truth inside a world of artificiality. This emotionally fraught creation, along with the more expected spaceship battles and robot hijinks, would earn *Rise of Skywalker* Oscar nominations for sound editing and visual effects.

One early decision Abrams made was to write out Billie's character Lieutenant Connix. No way did anyone want to force her to play invented scenes against what would be an automaton of her dead mother. But when they asked Billie if she wanted to be part of this process, she said yes. She'd made tougher decisions that that. "And so there are moments where [mother and daughter are] talking; there are moments when they're touching," Abrams said. "Touching" was right on the money. "There are moments in this movie where Carrie is there, and I really do feel there is an element of the uncanny, spiritual, you know, classic Carrie, that it would have happened this way, because somehow it worked. And I never thought it would."

Dialogue scenes with Carrie were scoured: a clip of her saying "always," another of her saying "never underestimate a droid," then "Don't tell me what things look like; tell me what they are." Plenty of good lines couldn't be made germane to the *Rise of Skywalker* plot. An old editor's trick for getting genuine emotions was also used: Abrams had editors pull footage from before and after each of Carrie's take. This gave them more precious usable seconds of Carrie emoting.

One flashback scene was written that featured 1980s-vintage Luke and Leia in training. Mark played himself, and was digitally de-aged down to about 30. Billie agreed to play Leia. Editors found a shot from *Return of the Jedi,* and superimposed a Reagan-era Leia face over Billie. Even if Carrie had been around, this may have been how such a scene was created.

But all the princess' horses and all the princess's men couldn't solve one now-almost-unspeakable problem: the original performance. Leia's cut *Force Awakens* scenes weren't entirely cut to increase the impact of Leia showing up later on. They were cut because it's not her best work. Carrie's early line deliveries were often flat, with low energy. For all they had changed Leia to better fit Carrie, Carrie couldn't always change herself to fit Leia. This had been her first serious acting assignment in ages. She became notably better at *The Force Awakens'* end, and in subsequent performances.

As in *Force Awakens*, the Leia of *Rise of Skywalker* most comes to life when she's talked about, when we see what she means to other characters. Poe Dameron, Maz Kantana, Lando Calrissian, and even the ghost of Luke all give Leia a Jedi glow-up. For all they inspire others, she's the person inspiring *them*.

But key scenes are still missing. This is a film trilogy about a mother and a son—Leia and Kylo Ren—yet the characters never share screentime. Ren was written as consumed with father (and grandfather) issues, so perhaps that's why he never breaks the seal on his mommy issues. But Leia should be more affected by his victims. Her only child is hunting and killing all of her friends, enslaving the galaxy, and murdered her husband. A little parental guilt might be called for.

Some completed scenes were not included in the final film because the paste-up job was too apparent. They "turned out to not meet the standard of photorealism that [we'd] hoped for," co-screenwriter Chris Terrio explained. This caused one more flaw in a film built, like a donut, around a missing center. Since many of the not-up-to-snuff scenes involved Leia talking with Kelly Marie Tran's Rose Tico, Rose's role in the film shrunk. A prominent costar of *Last Jedi* become accidentally absent.

Audiences discovered Leia's fate on December 19, 2019, when *Star Wars: Episode IV: The Rise of Skywalker* opened. The film's crawl opens with "The dead speak!" a 30-foot-high wink at the audience about Carrie's post hoc performance.

But all the focus on making the dead speak seems to have leaked into the rest of the story. Emperor Palpatine has resurrected himself, and is the one broadcasting a message of fear instead of hope to the galaxy. Chewbacca is mourned after his spaceship explodes—but then it turns out he survived. Threepio has his memory banks irreversibly wiped— and then gets rebooted back to normal. Leia used her nascent Force powers to reach out to Kylo Ren from worlds away, and calls him Ben before the effort kills her. Ren himself then dies, and is immediately resurrected, and then dies again. Han Solo appears via memory to scold his prodigal son, Luke returns via blue ghost, then he and Leia return one last time, as supportive spectral visions. Rey adopts the last name of

Skywalker: "she's the only person in the galaxy who was trained by two Skywalkers: Luke and Leia," Chris Terrio pointed out.

That was a month of Easter Sundays' worth of death and rebirth. Audiences ended up feeling manipulated by story beats that kept undoing bold decisions. *Seven different times* characters seemingly perish, only to be shown as still alive. The only ones who don't return are Palpatine—a *Star Wars Greatest Hits™* villain brought back to fill the void left by Snoke—and Leia herself.

Rise of Skywalker, besides earning its yearly billion dollars at the box office, was also a Carrie Fisher memorial of sorts. Here was a celebration for a woman gone too soon, here is how much she meant to all around her. And how much she is missed.

Carrie, the woman who never quite found her place in the world, turned out to be irreplaceable. A thousand people bent over backwards to try to do what she could have done with a scowl, a sigh, and a what-the-hell grin. In that way it's the perfect tribute: a calamitous sendoff for a calamitous person. *Rise of Skywalker* tries way too hard to please, to give you everything you ever wanted save for the one thing you want, the one thing it can't give you.

Rise of Skywalker was a perfect tribute in another way, the way that you miss a coworker when the office falls apart in their absence. Todd Fisher had been vocal about how the final Skywalker Saga film needed to have Carrie in it as Leia. For all the time working and reworking the Leia footage, trying to make do without Carrie Fisher the *actress*, the person best suited to fix the film was Carrie Fisher the *script doctor*.

This task was collage-art challenge like none other: writing a whole performance from leftovers and outtakes. Carrie had a sixth sense for how much treacle an audience could stand without gagging. How many characters could return from the dead before *Rise of Skywalker* turned farcical. How to honor her fictional doppelganger without tossing her up onto a pedestal. Carrie, who lived with "Pam" and "Roy" in her head, knew how to portray the balance between light and dark. How we're all living with it, trying to be good and be ourselves at the same time. How audiences will accept disappointments if they reflect reality.

Good stories give audiences what they want, great stories give them what they need. Some stories may have downbeat endings, but every good story's ending is unhappy, because it's over.

Every person lives a lifelong story, one where the final chapter has already been written. The question is how you fill up the pages of your life before you arrive at that final chapter. It won't all be parties, victories, and celebrations. Only in movies is there a princess to pin a medal on you for a job well done. In the real world, the struggle *is* the award. Never giving up feels a whole lot like winning.

On screen and off, in media and in reality, Carrie Fisher told us that, over and over. And she could have told us that one last time, if only her life's sentence had run on a bit longer.

Epilogue

Many extended families are held together by a single person. This person arranges the holiday reunions, passes on family updates, maintain the Christmas card list. When they leave, if no one else steps up, families can grow distant.

Or adversarial.

Six and a half years after she died, Carrie Fisher was given a star on the Hollywood Walk of Fame. It was on May 4, 2023—"May the Fourth" had been christened Star Wars Day. JJ Abrams and Bryan Lourd attended, C3PO and R2D2 served as escorts, and Billie Lourd and Mark Hamill spoke. Billie wore a dress with Princess Leia on it.

Carrie siblings weren't there. Billie hadn't invited them. Todd, who campaigned for years to get Carrie a star, said he was puzzled. Joely and Tricia made a joint Instagram post saying they were also disappointed.

Billie explained why in a statement to the press: it was because they'd written tell-alls. "Days after my mother died," she said, "her brother and her sister chose to publicly process their grief and capitalize on my mother's death, conducting multiple interviews and selling individual books for a lot of money, with the death of my mother and my grandmother as subjects."

"This was a conscious decision on my part to break a cycle with a way of life that I don't want to be a part of for myself or my children," she said. Carrie had lived her life in the spotlight: her siblings had followed suit. Billie would now take after her father, and cherish privacy over publicity.

"I have now passed the torch—or in this case, lightsaber—on to my two children," she said. "I feel so lucky that even though they won't get to meet my mom, they will get to know a piece of her through Leia."

We will always know Leia: knowing Carrie may become tricker.

247

"A person named Sheila Weller has taken it upon herself to sell and write an unauthorized biography based on my daughter's mother, Carrie Fisher." This statement of Bryan Lourd's ran in *Variety* in late 2019.

Bryan—who later that month would close a $400 million equity deal with his agency CAA—rarely made public statements. He didn't need to: his actions spoke for him. But he had read an excerpt of Weller's biography, *Carrie Fisher: A Life on the Edge*, that ran in *LA Magazine* the previous weekend. It was about her brutal last days, a time no one who was there wanted to revisit. Bryan and BIllie had turned down interview requests.

"For all the fans and friends of Carrie," he continued, "I just thought it necessary that you know this information before you decide to purchase this book or consider what is being said in the upcoming interviews and press Ms. Weller will do when trying to sell it. To be clear I haven't read the book. The only books about Carrie Fisher worth reading are the ones Carrie wrote herself. She perfectly told us everything we needed to know."

Bryan's thumb on the scale worked: Weller's book, for which she was given a healthy advance, did not receive the expected barrage of media coverage. This may have been an edict from upper management: few media elites want to get on Bryan's bad side.

If the lifetime of Carrie's habitual oversharing has made Bryan and Billie fanatical about privacy, it's understandable. But Carrie lived her life in public: that was where millions of *Star Wars* fans began to love and respect the woman behind Leia. And his statement that Carrie's books "perfectly" capture her life is a stretcher. Her first four books were fiction.

"[I]f I didn't write about it, someone else would," Carrie wrote, of revealing her private secrets. She meant a proper biographer, someone like Sheila Weller. Weller talked to dozens of Carrie's friends to put together her book. This is how traditional biographers work: you accrue as many new details as you can.

I have done something different with *Your Worshipfulness*. I have talked to no one in Carrie's inner circle of friends and family, no one at all in fact. Everything in this book was already public record, from her idle chat to her deepest thoughts. Call it a tell- *some*: I've left out quite a few public details that seemed too personal or intrusive.

This is my compromise, to serve a woman who overshared, a world that loves dirty laundry, and a family who wants privacy. It's intended as a celebration, of a woman whose star burned brightly, of a woman who knew what that meant.

* * *

There's an upside and a downside to not talking to people, Kitty Kelley-style, to get the good stories. The downside is you miss out on all the good conversation. Kitty Kelley herself has chastised me on this approach. On the upside, I got to read a lot.

JW Rinzler's magnificent three-volume trilogy— *The Making of Star Wars* and his follow-up volumes on *Empire Strikes Back* and *Return of the Jedi*—are the closest thing a researcher like me has to a time machine. I've necessarily told the *Star Wars* story from Carrie and Leia's perspectives, but the full *Star Warts*-and-all backstory deserves to be read on its own.

Carrie's four novels, *Postcards from the Edge, Surrender the Pink, Delusions of Grandma*, and *The Best Awful*, are written in code. Often it's a code as easy as a game on a kid's placemat. Some references were and still are mysteries. And some, of course, are actual fiction: hopefully Carrie was never handcuffed to a cactus, the way Suzanne was. I've included passage when one of Carrie's doppelgangers' thoughts seemed informed by her own life.

Carrie's family was a writing family; her mom had three books under her belt (*Debbie: My Life* in 1988, *Unsinkable* in 2013, and *Make 'Em Laugh* in 2015). Her brother, half-sister, and father all wrote as well: Todd Fisher wrote *My Girls* in 2018, Joely Fisher wrote *Growing Up Fisher* in 2017, and Eddie wrote *Been There, Done That* in 1999. Some of their stories about life with Carrie can be found here. Again, I left some of the gnarlier stories out.

For better or worse, Carrie Fisher's life was an open book. Her life was at times a page turner, a pot boiler, a mainstream novel, a comedy, a tragedy, a play, a screenplay, and a good old-fashioned sci-fi yarn. Her book is done, and it's too late to close it now. But it's a hell of a read. And full of sentences.

Acknowledgements

Thanks to Amy Reeder, Natasha from Reddit, Caseen Gaines, Karen J. Abraham, Ali Rosenthal, Joe Perry, and Lori Perkins.

Thanks especially to early readers Brian Sayles, Cindy Ryan, and Sean Ryan. Brian caught one instance of not "Poe Dameron" but "Cameron Poe" that puts me in *Star Wars* jail alongside those who spell Wookiee with only one "e." Speaking of Wookiees, Sean saved you the reader from terrible jokes of mine that would be a reach for Chewbacca. And Cindy made me repeatedly aware the point of Carrie's story should not ever be my verbal flourishes.

Despite their best efforts, any mistakes left in the book are entirely mine.

This book originated as a Kickstarter. Thank you to everyone who pledged, everyone who reposted, everyone who passed the word along.

For Riverdale Avenue Books, thanks to Lori Perkins and David Valentin: for Tantor Media thanks to Brittany Wilson.

Most people in my everyday world don't know (or care!) that I'm a writer. They think of me as the husband to Cindy and father to Sylvia and Holly. That's who I think of myself as, as well.

Finally, thanks to anyone who's ever worn space buns, or dressed up as Leia on Halloween, or cosplayed as Leia. She's a character with 13 minutes of screentime in a 1970s movie. All of you, all of us, made her more than that.

Bibliography

Biskind, Peter. *Easy Riders, Raging Bulls: How the Sex-Drugs-and-Rock 'N' Roll Generation Saved Hollywood.* Simon & Schuster; New York: 1998.

Bluth, Don. *Somewhere Out There: My Animated Life.* Smart Pop; New York: 2022.

Bonca, Cornel. *Paul Simon: An American Tune.* Rowman & Littlefield Publishers; New York: 2014.

Bouzereau, Laurent and Duncan, Jody. *Star Wars: The Making of Episode I - The Phantom Menace.* Del Rey; New York: 1999.

Carlin, Peter Ames. *Homeward Bound: The Life of Paul Simon.* Thorndike Press; New York: 2016.

Champlin, Charles. *George Lucas: The Creative Impulse.* New York; Harry N Abrams: 1997.

Eliot, Marc. *Paul Simon.* New York; John Wiley: 2010.

Gross, Edward and Altman, Mark A. *Secrets of the Force; The Complete, Uncensored, Unauthorized Oral History of Star Wars.* St. Martin's Press; New York: 2021.

Harris, Mark. *Mike Nichols: A Life.* New York; Penguin Press: 2021.

Hilburn, Robert. *Paul Simon: The Life.* New York; Simon & Schuster: 2018.

Hill, Doug and Weingrad, Jeff. *Saturday Night: A Backstage History of Saturday Night Live.* Beech Tree Books; New York: 1986.

Hirsch, Paul. *A Long Time Ago in a Cutting Room Far Far Away... My Fifty Years Editing Hollywood Hits—Star Wars, Carrie, Ferris Bueller's Day Off, Mission: Impossible, and More.* Chicago, IL; Chicago Review Press International: 2020.

Iger, Bob. *The Ride of a Lifetime: Lessons Learned from 15 Years as CEO of the Walt Disney Company.* Random House; New York: 2019.

Kaminski, Michael. *The Secret History of Star Wars: The Art of Storytelling and the Making of a Modern Epic*. Legacy Books Press; Kingston, Ontario: 2008.

Fisher, Eddie, with Fisher, David. *Been There, Done That: An Autobiography*. St. Martin's Press; New York: 1999.

Fisher, Todd. *My Girls: A Lifetime with Carrie and Debbie*. William Morrow: New York: 2018.

Fisher, Joely. *Growing Up Fisher: Musing, Memories, and Misadventures*. William Morrow; New York: 2017.

Jones, Brian Jay. *George Lucas: A Life*. Little, Brown; New York: 2016.

Marshall, Penny. *My Mother Was Nuts*. New Harvest; New York: 2012.

Miller, Craig. *Star Wars Memories: My Time in the (Death Star) Trenches*. Fulgens Press; 2019.

Miller, James Andrew. *Powerhouse: The Untold Story of Hollywood's Creative Artists Agency*. Custom House; New York: 2016.

Pollock, Dale. *Skywalking: The Life and Films of George Lucas*. New York; Harmony Books: 1983.

Reynolds, Debbie. *Debbie: My Life*. William Morrow; New York: 1988.

Reynolds , Debbie and Hannaway, Dorian. *Unsinkable: A Memoir*. William Morrow; New York: 2013.

Rinzler, JW. *The Making of Star Wars: The Definitive Story Behind the Original Film*. Del Rey; New York: 2007.

—. *The Making of Star Wars; The Empire Strikes Back*. Del Rey; New York; 2010.

—. *The Making of Star Wars: Return of the Jedi*. Del Rey; New York; 2013.

—. *The Making of Star Wars, Episode III - Revenge of the Sith*. LucasBooks; New York: 2005.

Taylor, Chris . *How Star Wars Conquered the Universe: The Past, Present, and Future of a Multibillion Dollar Franchise*. Basic Books; New York: 2014.

Annotations

p10: "There was a very mature streak than ran through Carrie," George said. — *Conver-sations from the Edge with Carrie Fisher*, "George Lucas." Aired January 30, 2002.

P16: "You know that term 'I could care less?'" Carrie said, years alter. "I could. I could care a lot less." — *PrimeTime Thursday*, Aired December 21, 2000.

P18: "The UK grudgingly agreed, after being told that Peter Cushing and Alec Guinness were the leads, and that Carrie, Mark, and Harrison were in smaller roles." — Edward Gross and Mark A Altman, *Secrets of the Force.*

P21: Carrie, with shoulder-length hair down, playing princess dress-up with the uninhibited glee of a five-year-old. — JW Rinzler, *The Making of Star Wars.*

P21: Carrie joked that she knew something new about Leia now: her favorite color. — JW Rinzler , *The Making of The Empire Strikes Back.*

P23: She hated it—"you don't put a wide hairstyle on an already wide face!"—but hating it would get her fired, she felt. "It's nice, really nice," she lied. — *CFTE.*

P25: Executives thought they could save some runtime and budget by telling George to end the movie with Leia being saved, but George refused to cut the Death Star dogfight attack. — *Light and Magic*, Episode 1.

P37: This was not the film: it was at best 30% of the real movie he was making. — Peter Biskind, *Easy Riders, Raging Bulls.*

P40: "I was sort of sorry we got it right on the first take," Carrie said, afterward. "I wanted to do it again." — *Secrets of the Force.*

P44: Mark heard a rumor the trailer was playing up in Westwood, so he and Carrie drove up there. — *Secrets of the Force.*

P47: Steven Spielberg offered to handle second-unit directing, but George didn't want the help. —Biskind.

P48: Harrison, who had the most experience with the press, would grade Carrie and Mark after each session, as if he were their publicity teacher. — *Rolling Stone, 1980.*

P54: "I'm glad I didn't do *Star Wars* because it was a nothing part. I would not want to get famous because of that movie." — Biskind.

P55: In the future Lucasfilm would purposefully try to hire female ILM employees, just to reduce the grossness quotient. — *Making of ESB.*

P58: "I was actually more interested in the character of Leia than I was with Luke," Foster said. — *Secrets of the Force.*

P63: Because it was the Holiday Special she had pitched singing a Christmas carol, and because she was Carrie she wanted it to be Joni Mitchell's "River," the saddest Christmas song ever written. — *Secrets of the Force.*

P67: "The only way I can do it," he said, "is to create a company that will generate profits." — *Making of ESB.*

P72: (A reporter snuck onto the set and pressed Carrie for plot details. This level of hounding was new to her, and despite the reporter being female, she said it felt like an assault.) — *Making of ESB.*

P74: She teased Harrison for not having a puzzle with his face on it, the way Luke and Leia did. — *Making of ESB.*

P74: She would fall asleep on set, mix up her human and robot costars, and dream of cyborgs and androids. — *Rolling Stone.*

P74: "So I had these violent nightmares, dreams where you keep trying to impose your reality and you can't. It gets you crazy." — *Making of ESB.*

P77: "Well, Harrison came over," Carrie said, "and the Rolling Stones came over, I think we stayed up most of the night." — *Making of ESB.*

P79: "I think she hides it. It's not stylish to be that dedicated." — *Making of ESB.*

P81: ...Carrie had bodyguards on set for her final few days of filming. — *Making of ESB.*

P83: Marketing was also aided by dumpster-diving thieves, who would grab bits of rubbish from ILM, including snippets of film, and sell them to magazines as sneak peeks. — *Making of ESB.*

P83: Carrie did one interview in a room filled with merchandize from the first film, the sci-fi equivalent of a doctor's ego wall. — *Making of ESB.*

P83: She described herself as "a strong girl with a low voice and self-righteous nature." — *Rolling Stone.*

P84: "It's very childlike so you can be very childlike." — *Making of ESB.*

P85: Dan got her to stop using cocaine: she was energetic enough without it. — *Primetime.*

P86: Right after that she went clothes shopping for Danny; if they were going to be together, she wanted him to look good. Plus, retail therapy is better than no therapy. — Penny Marshall, *My Mother Was Nuts!*

P87: She couldn't even go to sleep without pills. — *Primetime.*

P89: At parties she'd go through people's medicine cabinets, claiming to be Robin Hood "taking from the straight, and giving to the potentially stoned." — *Primetime.*

P89: Both *Star Wars* and *American Graffiti* had been films "where people felt better coming out of the theater than when they went in." — Biskind.

P90: Harrison joked that the even without a proper ending, the film had "at least $11 worth of entertainment." — JW Rinzler, *The Making of the Return of the Jedi.*

P91: "I talked about the way that Carrie Fisher was portrayed—she meant a lot to me in *Star Wars*—that she was this perfect little doll-like creature, and how terrific it was." — Making of *ROTJ.*

P95: ..."PLEASE... NO SLEEZY [sic] GEEKS TODAY." — *Light and Magic*, Episode 4.

P96: "I may have been naïve," he said later, "but I sort of missed that angle." — *CFTE.*

p100: When he found out he had publicly contradicted Marquand on set, he let the matter go. — *Making of ROTJ.*

p100: Carrie, though, did the scene George's way. — Dale Pollock, *Skywalking.*

p102: "When in doubt, I floor it," John had said, "I let my lifestyle play itself out." And it did. — *SNL book.*

p105: She'd organize parties of people going on trips. They might freak out, but for her, she wasn't going anywhere her brain didn't already take her every day. — *Primetime.*

p108: She joked that people who talked to her must have heavy hair, since they'd always tilt their head as they asked "How are you?" — *Primetime.*

p118: "My mother," Carrie joked, "was the only person I know who had a nervous breakdown without getting nervous or breaking down: she just moved right through it." — *The Arsenio Hall Show,* October 18, 1991.

p123: That was the rationalization, at least: better a junkie than crazy. — *Primetime.*

p145: This sort of work helped the director make their own choices for scenes, and feel more ownership. — Don Bluth, *Somewhere Out There.*

p171: Carrie had recently saved George from a drunk indie director who accosted him at a party, saying that George had single-handedly ruined serious filmmaking. — *CFTE.*

p182: When asked to sign her name, she put a pen in her left hand, and very slowly and deliberately wrote the word "SHAME." — *Primetime.*

p184: The elaborate 'do was meant to suggest that Leia's hairstyle was actually a toned-down tribute to her late mom. — *CFTE.*

p231: "She will always be an icon as Leia," costar Kelly Marie Tran said, "but also as Carrie." — *Secrets of the Force.*

Websites

Asher-Perrin, Emmet. "Do not read the *Empire Strikes Back* novelization, it will only make you sad." *Tor.com.* Published December 3, 2015. https://www.tor.com/2015/12/03/do-not-read-the-empire-strikes-back-novelization-it-will-only-make-you-sad/ Accessed July 10, 2020.

Audio released of Carrie Fisher emergency call. *Washington Post.* Published December 24, 2016. https://www.washingtonpost.com/videoentertainment/audio-released-of-carrie-fisher-emergency-call/2016/12/24/721ccec2-ca05-11e6-acda-59924caa2450_video.html?utm_term=.4f2ee52daa01 Accessed July 10, 2020.

Bell, BreAnna. CAA's Bryan Lourd Disavows Upcoming Carrie Fisher Biography. *Variety.* Published October 24, 2019. https://variety.com/2019/biz/news/bryan-lourd-disavows-carrie-fisher-biography-billie-1203382838/ Accessed July 10, 2020.

Beadle, Esther. Thank you, Carrie Fisher. *On the Borderlines.* Published https://ontheborderlines.wordpress.com/2017/01/14/thank-you-carrie/ Accessed July 10, 2020.

Bendix, Trish. Penny Marshall Was a Lesbian Icon, Even If She Wasn't Gay. *Into More.* December 18, 2018. https://www.intomore.com/culture/penny-marshall-was-a-lesbian-icon-even-if-she-wasnt-gay Accessed July 10, 2020.

Betzen, Nathan. Kodi v18 – 'Leia.' *Kodi.tv.* Published January 9, 2017. https://kodi.tv/article/kodi-v18-leia Accessed July 10, 2020.

Bevil, Dewayne and the Orlando Sentinal. Mark Hamill's role in new *'Star Wars'* movie began with lunch in Orlando. *Orlando Sentinel.* Published May 16, 2014. Accessed July 10, 2020.https://www.orlandosentinel.com/travel/attractions/the-daily-disney/os-disney-star-wars-mark-hamill-20140516-story.html Accessed July 10, 2020.

Blas, Lorena. Carrie Fisher's frequent companion: French bulldog Gary. *USA Today.* Published December 27, 2016. https://www.usatoday.com/story/life/people/2016/12/27/carrie-fishers-frequent-companion-french-bulldog-gary/95880672/ Accessed July 10, 2020.

Blauvelt, Christian. *Star Tours* jumps to lightspeed: Exclusive video of Disney's reboot of the classic Star Wars. *Entertainment Weekly.* Published May 19, 2011. ridehttps://ew.com/article/2011/05/19/star-tours-disney-star-wars-video/ Accessed July 10, 2020.

Breznican, Anthony. "Meet Fred Roos, the man who discovered two Han Solos." *Entertainment Weekly.* Published May 11, 2016. https://ew.com/article/2016/05/11/meet-man-who-discovered-two-han-solos/ Accessed July 10, 2020.

Britton, Luke Morgan. "Watch 'Rogue One' young Princess Leia actress discuss role and Carrie Fisher's death in first interview." *NME.* Published March 14, 2017. https://www.nme.com/news/film/rogue-one-young-princess-leia-actress-video-interview-2016908 Accessed July 10, 2020.

Brand, Russell. Russell Brand on Amy Winehouse: 'We have lost a beautiful, talented woman.' *The Guardian.* Published July 24, 2011. https://www.theguardian.com/music/2011/jul/24/russell-brand-amy-winehouse-woman Accessed July 10, 2020.

Bruss, Kelley. "Pursing justice." Furman University. Published April 9, 2018. https://news.furman.edu/2018/04/09/pursuing-justice/ Accessed July 10, 2020.

Busis, Hillary. Carrie Fisher Had Just One Request for Her Obituary. *Vanity Fair.* December 27, 2016. https://www.vanityfair.com/hollywood/2016/12/carrie-fisher-dies-strangled-by-bra-wishful-drinking Accessed July 10, 2020.

Byrne, Suzy. Carrie Fisher's L.A. Mansion Was Home to Many. *Yahoo Entertainment.* Published December 28, 2016. https://www.yahoo.com/entertainment/carrie-fishers-l-a-mansion-was-home-to-many-204951889.html Accessed July 10, 2020.

Cagle, Jess. Whoopi Goldberg duels with Disney. *Entertainment Weekly.* Published May 29, 1992. https://ew.com/article/1992/05/29/whoopi-goldberg-duels-disney/ Accessed July 10, 2020.

Caldwell, Carol. Girls on wheels: Penny Marshall and Carrie Fisher forever. *Jezebel.* https://jezebel.com/girls-on-wheels-penny-marshall-and-carrie-fisher-forev-1831256924 Accessed July 10, 2020.

Cameron, Brian. Roger Christian remembers Carrie Fisher. *Jedi News*. Published December 31, 2016. https://www.jedinews.com/film-music-tv/articles/roger-christian-remembers-carrie-fisher/ Accessed July 10, 2020.

Camus, Alyson. Harper Simon Wrote 'The Shine' With Carrie Fisher. *Rock NYC*. Published January 3, 2017. https://rocknyc.live/harper-simon-wrote-the-shine-with-carrie-fisher.html Accessed July 10, 2020.

Carrie Fisher: A Force for good. https://ibpf.org/learn/resources/blog/ Accessed July 10, 2020.

Carrie Fisher took cocaine on *Star Wars* set. *The Telegraph*. Published October 11, 2010. https://www.telegraph.co.uk/culture/film/film-news/8057776/Carrie-Fisher-took-cocaine-on-Star-Wars-set.html Accessed July 10, 2020.

Carrie Fisher: the high school dropout goes back to college. Knight-Ridder Newspapers. Published May 29, 1978. https://news.google.com/newspapers?nid=950&dat=19780529&id=P11 QAAAAIBAJ&sjid=i1gDAAAAIBAJ&pg=3813,3109244 Accessed July 10, 2020.

Carrie Fisher's Weight Loss: ' *Star Wars*' icon loses 30 pounds on new diet. HuffPost. Published May 12, 2011. https://www.huffpost.com/entry/carrie-fishers-weight-loss-30-pounds_n_861197 Accessed July 10, 2020.

Carrison Timeline/Masterpost. Published November 20, 2016. https://harryandcarrison.tumblr.com/post/153449316305/carrison-timelinemasterpost. Accessed July 10, 2020.

Chitwood, Adam. ' *Star Wars: The Force Awakens*': 28 Things We Learned from J.J. Abrams' New Commentary. *Collider*. Publisher November 14, 2016. https://collider.com/star-wars-the-force-awakens-trivia/#rey-finn Accessed July 10, 2020.

Conrad, Peter. *Shockaholic* by Carrie Fisher – review. *The Guardian*. Published November 10, 2011. https://www.theguardian.com/books/2011/nov/10/shockaholic-carrie-fisher-review Accessed July 10, 2020.

Cronin, Brian. Movie Legends Revealed | Did Carrie Fisher Have a Career as a Script Doctor? *CBR*. Published August 26, 2015. https://www.cbr.com/movie-legends-revealed-did-carrie-fisher-have-a-career-as-a-script-doctor/ Accessed July 10, 2020.

Davids, Brian. 'Star Wars' Actor Greg Grunberg Pours Cold Water on

'Rise of Skywalker' Director's Cut. *Hollywood Reporter.* Published March 20, 2020. https://www.hollywoodreporter.com/heat-vision/star-war-greg-grunberg-debunks-rise-skywalker-directors-cut-1285724 Accessed July 10, 2020.

Desta, Yohana. Carrie Fisher's Fascinating Romances: Paul Simon, Dan Aykroyd, Harrison Ford, and a U.S. Senator. *Vanity Fair.* Published December 28, 2016. https://www.vanityfair.com/style/2016/12/carrie-fisher-relationships Accessed July 10, 2020.

Dougherty, Margot. Looking back on EW's 1990 interview with Carrie Fisher. *Entertainment Weekly.* Published December 29, 2016. https://ew.com/news/1990/09/28/carrie-fishers-roles-actress-writer-and-daughter/ Accessed July 10, 2020.

Dulin, Dann. In bed with Carrie Fisher. *A&U Magazine.* Published April 1998. https://aumag.org/2015/12/29/carrie-fisher/ Accessed July 10, 2020.

Felsenthal, Julia. Why Carrie Fisher's new memoir will appeal to more than just *Star Wars* fans. *Vogue.* Published November 22, 2016. https://www.vogue.com/article/the-princess-diarist-carrie-fisher-review Accessed July 10, 2020.

Fisher, Carrie. Screech and Tell. *New York Times Magazine.* Publisher September 25, 2005. https://www.nytimes.com/2005/09/25/travel/tmagazine/screech-and-tell.html Accessed July 10, 2020.

Gardner, Chirs. Carrie Fisher on Robin Williams: He Opened Up to Me About Bipolar Disorder. *Hollywood Reporter.* Published August 13, 2014. https://www.hollywoodreporter.com/news/carrie-fisher-robin-williams-he-725201 Accessed July 10, 2020.

Gleiberman, Owen. Review: " *Morning Glory.*" *Entertainment Weekly.* Published November 12, 2010. https://ew.com/article/2010/11/12/morning-glory-3/ Accessed July 10, 2020.

Goldstein, Joelle. Carrie Fisher's Beloved French Bulldog Gary Retires to Florida 2 Years After the Actress' Death. *People Magazine.* Published January 9, 2019. https://people.com/pets/carrie-fisher-beloved-dog-gary-retires-florida/ Accessed July 10, 2020.

Goldstein, Patrick. The Force never left him. *Los Angeles Times.* Published February 2, 1997. https://www.latimes.com/archives/la-xpm-1997-02-02-tm-24513-story.html Accessed July 10, 2020.

Good Housekeeping Features Team. 'I'm in a business where the only things that matter are weight and appearance.' *Good Housekeeping.* Published July 12, 2015. https://www.goodhousekeeping.com/uk/lifestyle/a558228/carrie-fisher/ Accessed July 10, 2020.

Good Morning America. Rare and exclusive, behind the scenes look at ' *The Empire Strikes Back'.* Published December 15, 2020. https://www.goodmorningamerica.com/culture/video/rare-exclusive-scenes-empire-strikes-back-74735668 Accessed December 15, 2020.

Harrison, Ellie. James Blunt on his "American mother" Carrie Fisher: I lived in a madhouse with her. *Radio Times.* Published February 20, 2017. https://www.radiotimes.com/news/2017-02-20/james-blunt-on-his-american-mother-carrie-fisher-i-lived-in-a-madhouse-with-her/ Accessed July 10, 2020.

Here's why Carrie Fisher won't get trump's star on the Walk of Fame. *Los Angeles Times.* June 6, 2019. https://www.latimes.com/entertainment/movies/la-et-mn-carrie-fisher-mark-hamill-walk-of-fame-star-astarforcarrie-20190619-story.html Accessed July 10, 2020.

Heyman, Jessie. Carrie Fisher Loses 50 Pounds on Jenny Craig; 'Star Wars' Actress Reaches Weight Loss Goal (PHOTOS). *HuffPost.* Published September 2, 2011. https://www.huffpost.com/entry/fisher_n_947127 Accessed July 10, 2020.

Holmes, Adam. Star Wars: The Rise Of Skywalker VFX Reel Shows How Carrie Fisher Was Brought Back. *Cinema Blend.* Published February 4, 2020. https://www.cinemablend.com/news/2489633/star-wars-the-rise-of-skywalker-vfx-reel-shows-how-carrie-fisher-was-brought-back Accessed July 10, 2020.

Hirschberg, Lynn. The Controversy Over Bob Woodward's Belushi Bio ' *Wired'. Rolling Stone.* September 27, 1984. https://www.rollingstone.com/culture/culture-news/the-controversy-over-bob-woodwards-belushi-bio-wired-37163/ Accessed July 10, 2020.

Kittannning Leader Times. Published December 26, 1978. https://newspaperarchive.com/kittanning-leader-times-dec-26-1978-p-23/ Accessed July 10, 2020.

Knight, Richard Jr. Carrie Fisher's razorlike wit dissects her various realities. *Chicago Tribune.* December 19, 2008.

https://www.chicagotribune.com/news/ct-xpm-2008-12-19-
0812170618-story.html Accessed July 10, 2020.

Lenker, Maureen Lee. Anastasia composers tell the stories behind the film's
most beloved songs. *Entertainment Weekly.* Published November 21,
2017. https://ew.com/movies/2017/11/21/anastasia-songs-lynn-ahrens-
stephen-flaherty/ Accessed July 10, 2020.

Leonard, Elizabeth. "Carrie Fisher reveals she had an affair with Harrison
Ford on *Star Wars*: 'It Was So Intense.'" *People.* November 15, 2016.
https://people.com/movies/carrie-fisher-reveals-affair-with-harrison-
ford-star-wars/ Accessed July 10, 2020.

Levy, Nicole. PHOTOS: when Carrie Fisher lived in New York City. *DNA
info.* Published December 27, 2016. https://www.dnainfo.com/new-
york/20161227/times-square-theater-district/carrie-fisher-death-paul-
simon-broadway-photos-manhattan-apartment-obituary/ Accessed July
10, 2020.

Lewis, Andy; Malach, Hannah; Zukin, Meg. "'*Powerhouse*': Counting
Who is Quoted Most in the CAA Story." *The Hollywood Reporter.*
Published August 10, 2016.
https://www.hollywoodreporter.com/bookmark/powerhouse-counting-
who-is-quoted-918852 Accessed July 10, 2020.

Lewis, Dennis. The dead gay Republican in Carrie Fisher's bed. *Narkive
Newsgroup Archive.* Published 2005.
https://soc.motss.narkive.com/XOilyTwK/the-dead-gay-republican-in-
carrie-fisher-s-bed Accessed July 10, 2020.

Littleton, Cynthia. "'*These Old Broads*' director recalls Carrie Fisher's
'love letter' to Debbie Reynolds." *Variety.* December 27, 2016.
https://variety.com/2016/tv/news/carrie-fisher-debbie-reynolds-
elizabeth-taylor-these-old-broads-1201948862/ Accessed July 10, 2020.

Lourd, Billie. Billie Lourd on Becoming the Keeper of Princess Leia. *Time*
magazine . Published November 7, 2019.
https://time.com/5720323/billie-lourd-princess-leia-essay-carrie-fisher/
Accessed July 10, 2020.

Lussier, Germain. Meet the Actress Who Had to Don Princess Leia's Buns
in *Rogue One.* Gizmodo. Published March 14, 2017.
https://io9.gizmodo.com/meet-the-actress-who-had-to-don-princess-
leias-buns-in-1793257284 Accessed July 10, 2020.

Ma, Lybi. "Interview: The Fisher queen." *Psychology Today.* Published
November 1, 2001.

https://www.psychologytoday.com/us/articles/200111/interview-the-fisher-queen Accessed July 10, 2020.

Malarte, Jules-Pierre. Richard Marquand interview: *Return Of The Jedi, Star Wars*. Den of Geek. Published June 25, 2013. https://www.denofgeek.com/movies/richard-marquand-interview-return-of-the-jedi-star-wars/ Accessed July 10, 2020.

Mansfield, Stephanie. Carrie Fisher's candid confessions. *Washington Post.* Published August 13, 1987. https://medium.com/thewashingtonpost/carrie-fishers-candid-confessions-2d4bf2bb1355 Accessed July 10, 2020.

Marchese, David. Meg Ryan on romantic comedies, celebrity and leaving it all behind. *New York Times Magazine*. Published February 15, 2019. https://www.nytimes.com/interactive/2019/02/15/magazine/meg-ryan-romantic-comedy.html Accessed July 10, 2020.

McGovern, Joe. Read how Debbie Reynolds and Carrie Fisher connect to *EW*'s latest True Crime feature. *Entertainmnet Weekly.* Published October 4, 2017. https://ew.com/news/2017/10/04/true-crime-debbie-reynolds-connection/ Accessed July 10, 2020.

McLuskey, Megan. A Baby Named After 'General Leia' Kicked Off a Star Wars Debate Over Whether She Was Better as a Princess. *Time* magazine . Published December 12, 2018. https://time.com/5477733/princess-leia-star-wars-debate/ Accessed July 10, 2020.

McNamara, Jonathan. "Carrie Fisher on *Spy in the House of Me*, Tinkerbell and being the movie industry's best script doctor." *Phoenix New Times.* April 29, 2008. https://www.phoenixnewtimes.com/news/carrie-fisher-on-spy-in-the-house-of-me-tinkerbell-and-being-the-movie-industrys-best-script-doctor-6636095 Accessed July 10, 2020.

McNamara, Mary and Neuman, Johanna. Even in death, lobbyist is a complicated case . *Los Angeles Times.* Published April 30, 2015. https://www.latimes.com/archives/la-xpm-2005-apr-30-me-fisher30-story.html Accessed July 10, 2020.

Message board – Agnes of God. *BroawayWorld.com.* Posted August 29, 2012. https://www.broadwayworld.com/board/readmessage.php?thread=1047 828&page=3 Accessed July 10, 2020.

Message board. Did Carrie Fisher do ghost scriptwriting work on *Phantom Menace*? Published June 28, 2010.

https://boards.theforce.net/threads/did-carrie-fisher-do-ghost-scriptwriting-work-on-phantom-menace.31040423/ Accessed July 10, 2020.

Message board: Why did Lauren Bacall refuse to do *These Old Broads*? *Data Lounge.* Published April 15, 2018. https://www.datalounge.com/thread/21004583-why-did-lauren-bacall-refuse-to-do-these-old-broads- Accessed July 10, 2020.

Meyers, Kate. Pilots inspired by ' *Ghost.' Entertainment Weekly.* Published April 5, 1991. https://ew.com/article/1991/04/05/pilots-inspired-ghost/ Accessed July 10, 2020.

Miller, Mike. Carrie Fisher's Death: How Dangerous Is Sleep Apnea? *People Magazine.* Published June 17, 2017. https://people.com/celebrity/carrie-fishers-sleep-apnea-deadly/ Accessed July 10, 2020.

Movies News Desk. Carrie Fisher and Debbie Reynolds Property Auction Grosses Over $2 Million. *Broadway World.* Published October 11, 2017. https://www.broadwayworld.com/article/Carrie-Fisher-and-Debbie-Reynolds-Property-Auction-Grosses-Over-2-Million-20171011 Accessed July 10, 2020.

Moye, Clerence. ' *Star Wars'* Screenwriter Chris Terrio on Ending the 42-year 'Skywalker' Saga. *Awards Daily.* Published December 30, 2019. https://www.awardsdaily.com/2019/12/24/star-wars-screenwriter-chris-terrio-on-ending-the-42-year-skywalker-saga/ Accessed July 10, 2020.

Mozingo, Joe; Karlamangla, Soumya; Winton, Richard. "Carrie Fisher opened up about her demons — and knew she wouldn't have a Hollywood ending." *Los Angeles Times.* Published June 20, 2017. https://www.latimes.com/local/lanow/la-me-carrie-fisher-addiction-20170620-story.html Accessed July 10, 2020.

Mychaskiw, Marianne. We want to frame Carrie Fisher's makeup chart from *Star Wars. In Style Magazine.* Published January 5, 2017. https://www.instyle.com/news/carrie-fisher-princess-leia-star-wars-makeup-face-chart Accessed July 10, 2020.

Natalie Portman: Forbidden Love. *StarWars.com.* https://web.archive.org/web/20050630014030/http://www.starwars.com/episode-ii/bts/profile/f20020827/indexp2.html Accessed July 10, 2020.

Parker, Ryan. Harrison Ford Remembers Carrie Fisher During Mark Hamill's Walk of Fame Star Ceremony. *Hollywood Reporter.* March 8, 2018. https://www.hollywoodreporter.com/heat-vision/harrison-ford-remembers-carrie-fisher-mark-hamills-walk-fame-star-ceremony-1093171 Accessed July 10, 2020.

Pate, Brian. Carrie Fisher cancels Emerald City Comicon 2013 appearance. Published February 27, 2013. http://www.conventionscene.com/2013/02/27/carrie-fisher-cancels-emerald-city-comicon-2013-appearance/ Accessed July 10, 2020.

People Staff. A Dear Friend Remembers How Carrie Fisher Became a Novelist. *People Magazine.* Published January 13, 2017. https://people.com/movies/paul-slansky-remembers-how-carrie-fisher-became-a-novelist/ Accessed July 10, 2020.

Pressberg, Matt. Carrie Fisher, Debbie Reynolds Funeral Features Dancing, Droids and a Standing Ovation. *The Wrap.* Published March 25, 2017. https://www.thewrap.com/carrie-fisher-debbie-reynolds-funeral-features-dancing-droids-and-a-standing-ovation/ Accessed July 10, 2020.

Ragogna, Mike. That "St. Judy's Comet" Kid: A Dinner Conversation With Harper Simon. *HuffPost.* Published May 14, 2010; updated December 6, 2017. https://www.huffpost.com/entry/emthat-st-judys-comet-kid_b_576000 Accessed July 10, 2020.

Ratcliffe, Amy. *THE LAST JEDI* Has New Space Jewelry Because of Carrie Fisher. *Nerdist.* Published November 5, 2017. https://nerdist.com/article/star-wars-the-last-jedi-carrie-fisher-space-jewelry-rian-johnson/ Accessed July 10, 2020.

Reyes, Jenna. Carrie Fisher and Sharon Horgan Talk About How the *Star Wars* Star Joined *Catastrophe.* *Vulture.* Published April 20, 2016. https://www.vulture.com/2016/04/how-carrie-fisher-joined-catastrophe.html Accessed July 10, 2020.

Robinson, Joanna. How Carrie Fisher Became the Surprising Face of the Rebellion Against Trump. *Vanity Fair.* Published January 23, 2017. https://www.vanityfair.com/style/2017/01/carrie-fisher-todd-fisher-womens-march-donald-trump Accessed July 10, 2020.

Rossen, Jake. The dark side: an oral history of *The Star Wars Holiday Special.* *Mental Floss.* Published November 18, 2019. http://mentalfloss.com/article/72863/dark-side-oral-history-star-wars-holiday-special Accessed July 10, 2020.

Sammons, Eric. Why Princess Leia Is The Archetypal Strong Woman Female Leads Can't Replicate. *The Federalist.* https://thefederalist.com/2016/12/30/princess-leia-archetypal-strong-woman-female-leads-cant-replicate/ Accessed July 10, 2020.

Sciretta, Peter. "Carrie Fisher, Script Doctor: Her Unknown Legacy Examined." *SlashFilm.* December 29, 2016. https://www.slashfilm.com/carrie-fisher-script-doctor/ Accessed July 10, 2020.

Serna, Joseph and Winton, Richard. Carrie Fisher's autopsy reveals cocktail of drugs, including cocaine, opiates and ecstasy. *Los Angeles Times.* Published June 19, 2017. https://www.latimes.com/local/lanow/la-me-ln-carrie-fisher-autopsy-report-20170619-story.html Accessed July 10, 2020.

Shapshay, Mara. Carrie Fisher saved my life. *Los Angeles Magazine.* Published January 12, 2017. http://www.lamag.com/culturefiles/carrie-fisher-saved-life/ Accessed July 10, 2020.

Snierson, Dan. Q&A with ' *Catastrophe'* stars Rob Delaney, Sharon Horgan. *Entertainment Weekly.* July 7, 2017. https://ew.com/article/2015/06/27/catastrophe-rob-delaney-sharon-horgan-amazon/ Accessed July 10, 2020.

Solan, Colin. CA – Princess Leia signs. *Convention Scene.* Published January 17, 2012. http://www.conventionscene.com/2012/01/17/ca-princess-leia-signs/ Accessed July 10, 2020.

Spector, Nicole. Carrie Fisher Taught Me How to Live. *Vogue.* December 29, 2016. https://www.vogue.com/article/carrie-fisher-life-advice Accessed July 10, 2020.

Staba, David. Hollywood Kid Carrie Fisher and Her Best Awful. *BP Hope.* Published Fall 2004. https://www.bphope.com/hollywood-kid-carrie-fisher-and-her-best-awful/ Accessed July 10, 2020.

Steinberg, Don. Help me, Obi-Wan: Carrie Fisher's private philosophy coach. https://www.newyorker.com/culture/culture-desk/help-me-obi-wan-carrie-fisher-private-philosophy-coach Published December 11, 2017. Accessed April 4, 2023.

Stevenson, Laura. "Now Carrie Fisher will have to title Her Autobiography 'daughter of *Star Wars.'*" *People.* Published June 20, 1977. https://people.com/archive/now-carrie-fisher-will-have-to-title-her-autobiography-daughter-of-star-wars-vol-7-no-24/ Accessed July 10, 2020.

Swartz, Tracy. How Carrie Fisher and Dan Aykroyd's love blossomed in Chicago. *Chicago Tribune.* Published January 25, 2017. https://www.chicagotribune.com/entertainment/ct-carrie-fisher-death-dan-aykroyd-20170125-story.html Accessed July 10, 2020.

Telegraph Reporters. "New study shows just how rarely women appear in *Star Wars.*" *The Telegraph.* Published June 1, 2018. https://www.telegraph.co.uk/films/2018/06/01/new-study-shows-just-rarely-women-appear-star-wars/ Accessed July 10, 2020.

Tramel, Jimmie. Pop culture: Creative force was strong in multitalented Carrie Fisher. *Tulsa World.* Publisher December 29, 2016. https://www.tulsaworld.com/entertainment/pop-culture-creative-force-was-strong-in-multitalented-carrie-fisher/article_232b4b0c-3ef0-57cd-82ff-bb9fa8b2de29.html Accessed July 10, 2020.

Vary, Adam, B. The Crazy Story of How " *Clue*" Went From Forgotten Flop To Cult Triumph. Buzzfeed. Posted September 2, 2013. https://www.buzzfeed.com/adambvary/something-terrible-has-happened-here-the-crazy-story-of-how#.qaydqAm5K Accessed July 10, 2020.

Waver, Hilary. Sean Lennon Remembers His Friend Carrie Fisher Through His Music. *Vanity Fair.* March 10, 2017. https://www.vanityfair.com/style/2017/03/sean-lennon-remembers-friend-carrie-fisher-in-song Accessed July 10, 2020.

Weaver, Hilary. Debbie Reynolds protected and preserved Hollywood's most precious relics. *Vanity Fair.* Published December 29, 2016. https://www.vanityfair.com/style/2016/12/debbie-reynolds-protected-and-preserved-hollywoods-most-precious-relics?verso=true Accessed July 10, 2020.

Whitbrook, James. How Lucasfilm Made *The Last Jedi's* Leia Hologram Sound Authentically Crummy. *io9.* Published February 26, 2018. https://io9.gizmodo.com/how-lucasfilm-made-the-last-jedis-leia-hologram-sound-a-1823321240 Accessed July 10, 2020.

White, Timothy. " *Star Wars*: Slaves to the Empire." *Rolling Stone.* Published July 24, 1980. https://www.rollingstone.com/culture/culture-news/star-wars-slaves-to-the-empire-61931/ Accessed July 10, 2020.

Whittaker, Alexandra. Carrie Fisher's Daughter Billie Lourd Tells the Story of Her Mom's Tattoo Gone Wrong, and It's Classic Carrie. *In Style Magazine.* Published October 26, 2017. https://www.instyle.com/news/carrie-fisher-billie-lourd-tattoo Accessed July 10, 2020.

When Debbie Reynolds and Carrie Fisher simultaneously starred on Broadway. *Playbill.* March 1983. https://www.playbill.com/article/when-debbie-reynolds-and-carrie-fisher-simultaneously-starred-on-broadway Accessed July 10, 2020.

About the Author

Jeff Ryan is the author of the #1 bestseller *Super Mario: How Nintendo Conquered America; A Mouse Divided: How Ub Iwerks Became Forgotten and Disney Became Uncle Walt* and *Father and Son Issues: The Secret History of Spiderman* (also published by Riverdale Avenue Books).

Other Riverdale Avenue Books You Might Like

You're Gonna Make It After All:
The Life, Times and Influence of Mary Tyler Moore
By Marc Shapiro

Elvis Forever:
Looking Back on the Legacy of the King
By Boze Hadleigh

The Binge Watcher's Guide to Doctor Who:
A History of Doctor Who and the First Female Doctor
By Mackenzie Flohr

The Binge Watcher's Guide to the Films of Harry Potter:
An Unauthorized Guide
By Cecilia Tan

The Binge Watcher's Guide to The Handmaid's Tale:
An Unofficial Companion
By Jamie K. Schmidt

The Binge Watcher's Guide to Black Mirror:
An Unofficial Companion
By Marc W. Polite

The Binge Watcher's Guide to The Twilight Zone:
An Unofficial Journey
By Jason Trussell

The Binge Watcher's Guide to The Golden Girls
By Marissa DeAngelis

The Binge Watcher's Guide to Supernatural:
An Unofficial Companion
By Jessica Mason

The Binge Watcher's Guide to The Twilight Saga
An Unofficial Companion
By Rachel Zimny

The Binge Watcher's Guide to the Marvel Universe
An Unofficial Companion
By Jessica Mason

www.ingramcontent.com/pod-product-compliance
Lightning Source LLC
Chambersburg PA
CBHW070024100426
42740CB00013B/2590